WHAT PEOPLE ARE SAYING . . .

Mr. Kaye's books answer clearly and concisely the "what to do" and "how to do" type questions that haunt clients in the areas of estate and financial planning. If true genius can be defined as the ability to reduce complex problems to easily understandable concepts, Mr. Kaye has achieved that status.

Richard Creange
New York, NY

Mr. Kaye's concepts are so extraordinary they have completely changed the way I use life insurance in my estate planning.

Mark Papalia, CLU, ChFC, CFP • Papalia Financial Services, Inc.
Danville, PA

Barry Kaye is inspiring! Of all the seminars I have attended, he is the best I have ever seen.

Michael Hebner, First Vice President • Roney & Co.
Flint, MI

The life insurance industry owes Mr. Kaye an immense debt of gratitude for placing the significance of life insurance in the forefront of people's financial and estate plans through his creative and personal investment where the industry has been the beneficiary at large.

Bijan Nahai • Nahai Insurance Services
Beverly Hills, CA

After 30 years I have come to the conclusion that for income, estate and gift tax purposes Barry's wealth creation and optimization methods really work and fully deliver on promises.

Ralph S. Adorno, C.L.U. and Associates
New York, NY

Barry is right! After 30 years with the Internal Revenue Service, Estate and Gift Tax Department, I am convinced that the best estate planning is *life insurance planning,* carefully implemented to avoid estate taxation.

Stephen L Diamond, J.D.
Los Angeles, CA

Mr. Kaye, you are an inspiration to my business and me. The conviction with which you practice invigorates the entire industry.

Lynne Rosenberg-Kidd • Innovative Solutions • Transamerica
Los Angeles, CA

Thank you Mr. Kaye! Your systems and methods have changed my life.

Mitchell Cohen
Encino, CA

Mr. Kaye, you amaze me! Thank you for showing me the power.

Jesse Savage • American Express • IDS
Las Vegas, NV

Barry, you are the greatest! Because of you I have completely changed the way I look at life insurance.

Bob Kersting, Jr. • John Hancock Agency
Phoenix, AZ

Barry, your innovative concepts and your wealth transfer techniques are absolutely incredible. You are the ultimate maverick in a sea of conventional wisdom. Your conviction and passion are truly evangelical.

Martin Greenberg, Chairman • Total Financial & Insurance Services
Los Angeles, CA

Mr. Kaye, you're my hero! I was an accountant who didn't know. Now I see the light.

David Owens, CPA
Readfield, ME

DIE RICH 2

BOOKS BY BARRY KAYE

$2,700,000 In My First Year (1963)

How to Save a Fortune on Your Life Insurance (1980)

Save a Fortune on Your Estate Taxes (1990)

Die Rich and Tax Free (1994)

Live Rich (1996)

The Investment Alternative (1997)

Die Rich 2 (2000)

DIE RICH 2

The Absolute Bottom Line on Wealth Creation and Preservation

Barry Kaye

FHA Publishing

ISBN: 1-930286-00-7

Printed in the United States of America

00 01 02 03 5 4 3 2 1

Dedication

In the past I have dedicated my books to my beloved wife, Carole, who had made all things possible for me. In addition, I have named as inspirations my children, Alan, Howard, and Fern, and the people who work around me as well as the professionals who have learned from these books how to better implement my concepts. Lastly, but most importantly, I have dedicated my books to the public so that they might be better served by the professionals who have the obligation and responsibility to explore every possible option.

Since this is probably the ultimate compilation of all my books and ideas, and possibly the final book I will write on this subject, I can do no less than to rededicate my efforts to all those who have inspired and supported me in the past.

Acknowledgments

I want to say to Rhonda Morstein Gilligan, my contributing editor for the past ten years, that you are amazing. The understanding of my concepts that you have developed since we first worked together has enabled you to enhance them to a final optimum in Die Rich 2. I could never have done this without you and, once again, I express my appreciation for all the books that you have participated in, all the help you have provided me, and, most importantly, what your edited words have meant to other professionals and the public.

Thank you, congratulations–and all I leave unsaid.

Acknowledgements

Contents

From the Publisher

The author describes in this book many situations that he had available to him at the time it was written. Without knowledge of your specific requirements, the author and publisher disclaim any liability for loss incurred by use of any direct or indirect application of the material contained herein. These ideas and concepts are only a starting point — only by using the proper professionals can you determine the complete suitability for your situation as well as consummate the proper implementation of these methods for optimizing and preserving your wealth for your family. Any change in the basic assumptions described herein will alter the specific results or returns. However, in most cases, the results will still be superior to those realized through any other approach. Naturally, all results are also limited by the assumed solvency of the company or consortium of companies that you elect to utilize.

Since any reference to an internal rate of return must be based on an assumed interest rate and period of time, there can no such comparison made, due to the uncertainty of when death will occur. In all cases, the author has diversified his client's portfolio and in most cases utilized less than 10% of the client's assets in doing so. Since he never proposes any course of financial action that would adversely affect his client's lifestyle, the internal rate of return is irrelevant in the context these ideas and concepts will provide.

You should consult your attorney for the implementation of any legal papers, such as trust documents, that may be necessary for carrying out these ideas. Trust officers can further provide you with the necessary information relative to these documents.

Foreword

In 1980, I first introduced *How to Save a Fortune on Your Life Insurance*, which I wrote to address and correct many of the misconceptions people had about life insurance. I felt those fears and misperceptions were keeping large numbers of people from availing themselves of one of the best tools for wealth creation and preservation available. In that book, I set out to speak straight about the buying and selling of life insurance so that more people would feel comfortable taking advantage of this marvelous financial tool. At that time a much higher pricing structure was prevalent in the life insurance industry. This book helped bring about a reduced pricing of up to 50%.

In 1990, I followed up *How to Save a Fortune on Your Life Insurance* with *Save a Fortune on Your Estate Taxes*. By then, I was the leading proponent of the use of life insurance to discount estate tax costs and was fighting an often uphill battle against the preconceptions and conventional wisdom of the times.

My next book, *Die Rich and Tax Free*, launched the wealth creation and preservation industry, which has since grown to include innumerable attorneys, accountants, and financial planners who engage in the processes of using life insurance to improve the financial outcome for estates. Finally, the American public and professional financial industries were beginning to see that life insurance was not simply a means of replacing income for widows, nor even just a way to discount estate tax costs for the very rich. Life insurance was beginning to be seen as the best means to a highly optimized end.

In *The Investment Alternative*, I took life insurance one step further and showed it to be an integral and important part of any wisely diversified financial portfolio. New concepts depicted the ways in which life insurance outperformed investments, recaptured losses, and protected gains.

After more than five books, 24 newspaper and magazine articles, and 38 years of struggling to overcome prejudice, misinformation and skepticism, it seemed that I was finally being heard. More and more people were embracing my techniques and, as a result, creating and saving fortunes.

It was around this time that Worth magazine published an article entitled *Die Broke* by Mark Levine and Stephen M. Pollan that I took basically as a parody of *Die Rich and Tax Free*. Then, in 1998, the Die Broke article was expanded into a book by the same title.

Originally the idea of being the object of a parody was somewhat flattering. But my pleasure at the compliment quickly turned to distress as the content of both the article and the book were given serious consideration among the media and industry pundits. As a parody, the Die Broke material was clever and entertaining. As a serious plan for an individual's financial welfare I find it dangerous and ill-considered and I was surprised that Worth magazine, which bills itself as a magazine for financial intelligence, would print in apparent seriousness an article based on this premise.

The fact of the matter is that you can't die broke unless you're already broke. Or, as my wife very succinctly put it, "If you are rich, you can't die broke unless you're an idiot or a psychic."

Unless you know when you will die and how, unless you know for a fact that you will never need extended medical care, will never have to help your children through a tragedy, or will never want something more than you already have, you can't possibly die broke. As long as you are alive, there will be the necessity for money to support yourself. You could decide not to care about providing for your children or favorite charity and simply start spending all your principle with the intention of living the high life until you die. But what if you get unlucky and fail to die before your money runs out? Then you won't be dying broke, you'll be living broke. And very few advisors possessing real financial intelligence would advocate that.

Because of the damage done by the "die broke" fad, I felt it absolutely imperative to update my original Die Rich book in an effort to return the focus of estate planning to where it belongs — on giving people the ability to support, maintain, and enhance their current lifestyles while preserving for their loved ones a legacy of financial security. It is my hope that the concepts and principles contained within this book will help people live richer and die richer.

It will be interesting to see if Levine and Pollan can come up with any ways for people to die broker, thereby precipitating a Die Broke 2.

I have always espoused the idea that you must provide for your own welfare first before considering the needs of your children, charity, employees, etc. As much as you may want to take care of the people who are important to you, you only get one life. Your first and foremost responsibility is to live it to the fullest.

But I also believe in giving back. In making life better for those who come after you. I believe that our obligation to our children does not end with our deaths and that taking care of them from beyond the grave is one of the greatest means available for continuing a dynasty of love.

We are each of us more than just the expression of our own selfish desires and impulses. We are part of something bigger. We have the ability to have a profound and lasting effect on our families, community, and the society that allowed us to achieve our ambitions.

In my book, *Live Rich*, which I wrote in 1995 and released in

1996, I state that living rich means more than just being wealthy. *Live Rich* was written at the prompting of many people who read *Die Rich* and then wanted to know a better way of living rich. To live rich is to embrace life and live it to the fullest, to have a directed purpose, and to pursue it with vigor and determination. Yet, I also say, and still believe, that living rich is enhanced when you have the financial wherewithal to follow any dream and to live large and free of fear.

Now, in response to Levine and Pollan's Die Broke theories I have come to the realization of one more "live rich" tenet: He who lives rich, dies rich. Rich in the knowledge of having provided for his loved ones, rich in the knowledge that their welfare is secure, rich in the pride of having given back to his community, and rich in the special peace that comes from knowing he left behind a legacy characterized by more than selfish self-indulgence.

About the Author

Barry Kaye founded the Wealth Creation and Preservation industry, which today is a professional focus of countless attorneys, financial advisors, and life insurance salespeople. Between them, those engaged in the ever-burgeoning field have helped to preserve and create over $15 billion in saved estate tax costs and optimized assets for their clients.

Barry Kaye was also the catalyst for the development of the type of life insurance policy—the last-to-die, survivorship policy — that is the single most effective financial tool available for accomplishing these concepts and techniques.

Kaye is the author of the two all-time bestselling books on life insurance and estate planning. His first book, *How to Save a Fortune on Your Life Insurance*, was an immediate bestseller. His next book and videotape, *Save a Fortune on Your Estate Taxes*, was the all-time bestselling book in America on the subject.

In his latest book, *Die Rich 2*, Kaye expands upon his concepts, presenting new methods and utilizations to achieve even more impressive results. He also presents a thorough overview of the industry, going beyond theory to the nuts and bolts of making his plans work.

Kaye has also produced easy-to-understand videotapes outlining his dynamic techniques, entitled *Barry Kaye's Six Most Costly Mistakes Made By Those Worth $3 Million to $250 Million*, *Die Rich and Tax Free!*, his original 2½ hour seminar video, *Save A*

Fortune on Your Estate Taxes, Make Millions, Save Millions, and the most recent 3-hour seminar video, *Wealth Creation and Preservation*. He is frequently quoted in the national press and has appeared as the guest speaker on numerous radio and TV shows, including two appearances on the *Today Show*. He also appears at more than 100 seminars a year sharing his visionary ideas on how to create and preserve wealth and has already been booked for over 140 seminar appearances in 2000.

A native New Yorker who began his career as a radio and TV personality, Kaye joined New England Life as an insurance agent in 1962, immediately breaking all life insurance industry sales records for a first year agent. In 1966, he received his C.L.U. degree. Soon after, he was named a lifetime member of the Million Dollar Round Table Club and became one of the founders of the prestigious International Forum. In 1968, he established Barry Kaye Associates. His innovative use of life insurance earned him a reputation for creativity in the insurance field and his outstanding integrity and financial acumen resulted in astonishing success in his field. In 1982 he established Wealth Creation Centers nationwide. His success is legendary and unparalleled. He is probably the only insurance salesperson to ever lead 13 insurance companies during his career.

Kaye, who is listed in *Who's Who in America*, *Who's Who in the West*, and *Who's Who in Finance and Industry*, has served on the California Senate Advisory Commission on Life Insurance. A philanthropist who is well known for his outstanding contributions to charitable organizations, he is a member of the Board of Ben Gurion University and the City of Hope, one of the founders of La Societé and the Los Angeles Music Center, and former Vice Chairman of the Young Musicians' Foundation. He is the recipient of the Man of Hope award from the City of Hope for Founders of Diabetic Research (1976), the Menachim Begin Award for Israel Bonds (1977), and the Lifetime Achievement Award from Ben Gurion University of the Negev (1987). Using the techniques he developed and teaches for maximizing charitable contributions, Kaye also gifted the American College of Life Underwriters with over $1 million, the largest endowment in its history. He recently pledged stock to the American College to create a first-time ever Chair at any university for Wealth Creation and Preservation to teach how to preserve, create, and maximize wealth.

A devoted family man, Kaye's son Alan runs his Los Angeles office. His son Howard runs the Boca Raton office and daughter Fern runs the New York office. They all work with him as he travels the country speaking at seminars and spreading the wealth creation word. He is also cofounder, along with his wife, of *The Carole & Barry Kaye Museum of Miniatures*, which houses the largest collection of contemporary miniatures in the world and is located on famed Museum Row in Los Angeles.

Introduction

Barry Kaye does magic with money. He pioneered the Wealth Creation and Preservation industry and created many of the concepts now used by accountants, attorneys, financial planners, and insurance salespeople all across the country to maximize clients' assets and protect their estates.

In addition, Barry Kaye remains one of the foremost salespeople—perhaps in fact the leading salesperson—of individual life insurance products in the country through his nationwide network of Barry Kaye Associates participating brokers.

In six previous books, Barry has presented a wealth of information on the subject of life insurance as a crucial addition to any well-diversified portfolio. He has shown America that insurance is not a dirty word. Quite the opposite. Life insurance is a unique and magnificent financial tool that is often the only means to achieve the most optimized financial end.

In the beginning, both laypeople and professionals doubted Barry's vision. For years, life insurance carried some bewildering stigma. Yet Barry Kaye knew that the skepticism came from misinformation and misunderstanding rather than from reason. He knew that people's reluctance to accept the fact of their own mortality caused them to retreat from the benefits of life insurance. But all too often he was approached by people who came to the realization of death too late, after opportunity had passed. They came to him when they were old and sick and could no longer dismiss reality, wanting desperately to avoid the inevitable and protect their legacy for their heirs. His sorrow for the unnecessary waste of these people's resources, and his anger at a financial industry that turned up its nose at one of the most favorable solutions available for them, kept him flying in the face of conventional wisdom.

Now, the truth of Barry's vision is irrefutable and his ideas have been embraced by many of America's wealthiest individuals and most respected professionals. His techniques have proven themselves time and time again even as the dire, tragic outcomes of those who have shunned his methods have made headlines.

In this latest book, Barry presents a definitive compilation of materials developed over his 38 years as a wealth creation and preservation specialist.

The 12 Principles of Estate Preservation and Wealth Creation — Through the years of his involvement in the wealth creation and preservation industry, Barry Kaye has met the same resistance, been asked the same questions and overcome the same reluctance to believe, time and time again. As a result, he has formulated a distillate of the tenets of his techniques, a condensed "bible" that succinctly presents the foundation upon which all his creative concepts and incredible results are built.

Wealth Creation and Preservation — Nothing else compares to life insurance for most, if not all, estate tax cost discounting and legacy increasing goals. As he introduces the truths he has championed for so long, Barry compares conventional thinking and techniques against the outcomes resulting from his life insurance concepts.

Concepts — Barry Kaye's most valuable concepts updated to reflect current rates and costs and including several all-new strategies for estate tax cost discounting, financial optimization and maximization, and charitable giving.

Case Studies — 10 actual Case Studies in which Barry used a blend of techniques to create highly optimized results for his clients.

The Bottom Line on Insurance — When fully understood, the truth about life insurance's value for wealth creation and preservation is irrefutable. It is also quite simple. The truth about how and why life insurance works often surprises people who previously thought it to be complicated and mysterious. Barry explains:

- You Can Buy Insurance Even If You're Uninsurable
- The Real Truth About Replacement of Inefficient Policies
- Life Insurance Can Be Guaranteed
- Life Insurance is Not An Expense
- The Truth About "Based On Current Assumptions"
- How to Buy the Best Policy for Your Needs

Rates — As always, Barry includes all the information you'll need to calculate to your own situation each concept and strategy he presents. The rates presented are real, and although they don't represent a quotation — for that you must get examined — they are available as quoted under the assumed qualifications. Find out for yourself just how well these concepts can perform for the benefit of your loved ones.

DieRich2.com

If you find this book of interest, a visit to Barry's website is a must. There you'll find a resource-rich tool for understanding life insurance's many benefits and opportunities. The site plays host to a full reprinting of Barry's 25 Bottom Line columns, which first appeared in the Los Angeles Times and Forbes magazine. It presents his entire "Special Report" on *Clinton's Increased Exemptions* and how they impact your planning. It offers Barry's recommendations to some of the Forbes 400's richest Americans for estate maximization.

You can also find on the website an up-to-date listing of all the free seminars at which Barry will be appearing and a reservation form with which you can book your attendance.

As its newest feature, Barry's website has recently become fully interactive offering you the ability to customize many of his most popular and important concepts to your own exact situation. By entering your age, marital status and estate value in a secure, confidential environment, you can receive with absolutely no obligation an illustrated representation of how each of the fabulous concepts presented would work for you.

Visit the website today at ***www.DieRich2.com*** or call Barry Kaye directly at 800-DIE-RICH (800-343-7424) for any explanation or a personal consultation.

DIE RICH 2

The 12 Principles of Estate Preservation and Wealth Creation

Throughout my 38 years in the life insurance industry, I have encountered the same false impressions and the same misconceptions over and over among both the public and members of the insurance and general financial services industries. Because life insurance was originally packaged simply as a means of providing for a family in the event the breadwinner died prematurely, many people have had difficulty transitioning their thinking to realize the many other potentials it affords in the overall mix of financial planning.

As a result of all the times I have had to explain the same basics, I came to formulate a set doctrine intended to present as simply and succinctly as possible the key tenets for effective estate planning and wealth creation utilizing life insurance. These "12 Principles of Estate Preservation and Wealth Creation" are the proven nucleus of the methods and concepts that I will present throughout this book to maximize and optimize assets and help you die rich.

My concepts address the two basic areas of misunderstanding that seem to perpetually surround life insurance and interfere with its effective employment as a financial vehicle to discount estate tax costs and increase the legacy left to your heirs.

The first six principles address the proper inclusion and usage of life insurance in the overall financial planning mix:

1. **There is no reason to pay estate taxes when an insurance company can effectively pay them for you**. Estate taxes can claim up to 55% of estates valued at more than $3 million. Even after allowed exemptions, taxes can decimate wealth and leave your heirs struggling to liquidate assets to pay the government. Many strategies have been concocted to minimize taxes and we'll examine most of them later in this book. Some have limited value, some will be shown to be totally ineffective, and others can create a lot more problems than they solve. But all of them have one thing in common. Even after they have been executed, any money left in your estate at the time of your death will be subject to the up to 55% estate tax. Only if you give everything away before or at your death, leaving nothing for your own on-going support or for your heirs, can any of these methods protect your estate from estate taxes. But a life insurance policy, which comes to your heirs income and, if properly structured, estate tax free, can produce the funds needed to pay the estate taxes at as much as a 90% discount. The insurance proceeds pay the taxes. You retain your estate during your lifetime to provide for your welfare and pleasure. Upon your death(s), your estate passes to your heirs intact. I always refer to this as paying your estate taxes on a wholesale basis rather than retail.

2. **Paying the lowest tax is not the object of good estate planning. It is leaving the most money to your heirs or charity**. Along the same lines as the thinking that has led many people to simply accept the "necessary evil" of paying taxes, is a school of thought that suggests that your estate planning goal should be to "shelter" as much of your estate as possible in order to pay the lowest tax. But this is backward thinking. Reducing your estate to reduce your estate tax can also mean reducing the inheritance you leave to your heirs. Using life insurance, you can not only pay the estate taxes at a significant discount but maximize what you leave to your heirs as well. And generally the cost of the insurance is far less than the amount of property you would have to give away during your lifetime in order to reduce your estate tax cost the same amount. Plus, since estate taxes would reduce the value of your property by half, the leverage of life insurance can actually create up to 20 times more than your after-tax assets.

3. **The best estate plan is to effectively increase your exemptions beyond your assets so there is no tax to pay**. Most people begin their estate planning by adding up their assets and then subtracting the amount of their allowable exemptions. The amount that remains is the amount they believe they have to pay taxes on. To protect that amount for their heirs they then undertake any number and combination of convoluted legal plans and trusts. But using life insurance, estate planning is much simpler than that. Clearly, if the amount of your exemptions equaled the amount of your estate, you would have no further planning to do. Using life insurance, that is exactly what can occur. You add up your estate, purchase a life insurance policy with a death benefit equal to your estate tax exposure, and effectively exempt

your entire estate from estate taxes. The bottom line balances and the trusts and gifts and plans become obsolete.

4. **All estate planning is done backwards! You should buy insurance first, then see an attorney**. Traditionally, life insurance is the last thing considered, the afterthought to all other plans. This couldn't be more wrong or more backward. If you follow the conventional wisdom, you'll figure out your tax exposure, shelter as much money as you can to avoid taxes, and pay a small fortune along the way in attorney costs and maintenance fees. You'll wind up renting your own home back from the heirs you gifted it to or jointly owning the business you spent your life building or selling cherished possessions during your lifetime to limit the eventual tax implications for your children. Then, after all those plans are made, you'll look at what's left and consider buying insurance to protect it. This couldn't be more wrong. In almost every case I've seen, the bottom line works out much better if you undertake the process exactly opposite from the conventional wisdom. First, you should get a medical exam. Second, you should find out how much insurance you can buy given your age, finances, and rating. Only after you've bought insurance to protect as much of your estate as you possibly can should you start examining the remaining ramifications and making additional plans.

5. **Buying life insurance is not an expense**. There is no difference if, at your death, your heirs get a three to ten times return from your stocks, your real estate, or your life insurance. It has never failed to astonish me when people who balk at the "expense" of life insurance turn around and invest their money in the stock market in order to earn a return they hope will benefit their heirs. Life insurance is not an investment. But it is also not an expense. It is a financial vehicle

that produces a return in excess of what was paid for it. In fact, as we will see in the next chapter, life insurance outperforms investments in every major yardstick there is for growth, predictability, and security. Life insurance is an alternative to investments and acts to increase the value of your money many times over. The outlay required to create the return can not in fairness be considered an expense any more than the initial cost of a stock that earns appreciation is considered to be an expense.

Furthermore, you must always keep in mind that no matter what magnificent return your investments net, they will be subject to capital gains taxes during your lifetime or estate taxes as they are passed to your heirs. Any investment you make must earn double the return a life insurance policy will yield in order to stay equal at death (assuming you're in a 55% estate tax bracket.) The purchase of a stock or other commodity offers no guarantees of what it will return, could produce a loss, could require more time than you have to earn its potential, and is then fully subject to taxation. Life insurance offers a predetermined and often guaranteed return, never produces a loss, makes its full return available the day you purchase it, and is free of income tax and, if properly structured, estate tax. How then could you consider the purchase of the stock to be an investment but call the purchase of life insurance an expense? Many people say they don't want to leave more to their children, yet this seems only to apply to life insurance as they continue to make investments.

6. **Life insurance is simply another asset or commodity that further diversifies your portfolio**. Diversification is the key to a safe, well-managed portfolio. You would never put all your assets into one stock. You spread them around, investing some funds in dynamic growth vehicles, and some in safe

blue chips. You speculate with some, and put others into an IRA. In short, you cover yourself and minimize your risk while maximizing your potential. But any portfolio that doesn't include life insurance can not be considered to be truly safe or truly diversified. There is one thing all your investments — from the mavericks to the blue chips — have in common. They all need time to earn their returns. But life insurance produces its full return from the first day it is purchased. So only life insurance — the Investment Alternative — can offer immediate protection for your estate and heirs in the event tragedy occurs.

The second six principles examine the creative means available for paying for insurance to limit your outlay while achieving optimized results:

7. **Utilize the appreciation of your passive IRA by effectively increasing a $2 million IRA up to $38 million at your death**. Many wealthy people have funds in an IRA, pension, profit sharing plan, or annuity that constitute what I call "junk money". Other financial professionals call them "passive funds" or "excess funds", but the meaning is the same. They are funds for which the owner has no intended purpose or real need — funds that sit on the bottom of the owner's pile of money—and they are generally being held as a legacy for the owner's heirs. But what people fail to consider as they leave those funds to amass interest and grow, is that upon their deaths, as the funds pass to their heirs, they will be subject to estate taxes that can reduce them by more than half. Unneeded IRA funds can be far more effectively utilized as a means for paying for insurance protection. Even after paying the income taxes that may be due upon selling the asset, the remaining funds can be leveraged to produce an up to

10 times return that will come to your heirs income and estate tax free. This strategy can not only prevent the loss of up to 70% of the IRA, pension, or annuity asset to income and estate taxes, it can protect and optimize your entire estate for your heirs.

8. **Effectively increase your Municipal Bond yields from 5% to 15% utilizing the difference to buy life insurance**. We will examine this principle in more depth in the next chapter. However, it is important to note that while Municipal Bonds are income tax free, they are not estate tax free as they pass to your heirs. If you own Municipal Bonds the principal of which you are intending as a legacy, you may have within them the means to purchase life insurance that will greatly increase what your heirs receive without negatively affecting the income you receive. The bottom line is simple and clear. Many people can receive the exact same income on an after-tax basis as their bonds are currently producing tax free and still have enough cash left over to buy life insurance for the benefit of their heirs. If you were one of them, wouldn't you be foolish to do anything else?

9. **Review your insurance to possibly reduce the cost of existing policies or increase your death benefit for the same outlay**. Many people shy away from the very idea of replacing an existing insurance policy. Unfortunately, a few bad apples in the insurance industry who exploited customers' naivete for their own gain made headlines in recent years and called into question the whole question of replacement. But as I explain in the chapter entitled *The Bottom Line on Insurance* and demonstrate in the Case Study on page 192, there are many instances in which replacement is the wise, responsible course to follow. And in those instances, appro-

priate replacement of an obsolete policy can result in an increased death benefit and effectively "pay" for more coverage.

10. **Using tax deductible loans, you can pay for insurance that will effectively increase the value of your home up to ten times**. Conventional wisdom has long held that, as soon as you can afford to, you should live a debt-free life. But does that really make sense? Too often we accept the conventional wisdom without thinking it through and such is the case with this belief. In fact, as I demonstrate in the concept entitled *Convert Your Debts to Assets* on page 63, you can often use a debt to create a valuable asset. Consider this: a mortgage on your home can be tax deductible, so its real cost to you is about half the annual interest. Yet, the funds produced by mortgaging your home can buy life insurance with a net return of up to 10 times. The value of your home will ultimately be reduced by estate taxes so your mortgage-free property is really worth as little as half to your heirs, which makes the leverage of life insurance equal to a 20 times return. But a tax-deductible mortgage against it can produce the funds to pay for insurance that will protect not only its value, but also the value of your entire estate. Which makes more sense, the conventional wisdom or the bottom line thinking of my life insurance concepts?

11. **Borrow against your stocks, accrue interest, pay nothing until you die and then it is tax deductible**. If you could buy life insurance to create or preserve wealth for your heirs without it costing you a dime in your lifetime, would you do it? You can. If you're worth $3 million or more you undoubtedly have some significant amount of funds invested in stocks, bonds, or other commodities. Those investments can be one of the best sources of the funds to buy insurance. You

can take a loan against your investment assets for as little as 7% a year interest at current Libor rates. But with your stock and bond portfolio as collateral securing the loan, your stock brokerage firm won't require that you pay the interest or principal on the loan. You can simply accrue them both until your death. At that time, your heirs will have to repay both the loan principal and interest. The entire loan simply becomes a liability thereby reducing the estate thus reducing the estate taxes. In effect, this means Uncle Sam pays off half of all loans. This may seem like an unnecessary burden upon your heirs until you consider that you can use the borrowed amount to purchase life insurance that can produce as much as a ten times return. Even after paying back the interest and principal, your heirs will come out way ahead and it will never cost you a dime during your lifetime or negatively impact your own lifestyle.

12. **Simply pay insurance premiums from your own cash flow**. If it is really your intention to leave your heirs the most optimized legacy possible, buy insurance. As you will plainly see on the pages that follow, nothing else compares. With knowledgeable advise as to what policy to purchase on whom and how, the returns that life insurance produces and the terms under which it produces them are inarguably the single most effective means of maximizing your legacy.

When applied to the goals of estate planning, these "12 Principles" can serve as the guideline to the most cost-effective, efficient "Die Rich" techniques. We will be examining each of them in more detail on the pages that follow but if you take nothing else away from the reading of this book, take them right to your bottom line.

Wealth Creation

There are really only two purposes for money: to be spent and to be used to make more money. The first one always seems to take care of itself without any difficulty. The second is what this section of my book is about.

There are numerous ways available to accomplish the goal of increasing one's assets. They include savings and CD accounts, stocks, bonds, annuities, business interests, real estate and other investments. All of them have value and all of them have historical evidence to prove they work. Yet, as I touched upon in the previous chapter, they are all flawed in three important ways.

1. **Investments require time to grow**. Time you may not have. The best stock in the world isn't worth the paper the certificate is printed on if you die before it reaches its potential.

2. **Investments don't offer guaranteed returns**. No matter how educated, your guess is still a guess. You might win big. You might lose. But you can not plan with any certainty what the outcome will be.

3. **Investment earnings are subject to income taxes that can reduce them by up to one-third**. For every $3 step you take forward, you must be prepared to take a $1 step back. Furthermore, the $2 that is left is subject to estate taxes of up to 55% as it passes to your heirs when you die. They could ultimately get less than $1.

These three flaws are especially evident if any part of your investment strategy is intended to build up your estate for the ultimate benefit of your heirs. Without a guarantee of time to earn returns, without foreknowledge of what those returns may be, and faced with the certainty of taxes, any thought you have of using your investments to create a legacy for your heirs is nothing more than a wish and a hope.

The only financial vehicle available that successfully avoids these three pitfalls is the one that is most often overlooked: life insurance.

Life insurance was once thought of strictly as a means of replacing income in the event of the premature death of a breadwinner. But because it enjoys certain advantages that distinguish it from investments, in many instances life insurance is actually more perfectly suited to the goal of using money to make more money than is anything else available. It is these advantages that make life insurance the perfect investment alternative in any well-diversified portfolio intended to increase your legacy.

1. **Life insurance pays its stated return the very day it is purchased should the circumstances arise.** It doesn't need time to grow; its potential is fulfilled from the very beginning.

2. **Life insurance benefits are predetermined from the inception of the policy**. Although in some instances the amount of death benefit is 'based on current assumptions', it is still a more reliable outcome than almost any investment can offer. More importantly, the recent advent of guaranteed policies takes away all uncertainty. Plus, as I will detail later, any investment you make is also, in effect, 'based on current assumptions.'

3. **Life insurance benefits come to your heirs income tax free**. Life insurance is also an extremely easy asset to structure within an Irrevocable Trust so its proceeds will not be subject to estate taxes. These tax savings can total up to 70% of the asset's gross pre-tax value so they effectively increase the net return by as much as three times.

Some people try to answer the claims regarding life insurance's effectiveness by asserting that it is only of value in the event that the insured dies 'early'. And clearly, insurance's value to their heirs if they were to die tomorrow is incontrovertible. As we've just seen, nothing will produce the returns insurance does the very day after it is purchased. And since any of us could die tomorrow it seems clear to me that insurance is a must.

LIFE INSURANCE OUTPERFORMS YOUR INVESTMENT PORTFOLIO ... GUARANTEED

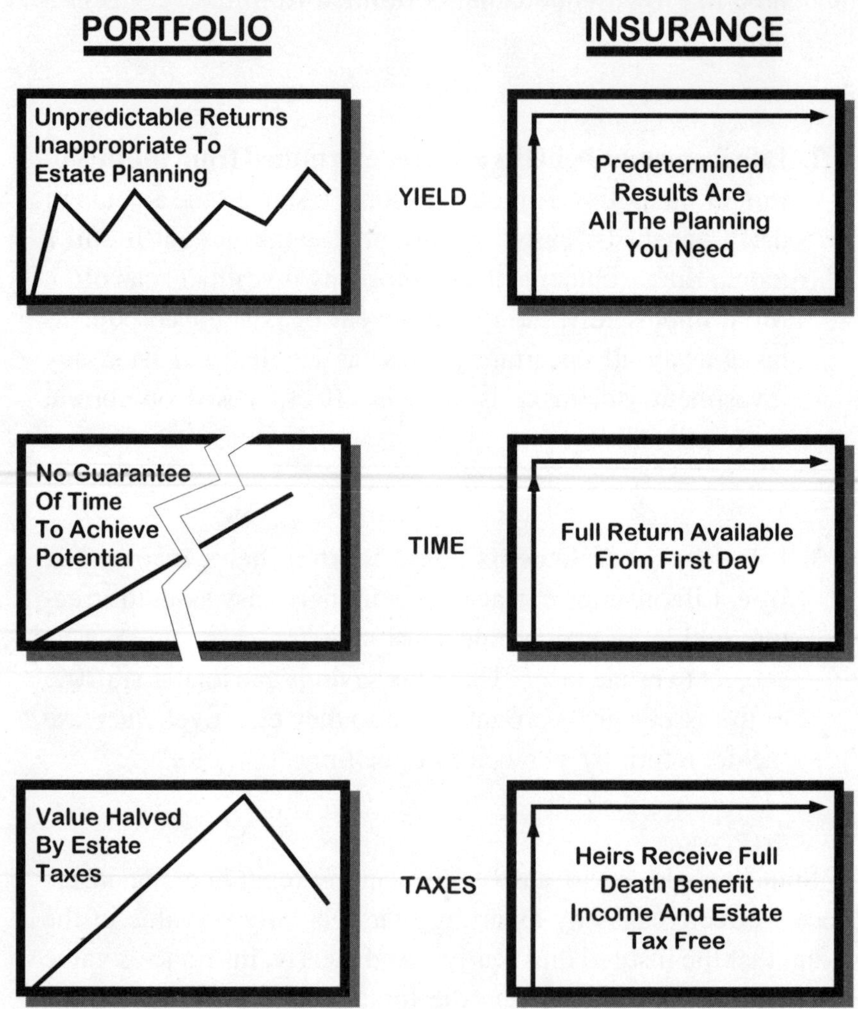

DIVERSIFY, REALLOCATE, MAXIMIZE USING THE INVESTMENT ALTERNATIVE

All figures are based on current assumptions. Charts are for illustrative purposes only.

But insurance is not only a good buy if you die early in the policy's life. The cash values that a universal life policy accrues, though not an investment or a savings plan, function in much the same way; they can be borrowed against or even withdrawn from the policy. This means that the value of the policy is not only vested in the short term 'hope' for an early death to best take advantage of the death benefit. The fact of the matter is, insurance compares extremely favorably throughout the course of your life against practically any bank or savings institution that holds people's money and returns them an increase in the form of earned interest. In fact, an insurance policy completely surpasses the bank return in value because it not only builds up this comparable cash value, but also has available the highly optimized death benefit against the eventual inevitability of your family's need of it.

Look at charts that follow on pages 45 and 46. They detail the course money takes when placed into a savings account versus when it is used to purchase insurance. The results of the comparison are very important.

In the beginning the savings account is worth more than the insurance policy. $1.05 million in the bank equates to a little over $800,000 in the policy. However, while the bank is about $250,000 ahead of the insurance policy while you're alive, should tragedy strike, the policy would immediately optimize and become worth $5.8 million more than the savings account.

Look how closely the insurance policy keeps pace with the savings account through the twelfth year. The gap between cash value and compounded savings gets narrower and narrower. Yet the only growth the savings offer is the interest, while the insurance continues to have in reserve a $6.85 million death benefit. Would you really prefer an additional $14,000 over a $6.85 million death benefit?

Now look at year thirteen. The insurance policy cash values have surpassed the compounded savings and the policy still has that $6.8 million death benefit waiting in reserve for the day it is needed.

By year twenty the policy has over $200,000 more in cash values than the savings account has earned. And the $6.85 million remains in reserve.

The policy continues to surpass the savings account through the thirty-second year by which time the owner is 92 years old. Do you think consideration of that death benefit might be in order now? The savings account contains about $4.76 million while the policy only has $4.75 million. But the policy still has the $6.85 million death benefit which, at age 92, has to be something the owner is thinking about.

Only if the owner lives to be 100 does the savings account surpass the insurance death benefit and then only by about $150,000. Is that extra $150,000 worth running the risk that you don't make it to age 100?

And now here's something that I hope will really make you understand the phenomenal nature of life insurance as an investment alternative. To be truly accurate, you must go back to the chart and cut all the savings account numbers in half.

As long as the funds held in the savings account remain within the estate of the owner, they will be subject to estate taxes as they pass on to his or her heirs. Those estate taxes will reduce them by as much of 55%. So the $7 million accrued in the savings account by year 40 will be reduced by about half to $3.5 million while the death benefit proceeds from the insurance, if they have been properly structured within an Irrevocable Trust or are owned by the children, will come to the heirs income and estate tax free. Pick any year and do the math. The results are unarguable. In every way and every sense, the life insur-

Savings Account vs. Insurance Policy

Age 60	Bank	Insurance	
Year	Life or Death at 5% Tax Free	In Life Cash Value	At Death Policy Pays
1	1,050,000	801,322	6,850,000
2	1,102,500	882,554	6,850,000
3	1,157,625	959,930	6,850,000
4	1,215,506	1,039,126	6,850,000
5	1,276,281	1,120,336	6,850,000
6	1,340,095	1,209,246	6,850,000
7	1,407,100	1,289,812	6,850,000
8	1,477,455	1,380,916	6,850,000
9	1,551,328	1,470,459	6,850,000
10	1,628,894	1,572,504	6,850,000
11	1,710,339	1,678,048	6,850,000
12	1,795,856	1,781,194	6,850,000
13	1,885,649	1,895,409	6,850,000
14	1,979,931	2,014,234	6,850,000
15	2,078,928	2,138,682	6,850,000
16	2,182,874	2,268,654	6,850,000
17	2,292,018	2,403,264	6,850,000
18	2,406,619	2,549,930	6,850,000
19	2,526,950	2,694,646	6,850,000
20	2,653,297	2,881,304	6,850,000

Bank money usually in estate and cut in half at death by estate taxes. Investment Alternative usually out of estate and tax free.

*All figures are based on current assumptions.

Savings Account vs. Insurance Policy

Age 60	Bank	Insurance	
Year	Life or Death at 5% Tax Free	In Life Cash Value	At Death Policy Pays
21	2,785,962	2,990,835	6,850,000
22	2,925,260	3,133,599	6,850,000
23	3,071,523	3,279,170	6,850,000
24	3,225,099	3,428,864	6,850,000
25	3,386,354	3,582,103	6,850,000
26	3,555,672	3,738,796	6,850,000
27	3,733,456	3,898,716	6,850,000
28	3,920,129	4,062,389	6,850,000
29	4,116,135	4,228,497	6,850,000
30	4,321,942	4,397,874	6,850,000
31	4,538,039	4,571,741	6,850,000
32	4,764,941	4,751,514	6,850,000
33	5,003,188	4,939,593	6,850,000
34	5,253,347	5,139,148	6,850,000
35	5,516,015	5,353,664	6,850,000
36	5,791,816	5,587,795	6,850,000
37	6,081,406	5,847,024	6,850,000
38	6,385,477	6,137,912	6,850,000
39	6,704,751	6,468,894	6,850,000
40	7,039,988	6,850,386	6,850,000

Bank money usually in estate and cut in half at death by estate taxes. Investment Alternative usually out of estate and tax free.

*All figures are based on current assumptions.

ance out performs the safe, conservative, solid financial vehicle of a bank savings account.

Clearly, life insurance is not merely a financial vehicle that protects one's economic life against death by producing benefits. It is an asset, a commodity that diversifies any financial portfolio. That life insurance has not traditionally been thought of in this way has led to numerous financial tragedies that are made even more tragic in that they could have been so simply avoided. Fortunately, in more recent times, acceptance of this uniquely valuable tool has grown and, as a result, wealth has been created and preserved for hundreds of thousands of families all across America.

Later in this book, I will share with you many of the techniques I have developed to utilize the unique potentials of life insurance to increase and preserve assets. You will see in both theory and application what life insurance can achieve and you will learn how it accomplishes its dramatic outcomes. Most importantly, you will learn to eschew the conventional thinking about life insurance and come to see the potentials and possibilities that characterize it.

I invite you to take any of the concepts and techniques presented in this book to your accountant, attorney, financial planner, and/or stockbroker for comparison of the outcome. Go with them to the bottom line result being sure to take into consideration the realities of time and taxes. See for yourself how, in every case in which your planning and intentions include leaving behind a legacy of protection and security for your heirs, the concepts here will be shown to be superior.

Most of all, I ask you to keep an open mind. I know that you probably have some deep discomfort with the topic of life insurance. Most of us for whom these concepts are of value come from a time in which the sale of life insurance was most often accomplished by pushy, overbearing, relentless salesmen who left their customers feeling like hunted prey. Furthermore, life insurance cannot be discussed without an admission of mortality, an admission that most of us would prefer not to have to make. We all know we will die someday. But few of us really want to sit and discuss the financial implications our deaths will have upon the world we leave behind.

Yet, our reluctance to face the truth won't prevent it. It will simply leave us unprepared and may jeopardize our good intentions for our families, friends, business associates, and charities. We can leave behind a diminished legacy, the remnants of our fear. Or we can die rich and leave behind an optimized estate, a testament to the power of our love and devotion to overcome our discomfort. The choice is simply that, a choice. I hope you make the right one. You are going to die whether you buy life insurance or not.

On the following pages, we will follow the course of money to compare what happens when conventional wisdom is applied to planning versus when my wealth creation methods are employed. We will examine several different scenarios for maximizing assets, converting losses into gains, and diversifying portfolios to achieve highly optimized returns.

For the sake of these examples, we will utilize two couples, the Smiths and the Joneses. The Smiths will follow the traditional path. The Joneses will utilize my creative techniques. While it might seem a simplistic or even "hokey" device, following them both to the bottom line we will clearly see the advantages life insurance as part of a diversified financial portfolio can yield. And I have no doubt that when you do that, you will definitely want to 'keep up with the Joneses'.

In the examples, we will assume both the Smiths and Joneses will be using last-to-die policies purchased on a one-pay basis and that they both qualify for Preferred rates. You can customize each example to your own situation by adding or subtracting zeroes as needed and rounding the numbers up or down. The Preferred rates that would apply at your age, marital status, and payment mode can all be found at the back of this book on the charts that begin on page 253. In addition, many of the examples given are available in a fully interactive state on my website at *www.DieRich2.com.* Simply select "Interactive Concepts" from the main menu and follow the instructions to see exactly how these concepts would apply to you.

All rates used in the examples are based on actual rates available through leading insurers. For the sake of simplicity, we assume returns of 10–to–1 for average age 60, 5–to–1 for average age 70, and 3–to–1 for average age 80 based on current assumptions of interest and mortality. [For a full explanation of how "Based on Current Assumptions" (BOCA) impacts an insurance policy, see pages 211–215.] Though guaranteed policies that avoid the "based on current assumptions" caveat are now available through many insurers, today's low interest rates allow us to use the less expensive BOCA rates in relative safety.

For more information on how to determine what payment option and policy type is best for you, see pages 232–247.

Many of the examples given have more than one option for how they are executed. Insuring your children for the benefit of your grandchildren will obviously yield greatly enhanced returns. Borrowing the money for the premium payments and/or gifting some or all of an asset's value to charity, will also alter your final outcome and tax ramifications. I will try to explore a range of available procedures. However it would be far too complicated to give every possible deviation within each individual example.

I recommend that once you understand how valuable these concepts can be, you consult your insurance specialist and a qualified attorney to review how best to apply them to your needs and goals.

In many examples in which loans are taken to pay for insurance premiums, I will state that "Uncle Sam repays half your loan." This refers to the fact that any loan outstanding against your estate at the time of your death reduces your estate by the loan amount. Since I generally assume your estate tax liability to be 55%, or approximately half, any amount by which your estate is reduced "saves" your heirs the 55% tax they would have had to pay on that amount had it remained in your estate. In this way, they "save" half the loan amount—an amount Uncle Sam can be thought of as paying. In effect, you have made all loans tax deductible at your death.

Simply demonstrated, if you have an outstanding $1 million loan against your $10 million estate at the time of your death, your estate value is decreased to $9 million. The estate taxes on $10 million would be about $5 million and your heirs would be left $5 million. But the estate taxes on $9 million are about $4.5 million, leaving your heirs $4.5 million. Without the loan, your heirs receive $5 million. With it, they receive $4.5 million. So, the cost of the $1 million loan to your heirs was only $500,000—Uncle Sam effectively paid half.

Estate taxes are $1.1 million on the first $3 million and then approximately 55% on any amount over $3 million. So, for example, a $6 million estate would face estate taxes of $1.1 million on the first $3 million and $1.65 million, 55%, of the second $3 million for a total of $2.75 million. Due to this method of calculation, estate taxes do not become a straight 55% until you reach an estate valuation of $24 million. For examples using less than $24 million, I have either stated the actual estate tax rate or simply utilized the actual estate tax amount, which you can find in the charts at the back of this book, beginning on page 253.

Please try to leave your preconceptions and misconceptions behind as you follow these examples through to their conclusions. Don't let misinformation, fear or unreasoned resistance dissuade you from an honest evaluation of the bottom line.

Though I have been credited with creating these concepts, in fact, I only discovered the basics and rearranged them to make it easier for you to understand. They exist not because I invented them, but because of the workings of simple mathematics and arithmetic. And mathematics don't lie. You will always find the truth at the bottom line.

Pension, Profit Sharing, 401(k), and/or IRA Maximizer

In this example, the Smiths and Joneses are average age 70 and therefore earning a 5–to–1 return on their insurance purchases. Both couples have an IRA worth $4 million as part of their $25 million estates. Both are in a 55% estate tax bracket and neither needs the income the IRA produces to fund their own lifestyle, consideration for which must come first in all planning. They are both intending the IRA to be part of the legacy they leave their heirs. Let's look at what happens when the Smiths hold their IRA for their heirs and the Joneses apply their IRA to a wealth creation technique.

The Smiths hold onto their IRA and leave it to their heirs after their deaths. Because an IRA is a tax-deferred asset, at that time the heirs will have to pay income taxes on the total fund. Assuming a 40% tax bracket for the heirs, those income taxes will equal $1.6 million. (This calcuation is always done in reverse.)

Estate taxes will claim 55% of the remaining $2.4 million asset value after income taxes have been deducted. That would equal about $1.32 million.

What remains for the Smiths' heirs? $1.08 million.

The Joneses, who also don't need their IRA income to protect their current lifestyle or provide for their future welfare, take a different course. They terminate their IRA now and pay the $1.6 million of income taxes. They gift $2.25 million starting immediately through 2006. In this manner they pay no gift taxes on the first $2 million. On the last $250,000 they pay about $150,000.

The trust buys a second-to-die life insurance policy on the Joneses. Receiving a 5–to–1 return, the policy yields $11.25 million for the heirs income and estate tax free.

At best, the Smiths' heirs receive $1.1 million. The Joneses receive $11.25 million.

Follow the course of money to the best bottom line:

THE SMITHS' IRA AT DEATH:		THE JONESES' IRA USED NOW:	
$ 4,000,000	IRA	$ 4,000,000	IRA
– 1,600,000	40% Income Tax	– 1,600,000	40% Income Tax
$ 2,400,000		$ 2,400,000	
– 1,320,000	55% Estate Tax	– 2,250,000	Buys Insurance*
$ 1,080,000	To Heirs	– 150,000	Gift Tax
		$ 0	
		+11,250,000	Death Benefit
		$11,250,000	To Heirs

*They gift $2.25 million starting immediately through 2006 and pay no gift taxes on the first $2 million. On the last $250,000 they pay about $150,000.

At average age 60, the insurance results are double those shown in this example and the Joneses' heirs receive $22.5 million. Even at exact age 80, this method yields $6.75 million for the Joneses' heirs, more than six times what the Smiths' heirs will receive.

At virtually any age, the insurance method yields significantly better returns than holding the IRA until death.

THE JONESES AT AGE 60:		THE JONESES AT AGE 80:	
$ 4,000,000	IRA	$ 4,000,000	IRA
– 1,600,000	Income Tax	– 1,600,000	Income Tax
$ 2,400,000		$ 2,400,000	
– 2,250,000	Buys Insurance*	– 2,250,000	Buys Insurance*
– 150,000	Gift Tax	– 150,000	Gift Tax
$ 0		$ 0	
+22,500,000	Death Benefit	+ 6,750,000	Death Benefit
$22,500,000	To Heirs	$ 6,750,000	To Heirs

*They gift $2.25 million starting immediately through 2006 and pay no gift taxes on the first $2 million. On the last $250,000 they pay about $150,000.

Of course, some people might be thinking about the potential growth that exists in the Smiths' IRA. The Joneses have cashed theirs out, it can't grow any further. That might be seen to be limiting the full potential return. But consider this. For the Smiths' $4 million IRA to be worth $11 million to their heirs, it would have to grow to $42 million during their lifetimes.

The $42 million IRA would be subject to income tax of 40%, which would reduce it $16.8 million to $25.2 million. After paying 55% estate taxes of $13.9 million, the heirs would receive $11.3 million.

The Smiths are 70 years old. Is it really likely that they will live long enough for their $4 million IRA to increase in value to $42 million in order to match the $11 million inheritance the Joneses are leaving for their heirs? Using life insurance, the Joneses have eliminated this element of time and risk. No matter how much time is left to them, they are secure in the knowledge that their heirs will receive an optimized $11 million.

A $4 million IRA has to grow to $42 million to yield $9 million after taxes:

$42,000,000	**IRA**
– 16,800,000	**40% Income Tax**
$25,200,000	
– 13,900,000	**55% Estate Tax**
$ 11,300,000	**Net To Heirs**

Of course, if you truly don't want to distribute your IRA to accomplish the optimized returns the Joneses' heirs will enjoy, there is still a way to maximize your IRA and increase what your heirs will receive.

Using the yearly appreciation earned by your IRA's principal, you can purchase an insurance policy for even more than $10 million without ever touching your original IRA principal. You can avoid all taxes at death by donating your IRA to charity or your own foundation.

But no matter what your preference, no matter how you look at it, the end result is greatly enhanced by the use of life insurance.

Municipal Bond Alternative

Many, if not most, people of significant affluence include in their portfolios some municipal bonds in order to take advantage of what they think of as their "tax free" nature. But municipal bonds are not tax free. They are income tax free, and that can be a valuable advantage. But they are still subject to up to 55% estate taxes.

For the sake of this example, we'll assume that both the Smiths and the Joneses have $30 million in municipal bonds as part of their overall estates. Both couples are average age 80 and enjoy the $1.5 million of tax free income their municipal bonds yield each year. They appreciate that they save $600,000 in income taxes on the return.

The Smiths use their annual $1.5 million income to support their lifestyle and accept as a necessary evil the eventual $16.5 million loss the asset will suffer upon their deaths. They would certainly like their heirs to inherit more than the $13.5 million that will remain, but they know of no other means for the same $30 million to produce the annual $1.5 million they need. They grin and bear the grim eventuality.

The Joneses follow a different course; one that allows them to retain the income they have come to rely upon and still pass almost the whole $30 million on to their heirs.

The Joneses sell their municipal bonds and use the money to buy an immediate annuity. Though their principle "vanishes" upon the purchase of the annuity, tax advantages in respect to the income it produces[1] create a highly optimized return. The Joneses' $30 million immediate annuity can be expected to return $3 million after taxes–twice the tax free return yielded by the municipal bond.

Keeping the same $1.5 million annual income that their municipal bonds were producing, the Joneses use the remaining $1.5 million of optimized annual income to purchase a last-to-die life insurance policy on themselves for the benefit of their heirs. Each year, they transfer $1 million to an irrevocable trust and pay $500,000 in gift taxes. The $1 million is used to purchase the insurance, which yields a death benefit of $33 million to their heirs, income and estate tax free. The heirs not only receive back the entire $30 million with no taxes due, but they receive an addi-

Using an immediate annuity, the Joneses retain their income and leave significantly more for their heirs.

SMITHS:		JONESES:	
$30,000,000	Municipal Bonds	$30,000,000	Immediate Annuity
x 5%	Tax Free Yield	x 10%	After Tax Yield
$ 1,500,000	Yearly Income	$ 3,000,000	Annual Income
		– 1,000,000	Transfer to Trust
$30,000,000	Municipal Bonds	– 500,000	Gift Tax
–16,500,000	Estate Tax	$ 1,500,000	Yearly Income
$13,500,000	To Heirs		
		$30,000,000	Municipal Bonds
		–30,000,000	Transfer to Annuity
		+33,000,000	Insurance Proceeds
		$33,000,000	To Heirs

[1] Because the government recognizes some portion of the income produced by an immediate annuity to be a return of principal, it taxes only the interest for life expectancy. This creates a significant opportunity for older people for whom income is more important than principal.

tional $3 million. They still come out way ahead of the Smiths' heirs who will lose $16.5 million to estate taxes and have only $13.5 million left.

If the Joneses don't need all the income their immediate annuity produces, they can increase their insurance purchase and create wealth beyond the original $30 million for their heirs. If they could diversify another $500,000 annually to this plan, they would pay an additional $175,000 in yearly gift taxes to transfer $325,000 to the trust to purchase another $10 million of insurance for their heirs. The heirs would inherit a total of $43 million tax free—$13 million more than the original $30 million.

Any funds not needed to support your lifestyle can be leveraged to achieve incredible results using life insurance.

JONESES:

$ 500,000	Used Per Year
– 325,000	Buys Insurance
– 175,000	Gift Tax
+10,000,000	Insurance Proceeds
$ 10,000,000	Available To Heirs Upon Death

Maximize the Value of Businesses and Real Estate

Many wealthy people earned their fortunes in businesses they created and grew. Some will pass those businesses on to their heirs. But for some that might not be an option. What do you do when your children aren't interested in the family business or the times have changed and it is no longer as profitable a venture as it once was?

At age 60, the Smiths have decided to sell their small chain of grocery stores that can no longer compete against the big chains and retire. At their peak, the stores made them rich and were valued at $20 million. Now they will be lucky to get $10 million.

At the same time, the Joneses have decided to sell a commercial strip mall they developed many years ago in a neighborhood that has since gone downhill. Also once worth $20 million, they are now being offered $10 million for the property.

The Smiths find a buyer and accept $10 million, resigning themselves to a $10 million "loss" over the business' peak value. After estate taxes, the Smiths' children will receive about $4.5 million. But what else can the Smiths do? The big chain is squeezing them out and things will only get worse if they don't accept this offer.

The Joneses accept the $10 million they are offered for their property and immediately transfer $1 million to an irrevocable trust for the purchase of life insurance. Since the $1 million falls within their Unified Gift and Estate Tax Credit, they pay no gift taxes on the transfer.

The trust buys a last-to-die life insurance policy on the Joneses with a $10 million death benefit.

The $9 million remaining from the sale price added to the $10 million death benefit equals $19 million. The Joneses have recaptured almost the full $20 million the property was worth at its peak.

Even after the remaining $9 million they received from the sale of the property is reduced by estate taxes to approximately $4.6 million[2], the Joneses' heirs' net inheritance attributable to the property sale is up to $14.6 million.

The net sales price is effectively tripled for your heirs using these "Die Rich" optimization techniques.

THE SMITHS' BUSINESS:		THE JONESES' REAL ESTATE:	
$10,000,000	Sale Price	$10,000,000	Sale Price
– 5,500,000	Estate Taxes	– 1,000,000	Insurance Premium
$ 4,500,000	To Heirs	$ 9,000,000	Remaining Asset
		– 4,400,000	Estate Taxes[3]
		+10,000,000	Insurance Proceeds
		$14,600,000	To Heirs

As an added benefit to this plan, Uncle Sam effectively pays for half the insurance premium.

The sales price of the property was $10 million, which after estate taxes would have been reduced by about half to $5 million, leaving $5 million. By making the $1 million insurance purchase,

[2] $4.6 million represents the estate taxes on $9 million if that amount represents the Joneses' total estate. If their property is part of a larger estate, taxes will be higher.

the $10 million is reduced to $9 million and the estate taxes are reduced to $4.4 million, leaving $4.6 million. The difference between the two results is only $400,000, not $1 million. The other $600,000 would have gone straight to the government so the purchase of insurance can not be considered to be a loss or expense.

Even though the insurance costs $1 million, estate taxes reduce the difference to the heirs to only $400,000. Uncle Sam effectively pays for half the premium!

THE SMITHS' ESTATE ASSETS WITHOUT INSURANCE:		THE JONESES' ESTATE ASSETS WITH INSURANCE:	
$10,000,000	Sale Price	$10,000,000	Sale Price
– 5,00,000	Estate Taxes	– 1,000,000	Insurance Premium
$ 5,000,000	To Heirs	$ 9,000,000	Remaining Asset
		– 4,400,000	Estate Taxes
		$ 4,600,000	To Heirs
		$ 5,000,000	To Smith Heirs
		– 4,600,000	To Jones Heirs
		$ 400,000	Net Cost for Insurance
		$ 4,600,000	After tax estate
		+10,000,000	Insurance Proceeds
		$14,600,000	Net To Heirs

Plus the Joneses' heirs still get $10 million of insurance!

Convert Your Debts to Assets

For a long time, conventional wisdom has held that, to the greatest extent possible we are better off living debt free. But, as is generally discovered to be the case with so much "common knowledge", when we rethink the accepted theory we find that it does not fully accommodate all the possibilities. In fact, there are occasions in which you can use your debts to make you even richer.

In this demonstration, we will use for our examples Mrs. Smith and Mrs. Jones, both 70-year-old widows and both of whom own homes worth about $500,000 as part of their $7 million estates.

Mrs. Smith used some of the insurance benefits she received upon her husband's passing to pay off the mortgage on the house. Now she owns it free and clear and is extremely pleased to be free of mortgage debt. She saves approximately $31,500 a year which is what a 7% mortgage on 90% of the home's value would cost. And she is pleased to know that the property will pass to her heirs without encumbrance. She is living the conventional wisdom oblivious to the fact that there is a better way that could net a far greater legacy for her children and make her house worth much, much more.

Mrs. Jones also owned her house outright without mortgage or encumbrance.

But she realized that as her $7 million estate is in an approximate 47% estate tax bracket, the home's value would be reduced by estate taxes of $235,000 when it passed to her heirs. The $500,000 asset she was so proud to own was really only worth $265,000 to her children. Dismayed by this reality, Mrs. Jones sought a means to maximize the house's worth. She took out a mortgage on the home for 50% of its value—$250,000. At 7% interest a year, the mortgage cost her $17,500. But because the home is her primary residence, she receives a mortgage interest credit on her income taxes, which cuts the net cost to less than $10,000 a year.

Mrs. Jones then used the $250,000 from the mortgage to buy a one-pay life insurance policy on herself with her children as beneficiaries. Even at 70 years old, she was able to get a policy for $1 million. For $10,000 a year net cost, Mrs. Jones' children will receive $1 million income and estate tax free.

Even after the Jones children pay off the $250,000 mortgage debt, they will still have $750,000. Plus, they will own the home, worth an additional $500,000, for a total of $1.25 million.

In addition, when they inherit the house, the outstanding $250,000 mortgage will lower its value from $500,000 to $250,000. Estate taxes on the $250,000 will only be $117,500 instead of the $235,000 Mrs. Smith's heirs will have to pay on the unmortgaged home they are to inherit. So the Jones children will 'save' an additional $117,500 in taxes.

Using your mortgage 'debt' you can vastly increase its value to your heirs'.

MRS. SMITHS' HOME:

$	500,000	Home Value
–	235,000	Estate Taxes
$	265,000	Value To Heirs

MRS. JONES' HOME:

$	500,000	Home Value
–	250,000	Mortgage
$	250,000	Remaining Asset
–	117,500	Estate Taxes
+	1,000,000	Insurance Proceeds
$	1,132,500	Value To Heirs

The bottom line is a net additional $867,500 to the heirs from the same house. Yet many people, still skeptical, are quick to point out that the woman must pay a net $10,000 per year on her mortgage. Let's take a look at that and, for the sake of simplicity, let's not take into account the fact that as she pays off the mortgage Mrs. Jones is paying off principal and interest so that the longer she lives the less her heirs will owe. Even setting that aside, if Mrs. Jones pays $10,000 a year for 10 years, she'll be 80 years old and her children will still net $767,500 more than the Smith children did. If Mrs. Jones lives to be 90, her mortgage will cost her $200,000, leaving a $667,500 gain for her heirs. If she lives to be 100, she'll probably have paid off the mortgage. Now her children will receive $300,000 less in proceeds from her estate. This will reduce her estate taxes by $141,000 so the real cost to the heirs is only $159,000. But they once again inherit a house that is worth its full, unmortgaged value of $500,000. Plus they still have a gain of $567,500 from the insurance proceeds.

Clearly the conventional wisdom is a lot more convention than it is wise. Living debt free may satisfy some outdated idea of what success is. But if you measure success in terms of the strongest bottom line for your children, you'll have to agree that it is just plain antiquated thinking.

Also, remember that to implement this method you wouldn't necessarily have to take a 50% mortgage on the house. If you want to pay less in annual mortgage costs, you could borrow 25% of the value of your home, or even just 10%. In this way, you can execute planning that is comfortable for your lifestyle. Of course, your heirs will receive less death benefit. However, I always make it a point to caution people not to sacrifice their own well-being for the sake of increasing their heirs' inheritance. Take care of yourself first — you only get one life and your first responsibility is to yourself. But beyond that, whatever you can do for your heirs should be maximized.

Of course, if you could afford to, you could take out a higher mortgage than 50%. With the tax advantages available for mortgage interest deductions, you might be able to afford the payments on a mortgage of 80% - 90% of your homes' value. In that case, you could almost double the amount of insurance you could purchase and truly create wealth for your loved ones.

I have deliberately shown this example using lower numbers but I do want to demonstrate the drama that can be achieved if your home is worth more and you can afford a higher mortgage.

If your house was worth $1 million and you took an 80% mortgage, you would have produced $800,000 which, when used to purchase insurance, could net your heirs $2.4 million - $8 million, depending on you and your spouse's average age. A $1.2 million mortgage against a $1.5 million home would produce between $3.6 million and $15 million. Will the real estate market ever increase your home's value by that much?

This technique for converting debts to assets can be used with collateral other than your home. While mortgages are a particularly attractive means for executing this concept because of the tax deductions allowed for mortgage interest, any loan that costs less than it nets can be optimized for your heirs in this way.

Maximize Gifts and Exemptions

After you attain a certain age and have amassed more than enough principal to provide for your welfare and enjoyment, most accountants will advise you to start depleting your estate by making yearly tax free gifts to your children in the maximum allowable amounts. There is some wisdom behind this strategy as every $10,000 gift you give decreases your estate and can save approximately $5,500 in estate taxes.[3] If you had three children and both you and your spouse gave them each $10,000 a year, each annual $60,000 in gifts could save as much as $33,000 in estate taxes. Over ten years, that could mean a significant tax savings of $330,000 going directly to your heirs instead of to the government.

But again, the conventional wisdom falls short of true optimization.

While $10,000 – $20,000 a year would undoubtedly be of value to your heirs, using that money to purchase a second-to-die life insurance policy on you and your spouse could net them far greater benefit.

Let's have the Smiths and Joneses demonstrate.

Both the Smiths and the Joneses average 60 years old. Both couples have two children and are worth $6 million. Both couples'

[3] Assuming your estate is in a 55% tax bracket.

estates are facing 45% estate taxes of $2.75 million which will deplete their children's inheritances and leave them only $3.25 million.

The Smiths' accountant advises them to each give both of their children the maximum allowable $10,000 gift per year. Doing so, the Smiths reduce their estate by $40,000 each year. Twenty years later, when they are both 80, their estate will have been reduced by $800,000. Their $5.2 million remaining estate will only be subject to estate taxes of 44% so their the total estate tax will be about $2.3 million, saving their heirs $400,000 in estate taxes.

While gifting does reduce estate tax, it doesn't begin to compare with the benefits of creating wealth.

TAXES WITHOUT GIFTING:		TAXES WITH GIFTING:	
$ 6,000,000	Estate Value	$ 6,000,000	Estate Value
X 45%		– 800,000	Gifts
$ 2,700,000	Estate Tax	$ 5,200,000	Adjusted Estate
		X 44%	
		$ 2,300,000	Estate Tax

The Joneses are also advised to each gift their two children $10,000 a year in order to remove that money from their estate for estate tax purposes. However, the Joneses gift the annual combined $40,000 to an Irrevocable Trust that uses the funds to purchase a second-to-die policy on the couple. At average age 60, the $40,000 in annual insurance premium purchases a policy with a $5 million death benefit. Now the Joneses enjoy double benefit from their gift. It still reduces their estate on a tax free basis by $800,000 over 20 years and saves their heirs $400,000 in estate taxes. But now it also produces an additional $5 million at a net cost of only $360,000.

Maximize your gifts to create significant wealth for your heirs.

THE SMITHS:		THE JONESES:	
$ 6,000,000	Estate	$ 6,000,000	Estate
$ 40,000	Annual Gifts[4]	$ 40,000	Annual Gifts
x 20	Years	x 20	Years
$ 800,000	Total Gifts	$ 800,000	Total Gifts
$ 6,000,000	Estate Value	$ 6,000,000	Estate Value
– 800,000	Total Gifts	– 800,000	Total Gifts
$ 5,200,000	Remaining Estate	$ 5,200,000	Remaining Estate
– 2,300,000	Estate Tax	– 2,300,000	Estate Tax
+ 800,000	Gifts	+ 5,000,000	Insurance Proceeds
$ 3,700,000	To Heirs	$ 7,900,000	To Heirs

[4] Based on $10,000 per parent for 2 children.

Would an extra $20,000 a year per child really be preferable to an ultimate gift of an extra $2.5 million per child?

Of course, if your children really need the financial help now, you could customize this program by diverting only a portion of the combined yearly gifts to the Irrevocable Trust for the purchase of insurance. The rest you could still gift directly to your children. In this way, four goals are achieved:

1. Your children get needed help now,
2. Your estate is reduced which saves them estate taxes later,
3. They have the proceeds of life insurance to pay the taxes with, and
4. Your gifts are optimized to yield a greatly increased inheritance.

For the absolute maximization of this concept, consider what can occur if you were to apply the same principles to your $675,000[5] lifetime gift exemption.

Many people hold onto their $675,000 exemption with the intent that it will help reduce estate tax costs at their deaths. In situations where the money may be needed in case of emergency or to help fund the couple's lifestyle, holding the exemption until death is probably the best course. However, if you can afford to gift your $675,000 individual exemption or $1.35 million combined exemptions during your lifetime(s), you have the means available to you to enact a fabulous feat of wealth creation.

Consider again the Smiths and Joneses each with their $6 million estates.

The Smiths plan to use their exemptions at death. They don't need the principal but they are investing it with the assumption that the earnings it generates will increase their estate for their heirs. The earnings produced by the remaining $4.65 million of their estate are used each year to fund their lifestyle.

If their $1.35 million earned 7% a year after tax for 20 years, it would grow to equal $5.4 million. At their deaths, the Smiths estate would be $10.1 million on which $5 million of estate taxes would be due. That would leave $5.1 million for their heirs.

The Joneses follow my "Die Rich" route. They use their combined $1.35 million exemptions now, transferring the funds to an Irrevocable Trust that purchases a one-pay last-to-die insurance policy on their lives. As they are 60 at the time of the purchase, they receive a 10–to–1 return of $13.5 million for their heirs.

Twenty years later, upon the deaths of their parents, the Joneses' heirs will receive their original $6 million estate minus the $1.35 million they transferred to the trust. That will leave them with $4.65 million. Taxes of $2 million will reduce the $4.65 million to

[5] In year 2000. Increasing to $1 million per individual and $2 million per couple in a marital situation by 2006.

$2.65 million. That $2.65 million will then be added to the $13.5 million of insurance benefit that the heirs will receive income and estate tax free for a total inheritance of $16.15 million.

The "Die Rich" technique more than triples the net amount of your gifts for your heirs.

THE SMITHS:		THE JONESES:	
$6,000,000 Estate		$ 6,000,000	Estate
		– 1,350,000	Exemption Transfer
$ 1,350,000	Invested	$ 4,650,000	Remaining Estate
x 20	Years of 7% Gain	– 2,000,000	Estate Tax
$ 5,400,000	Net	$ 2,650,000	Net Estate
+ 4,650,000	Static Estate	+13,500,000	Insurance Proceeds
$ 10,100,000	Total Estate	$ 16,150,000	To Heirs
– 5,000,000	Estate Tax		
$ 5,100,000	To Heirs		

Is there any real question which is the most effective plan? The Smiths' $5.1 million inheritance depends upon their $1.35 million investment earning 7% after tax every year for 20 years. The Joneses' $16.2 million inheritance is available immediately upon their deaths even if they die the very day after the insurance purchase is made.

This is another plan that can be executed in smaller increments as well. If transferring the $1.35 million combined exemptions depletes your principal beyond your comfort level, you can use only one $675,000 exemption and leave the other intact. Or you can use any other portion of one or both exemptions. Though the specific numbers change, the comparison remains exactly proportionate.

You can also improve this method for wealth creation. By 2006 your combined exemptions will be $2 million. At that time you will be able to remove $2 million from your estate with no gift taxes, thus allowing you to buy that much more insurance and creating even greater tax free leverage.

This is also a very effective means of optimizing your gifts for your spouse. You can buy insurance on you for the benefit of your spouse. Although at age 60 you won't receive the same 10–to–1 return on an individual policy that you can on a last-to-die policy, you will still be able to highly optimize the estate you leave your spouse.

How a Tax Can Become an Asset

On any estate worth more than $3 million estate taxes are inevitable and unavoidable.

The fact of the matter is that it is impossible to shelter all your money, and impossible to die broke unless you are prepared to live broke. There is only one exception to this rule and it is only a factor if you intend to leave your entire estate to charity. (If you do, you should be sure and read the concept entitled *Give Away Double Your Estate and Avoid All Estate Taxes* on page 127.)

Of course, there are a lot of ways you can minimize the impact estate taxes have on your estate, many of which are included in this book. But ultimately taxes are inevitable.

What if you could take your inevitable tax and turn it into an asset? Watch how the Joneses do it.

The Smiths just accept the fact of taxes hanging over their heads. They know that their $10 million estate is subject to $5 million of taxes and their heirs will only receive $5 million.

The Joneses, realizing that $5 million of their $10 million will also ultimately be forfeit to estate taxes, decide that they would rather turn that tax into an asset.

They diversify the $5 million from their estate. Having already used their existing exemptions, they use $3.3 million to fund an Irrevocable Insurance Trust and $1.7 million to pay the gift taxes on the transfer. The trust buys a last-to-die insurance policy on the Joneses for the benefit of their children. If the Joneses are average age 60, the insurance will ultimately produce $33 million for their heirs. If they are average age 70, the heirs will receive $16.5 million. And, if they are average age 80, the insurance proceeds will be $9.9 million which their heirs will receive income and estate tax free.

The Joneses $5 million tax liability is now a highly optimized asset producing a significant return. And you can do the same with any tax liability your estate is going to face.

The ultimate bottom line of wealth creation — additional funds for you and estate tax protection for your heirs, all at no cost!

THE SMITHS' TAX PAID AT DEATH:		THE JONESES' TAX USED NOW:	
$10,000,000	Estate	$ 10,000,000	Estate
– 5,000,000	Estate Tax	– 3,300,000	Transfer to Trust
$ 5,000,000	To Heirs	– 1,700,000	Gift Tax
		$ 5,000,000	Remaining Estate
		– 2,200,000	Estate Tax
		$ 2,800,000	Estate
		+33,000,000	Insurance*
		$35,800,000	To Heirs

*At average age 60.

Perhaps you are thinking that if your pending tax funds were left in your estate during your lifetime they could be invested in traditional growth vehicles and that the profit they reap will recover the tax loss for your heirs.

But consider this: any stock or other investment you buy would have to grow to more than 20 times its original value in order to net the same return after taxes for your heirs.

Suppose you had a $10 million estate facing $5 million of estate taxes. Left in your estate, the $5 million would have to grow to $75 million to produce for your heirs the same $33 million after taxes that life insurance will provide if you are average age 60, based on current assumptions. And, to really be fairly compared with life insurance, it would have to grow to that $75 million tomorrow to be available immediately should disaster require it.

Can you really think of a single investment vehicle that can produce that kind of a return that quickly? Even the fastest growing Internet stocks aren't producing returns like that. But life insurance can. And that's all you need to know in order to die rich.

Create Great Wealth for Your Heirs at Little or No Cost to You

One of the most common and, frankly, exasperating comments that people make when I present them with a life insurance solution for the realization of their financial goals for their children is that, "life insurance is too expensive."

I have never understood this thinking. To begin with, as I see it, life insurance doesn't "cost" anything at all. As I explain in depth later on in the chapter entitled *The Bottom Line on Insurance*, life insurance is not an expense. Although it is not an investment and differs from investments in several important ways, in this regard life insurance can be thought of as acting similarly to an investment. You pay money into your policy and the policy pays a return. We've already seen how, in fact, life insurance outperforms investments because its returns are predetermined, income tax free, and available immediately upon your death. If an investment that can not offer any of these certainties is not considered to be an expense, how can the purchase of life insurance be considered otherwise?

Furthermore, if purchased wisely, when you are in good health and still relatively young, life insurance can provide a 10–to–1 return[6], based upon current assumptions. Even at older ages, when the time remaining for an investment to grow is foreshortened, life insurance can still provide a 5–to–1[7] or 3–to–1[8] return. At age 80, will any investment you make have time to grow three times in value? More importantly, will it have time to grow the six times it would need to so that, after taxes, it can ultimately net the same three times return the insurance policy will if it has been properly structured in an irrevocable trust? Clearly, the answer is "no". So how then, with these kinds of returns, can the premium outlay needed to make the insurance purchase be considered an expense?

And yet, that life insurance is too expensive is still a common lament I hear from prospects. To help those people, I developed the following plan for borrowing away the cost of insurance so that wealth could be created for their heirs at little or no cost to them.

In reviewing their estate planning for their $25 million estate, the Joneses realized that their heirs would face $13.75 million in estate taxes reducing their inheritance more than half to $11.25 million. After evaluating many suggested courses of action, Mr. and Mrs. Jones recognized that the single best remedy for their impending loss was to buy a life insurance policy in the amount of the estate taxes.

At their average age of 60, a policy to produce the needed $13.75 million would cost $1.37 million, on a one-pay basis. But the Joneses were reluctant to part with that amount. Instead, using the strength of their investment portfolio as collateral, they borrowed the $1.37 million from their stock brokerage firm at 7.5% annually.

The annual interest cost for the $1.37 million loan was

[6] Based on a 60-year-old couple buying a second-to-die policy.

[7] Based on a 70-year-old couple buying a second-to-die policy.

[8] Based on an 80-year-old couple buying a second-to-die policy.

$103,125. Yet, in truth, the $103,125 wasn't simply supporting a loan of $1.37 million. It was funding the purchase of the life insurance policy that would ultimately provide $13.75 million to the Joneses' children and pay off their entire estate tax cost.

If the Joneses were to die tomorrow, their children would get the full $13.75 million death benefit and it would have cost the estate only $103,125. If they live ten more years, to their 70's, it will cost them $1 million. Yet, during all that time they will have the full use of their $1.37 million to invest and grow. Should they be fortunate enough to live to their 80's, the Jones would have paid $2 million. And still that $2 million will fund a death benefit of $13.75 million for their heirs—a more than six times return.

Without the purchase of life insurance, if you wanted to borrow to invest, you would introduce uncertainty and risk and that same $2 million would have had to grow to be worth more than $30 million in order to net, after estate taxes, the same $13.75 million for your heirs. And that doesn't even take any applicable income or capital gains taxes into consideration.

So, for an extremely minimal interest outlay of $103,125 a year, the Joneses protect their entire $25 million estate for their children.[9] To net the same $25 million without using this "Die Rich" concept, the Joneses estate would have to become worth about $57 million so that after estate taxes of $31.35 million the heirs would net $25.65 million.

[9] The Joneses' heirs will pay back the loan principal out of the insurance benefits they receive. This will ultimately reduce their final inheritance by $1.37 million. However, should the Joneses choose to, they can actually borrow an additional $137,500 at an additional cost of $10,312.50 per year and use that money to replace for their children the cost of the principal as well.

By borrowing the premium, you can create wealth for your family at greatly optimized rates.

THE JONESES:	
Estate	$ 25,000,000
Estate Tax	$ 13,750,000
Borrow	$ 1,375,000
Buys	$ 13,750,000 Insurance
Costs	$ 103,125 Per Year

If the Joneses' heirs didn't need all the money produced by the insurance policy to pay estate taxes, or if the Joneses bought more insurance than was needed for that one purpose, the rest would have been pure wealth creation. For a cost equivalent to 1/100th the ultimate return per year, the Joneses can provide financial well-being and security for their heirs.

At the bottom line of planning, the Joneses results look pretty terrific. But in truth, they're even better than they might seem at first glance. Remember: Uncle Sam pays off half of every loan.

At the time of their deaths, the Joneses have an outstanding loan against their estate of $1.3 million. This outstanding debt reduces their estate value from $25 million to $23.7 million. In turn, this reduces their estate taxes from $13.75 million to $13 million. This saves the heirs approximately $750,000 in estate taxes thereby effectively reducing the cost of the loan from $1.3 million to $550,000.

Every outstanding loan reduces the estate value, which reduces the estate taxes. Uncle Sam effectively repays half the loan principal!

WITHOUT THE LOAN:		WITH THE LOAN:	
$25,000,000	Estate Value	$25,000,000	Estate Value
– 13,750,000	Estate Taxes	– 1,300,000	Outstanding Loan
$11,250,000	To Heirs	$23,700,000	Remaining Asset
		– 13,035,000	Estate Taxes
		$10,665,000	To Heirs

The heirs receive half the loan in estate tax savings and receive back $13 million more in insurance!

Even with returns this good and the tax savings effected by the outstanding loan, there are still some prospects who say they don't want to pay out anything. They question why they should limit their lifestyles in any way in order to benefit children who will already be inheriting a significant amount of money. "Since the kids are the ones who will benefit," they say, "let the kids pay."

There is a way that this desire can also be achieved. Under the "Rule of 72," money doubles every ten years at 7% interest. Therefore, you can accrue the interest and pay nothing until death at which time the kids will pay the principal and the interest back. In this way, you can borrow the premium needed to purchase insurance for estate tax discounting or wealth creation without paying a dime throughout your lifetime. However, the kids still receive the leveraged advantage of life insurance.

Let's say the Joneses have an estate worth $15 million on which $8 million of taxes will be due. The Joneses are both 70 years old so their cost for $8 million of insurance will be about $1.6 million. At current rates of 7.5%, a loan against their portfolio for $1.6 million will cost $120,000 a year.

But the Joneses don't want to pay $120,000 a year. Much of their $15 million is tied up in property and other non-interest bearing assets so even though they look strong on paper, $120,000 would be a significant portion of their yearly cash flow. Still, the Joneses would just as soon not lose half their amassed estate to estate taxes.

The couple borrows $2.3 million from their stock brokerage firm. With it, they buy an insurance policy worth $11.5 million. The interest costs $172,500 a year at 7.5%, which the Joneses allow to accrue to the loan. They pay nothing.

When the Joneses die, their children use a portion of the insurance proceeds to pay the estate taxes. But the Joneses have wisely purchased more insurance than is needed for just that purpose. The rest reimburses the heirs for the cost of the loan and accrued interest.

If the Joneses live 10 years after they borrowed the money, their loan principal and interest will double to $4.6 million. At their deaths, that $4.6 million will reduce their estate from $15 million to $10.4 million. The estate taxes on their $10.4 million estate are about $5.2 million leaving $5.2 plus $11.5 million of insurance for a total inheritance of $16.7 million.

If the Joneses live 20 years, the loan will cost their heirs $9.2 million. Now their estate is reduced from $15 million to $5.8 million. Estate taxes on the $5.8 million adjusted estate are $2.6 million leaving only $3.4 million. However, with the addition of the $11.5 million of insurance benefits, their total inheritance becomes $14.9 million and they come out virtually whole. They inherit their parents' entire $15 million estate almost entirely intact and free from the ravages of estate taxation. And it didn't cost the Joneses a single dollar.

Even if the Joneses live into their 90's or to age 100, their heirs still come out better than if the policy hadn't been bought.

Mathematics don't lie. You can borrow away your tax and create wealth for your heirs, without it costing you a dime during your lifetime.

	10 YEARS	20 YEARS
Estate Value	$15,000,000	$15,000,000
Total Loan	– 4,600,000	– 9,200,000
Adjusted Estate Value	$10,400,000	$ 5,800,000
Estate Tax	– 5,200,000	– 2,600,000
Remaining Estate	$ 5,200,000	$ 3,400,000
Insurance Proceeds	+ 11,500,000	+11,500,000
To Heirs	$16,700,000	$14,900,000

Optimizing Junk Money

I first coined the term "junk money" in 1990 in my book *Save a Fortune on Your Estate Taxes*. At that time, I used the term to refer to an unneeded portion of a person's wealth that could be put to much better use funding the purchase of life insurance to pay estate taxes.

I still refer to unneeded and under-utilized money as "junk money". However, I have since expanded my recommendations for the used of these excess, discretionary, surplus funds.

Metaphorically speaking, junk money is made up of those bills sitting at the bottom of your pile of money. The ones you never spend. Often junk money is an annuity the income from which you don't need. It may be a savings account sitting in the bank earning its meager interest. It could be a CD or a T-bill. Basically, any liquid asset that is not being used to support your lifestyle and is not being optimized for your future or that of your heirs is junk money.

Yet, to the IRS those funds aren't junk money. As part of your estate they will be subject to the same up to 55% estate taxes as everything else. So the sad truth is that those junk bills are even junkier than you might have first thought. Not only aren't they doing anything useful, they will be devalued by as much as half at your death.

Watch what happens in one example of the course junk money

can take in an estate. There are several other examples and innumerable creative options available for optimizing these funds. In fact, the opportunities are simply too numerous to discuss in detail here. Hopefully, this one example should serve to demonstrate the general concept and provoke thought and discussion of the ideas. If the numbers are too large to apply to your situation, simply subtract a zero and everything will pro rata. This of course applies to all the concepts in this book and on my website.

The Smiths and Joneses are both worth $50 million. Both families live nice lifestyles and are able to indulge themselves. Yet, even so, both families have found that of the $3.5 million per year that their $50 million produces in interest[10] they only need about $3 million to cover their immediate needs and make sufficient provisions for their futures. They each have about $500,000 per year in unneeded income, which is produced by $10 million of "junk money"—neither the principal or interest it produces is needed or used, so it's junk.

At average age 70 and enjoying good health, the Smiths have every reason to believe they will live another 10 years. Based on a 7% return, the $10 million of excess funds sitting at the bottom of their pile will double over the next ten years to $20 million.

If the Smiths live another 20 years, to age 90, those junk funds will double again to $40 million.

Except for one thing which, by this point in the book, you should be anticipating. Estate taxes. The Smiths' estate is in the 55% estate tax bracket. So all their savings will be halved at their deaths. The $40 million of junk money will be subject to approximately $22 million of estate taxes, leaving their heirs $18 million. While this is not a bad outcome, there is a better way, as the Joneses will demonstrate.

The Joneses decide to use their extra $10 million to produce wealth for their heirs. They plan to use the $10 million now to

[10] Assumes a 7% annual return.

fund a "Die Rich" life insurance concept. Because $10 million exceeds their Unified Gift and Estate Tax Exemption, they pay $3 million in gift tax and transfer the remaining $7 million to an Irrevocable Trust, which buys a last-to-die insurance policy on the couple. At their average age of 70, the policy produces a 5–to–1 return of $35 million for their heirs, income and estate tax free, versus the $18 million that remains for the Smiths' heirs after taxes.

This is truly the bottom line on wealth creation. Money unneeded, unused, and facing devaluation by estate taxes is utilized to create a fortune for one's heirs.

But it doesn't stop there. There are numerous other means for customizing this program to produce an even greater legacy of wealth for your heirs.

The Irrevocable Trust could use just $3.5 million to buy an insurance policy on the Joneses. This would produce $17.5 million estate tax free for their children at their deaths. The remaining $3.5 million could then be used to purchase an insurance policy on the Joneses' children for the grandchildren. Assuming the Joneses' children are in their 40's, they could earn an incredible return of 28–to–1. That would mean a legacy of $98 million would be created for the benefit of their grandchildren with money the Joneses didn't need.

Of course, the Joneses trust could apportion the life insurance expenditure in any way that suited the family's needs. But in any case, their junk money has now been used to create a lasting legacy of financial security; they will truly "die rich".

Optimized junk money can more than double the legacy you leave your heirs.

THE SMITHS:		THE JONESES:	
$50,000,000	Estate	$50,000,000	Estate
–40,000,000	Needed Funds	–40,000,000	Needed Funds
$10,000,000	Junk Money	$10,000,000	Junk Money
X 10	Years at 7%	– 3,000,000	Gift Tax
$20,000,000	Net	$ 7,000,000	Transfer to Trust
X 10	Years at 7%	X 5	Insurance Return
$40,000,000	Net	$35,000,000	Net
–22,000,000	Estate Taxes	– 0	Estate Taxes
$18,000,000	To Heirs	$35,000,000	To Heirs

In the depiction of the course of money I used the figures that assume the Smiths lived for 20 years to help make the point that time is irrelevant in calculating returns and planning for your heirs. No matter the odds, the Smiths have no guarantee they will live twenty years, let alone more than that. Yet, if they don't live that long, their legacy to their heirs will be even less. The Joneses, on the other hand, will realize the exact same result whether they live another twenty years, another ten years, or, tragically, die tomorrow. No estate plan can be considered thorough or complete if its bottom line requires time that you simply may not have.

Guaranteed Returns Create Enormous Potentials

Recently some insurance companies have begun issuing policies that are completely guaranteed. Previously, all policies were "based on current assumptions". Their assumptions were influenced by market performance, insurance company costs, mortality statistics, interest, and dividends. As a result, it could happen that the premiums quoted when the insurance was purchased were not guaranteed. Additional premiums might be needed to support the desired death benefit or a lower benefit might ultimately be realized.

Rarely do changes in assumptions affect a policy to any substantial degree. However, toward the end of the 1980's when interest was unusually high, policy premiums were extremely low[11]. As interest dropped, many people found themselves having to pay more and greater premiums to sustain their coverage levels. This precipitated a belief on the part of the public that policies bought "based on current assumptions" were too dangerous and deceptive.

In today's world of low interest rates, I feel extremely confi-

[11] As insurance companies earn more interest with the premiums you pay them, prices for coverage go down. Conversely, when interest rates are low and insurance companies earn less, premiums are higher.

dent that premiums based on current assumptions are stable and safe. Nonetheless, there are people who will just never be comfortable with anything less than a guarantee. It was for them that the new policies were created.

In order to offer their guarantees, the new policies don't base their premiums on current market conditions. They basically adopt a 'worst case scenario' and base their rates upon it. In this way you know your rates will never go higher or your death benefit decrease.

As a general rule, I'm not a big fan of guaranteed policies. I have always believed that you were best served by buying the most insurance for the least amount of money. If conditions change and your premiums are no longer sufficient you can decide then whether to pay more into the policy in order to support the desired death benefit, or accept a lesser face amount. It is better, in my opinion, to put more money into the policy later on, if and when it is actually needed, than from the beginning when it is not. With the advent of "catch-up" provisions that let you make up any missed premium without any interest, this philosophy seems to me to be even more appropriate.

However, in addition to the peace of mind and stability of planning that guaranteed rates engender, there is one other benefit: These over-funded guaranteed policies can serve as a means of terrific wealth creation.

Because of the way insurance is priced, sold, and regulated, insurance companies are not free to simply set a price for their coverage. There must be a direct, mathematical correlation between the premium charged and the death benefit provided. The factors involved in the calculation must uphold an empirical relationship.

With the guaranteed contracts, that relationship is based upon the assumption of a worst case scenario. However, if the worst case scenario doesn't occur, then the relationship between the premiums paid and the death benefit provided breaks down. If this happens it will actually increase the death benefit or you can reduce the annual flexible premium.

It might be best understood if we follow the course of money using a traditional policy that is based on current assumptions in contrast with a guaranteed policy.

Both the Smiths and the Joneses have determined that they need $10 million of life insurance to provide for their loved ones and cover their estate taxes. The Smiths opt for a traditional policy with premiums that are based on current assumptions. Given their ages and health, they receive a 12–to–1 return on a one-pay policy. So for $833,333, the Smiths secure $10 million of life insurance based on current assumptions. They are aware that changes in interest rates or mortality statistics could impact their policy, requiring them to pay additional premiums or decreasing the ultimate death benefit. But they are confident any deviation will be minor and are willing to take the risk in order to get the most coverage for the least money.

The Joneses, on the other hand, prefer a guaranteed policy. They don't want to deal with additional premiums later on; they simply want to know exactly what their policy will cost and what it will yield. For the same $10 million of coverage, the policy costs $5 million, six times more than the Smiths' policy.

If assumptions remain the same throughout the Smiths' and Joneses' lives, at the time of their deaths the Smiths' heirs will receive $10 million, exactly as their parents had intended. However, the Joneses' heirs will receive $65 million, which represents the amount of insurance their $5 million would have bought based on the current assumptions. Since the worst case scenario never happened, the Joneses policy paid off based on the current factors.

Of course, if assumptions change, the Jones policy will never cost any more than they originally paid for it and the death benefit will never yield anything less than $10 million. The Smiths, however, could be faced with additional premiums. Should interest rates drop by a single percent, the same $10 million coverage that they bought for $833,333 would necessitate an additional $316,000 bringing the total cost to $1.15 million.

Clearly it is a matter of personal preference. For some people, the peace of mind of a guarantee coupled with the opportunity for tremendous increases makes a guaranteed policy worthwhile. Others prefer to get the most coverage for the least initial outlay and are prepared to risk that additional premiums might be needed.

The new type of "catch-up" policies provide a happy medium. The increase in premiums is far less than the guaranteed policies and are just slightly more than the policies based on current assumptions. However, you have the option to make up any needed premiums because of any change from the original assumptions to bring the policy back to the original assumptions. This happens simply by paying additional money and there is no interest charge for not having paid on that basis from the beginning.

This voids the greatly increased death benefits but it provides a much more reasonable premium with the same resulting guarantee.

Free Money

This is one of my all-time favorite concepts. It has been demonstrated in my previous books but absolutely bears repeating as it epitomizes the principles of wealth creation.

This concept uses a combination of financial vehicles to achieve its results. This type of blended creativity often accomplishes goals that no single investment, trust, or shelter can.

In addition to life insurance, this concept uses an immediate annuity to optimize the assets of an older client.

Like a life insurance policy, an annuity is a financial contract between you and an insurer. You pay money into the contract in the form of premiums and the contract accrues value based on the premiums and a specified amount of interest earnings. However, an annuity pays its benefits during your lifetime.

Most annuities are sold as retirement savings vehicles. Because their earnings are tax-deferred and the interest rates they offer are higher, at least initially, than those of the current markets, annuities can accumulate funds faster than other savings vehicles. But limiting thinking about annuities strictly as a means to save for retirement once again causes people to fall into a trap of conventional wisdom.

One type of annuity in particular, an immediate annuity, can be leveraged to become a superb wealth creation vehicle, as this concept will demonstrate.

An immediate annuity is one into which you place a single, usually large premium and it immediately begins paying you an income for life. There are two major reasons why an immediate annuity is superior for this purpose than any other income-producing vehicle. The first is that an immediate annuity enjoys tax advantages that greatly increase the percentage return you receive. The government views the income paid to you from your annuity as containing both a return of your own principal and interest. Only the interest portion is taxed so you receive a much higher net return until you have recovered all of your principal.

In addition, unlike a savings account or CD, the income promised you from your immediate annuity will never run out. Many people rely on a savings account to fund their lifestyles in their later years. But if those people outlive their planning they can wind up having to dip into principal to continue funding their needs. This depletion results in less income, which in turn necessitates more incursions into principal. If they live too long, they can find themselves without ample resources. But this can't happen with an immediate annuity. The risk of your outliving your principal is the insurance company's, not yours, and they will continue to pay you the promised income no matter how long you live.

Given these two advantages, an immediate annuity becomes a wonderful means for older people with significant estates to create wealth virtually out of thin air.

Mr. Jones is 85 years old. He has an estate worth $9 million, a significant portion of which is held in stocks and bonds. Mr. Jones' $9 million produces $450,000 a year interest earnings. While this amount is sufficient to support Mr. Jones' lifestyle, he'd like to have a little more income. However, he doesn't want to risk any of his principal; he wants the same guaranteed income, just more of it.

Mr. Jones borrows $2 million against his stock portfolio at 7.5% interest. The cost of the loan is $150,000 interest a year. Mr. Jones then uses the $2 million to purchase an immediate annuity, which, at his age and based on his life expectancy, yields $384,000 a year after tax. He uses $150,000 from the annual $384,000 to pay the interest on the $2 million loan. He then purchases a life insurance policy for $2 million at a cost of $160,000 a year. This policy will pay off the loan principal at his death and leave his estate intact for his heirs.

Do the math and you will realize that, as if by magic, Mr. Jones has created an extra $74,000 per year for himself with the exact same money. He gets to both live rich and die rich.

Creative use of insurance and annuities creates money out of thin air at older ages.

MR. JONES:		MR. JONES' ESTATE:	
$ 2,000,000	Loan	$ 9,000,000	Estate
X 7.5%	Interest Rate	– 2,000,000	Loan Principal
$ 150,000	Yearly Interest	$ 7,000,000	Net Estate
		+ 2,000,000	Insurance
$ 2,000,000	Immediate Annuity	$ 9,000,000	For Heirs
X 18.8%	Net Return		
$ 384,000	Yearly Return		
– 150,000	Loan Interest		
– 160,000	Insurance Cost		
$ 74,000	"Found" Money		

Not only that, but Mr. Jones has actually created a net gain for his heirs. Because the $2 million loan against his estate decreases his estate taxes by about $1 million, his heirs "save" $1 million and come out $1 million ahead. If he wanted to, or had need of more income for himself, Mr. Jones could choose to only purchase a life insurance policy for the net $1 million of estate taxes on that $2 million portion of his estate. His heirs will come out even and he will have $80,000 per year more.

Of course, Mr. Jones is not limited to a $2 million transfer to an immediate annuity. The formula works proportionately and each $1 million that he borrows and uses in this way will create an additional $80,000 of income for him. If he chooses, he can even take this concept to the next level of wealth creation by borrowing enough against his portfolio to protect his entire estate against depletion by taxes.

If Mr. Jones were to borrow $5 million from his stock brokerage firm at 7.5% yearly interest, it would cost him $375,000 a year. The $5 million, used to purchase an immediate annuity, would provide Mr. Jones with $960,000 each year of his life. From that, he could pay the $375,000 of loan interest and still have $585,000 remaining.

At his death, the outstanding $5 million loan will reduce Mr. Jones' estate to $4 million upon which approximately $1.65 million in estate taxes will be due. In addition, his heirs will need to repay the $5 million loan principal bringing their total tax and loan debt to $6.65 million. At age 85, Mr. Jones can purchase a life insurance policy worth $6.65 million for $325,000 a year. Even after paying the yearly insurance premium, Mr. Jones has an extra $260,000 a year. The heirs receive $7 million at his death. They pay off the $5 million of loan principal and the $1.65 million of estate taxes and inherit his entire estate intact. Meanwhile, Mr. Jones accomplished all of this without ever diminishing his principal or the $450,000 of yearly pre-tax income it produced during his lifetime. This is truly the ultimate bottom line of wealth creation.

The ultimate bottom line of wealth creation — additional funds for you and estate tax protection for your heirs, all at no cost!

MR. JONES:	
$ 9,000,000	Estate
$ 5,000,000	Loan
X 7.5%	Interest Rate
$ 375,000	Yearly Interest
$ 5,000,000	Immediate Annuity
X 18.8%	Net Return
$ 960,000	Yearly Earnings
– 375,000	Loan Interest
– 325,000	Insurance Cost
$ 260,000	"Found" Money

MR. JONES' ESTATE:	
$ 9,000,000	Estate Value
– 5,000,000	Loan for Annuity
$ 4,000,000	Remaining Estate
– 1,650,000	Estate Tax
$ 2,350,000	After-tax Estate
+ 7,000,000	Insurance
$ 9,350,000	To Heirs

This is truly living rich! And dying rich.

MR. JONES' ESTATE WITHOUT THIS "DIE RICH" TECHNIQUE:	
$ 9,000,000	Estate
– 4,500,000	Estate Taxes
$ 4,500,000	To Heirs

Build a 100-Year Tax Free Dynasty

Once you have provided for your children's continued financial welfare by optimizing and diversifying your estate to include life insurance, you might also want to consider how to best provide for your grandchildren. In the concept *Maximize Gifts and Exemptions,* I presented the technique for purchasing life insurance on the lives of your children for the ultimate benefit of your grandchildren. This is an excellent means of creating significant wealth. To do so, I recommend the use of life insurance within a Generation Skipping Trust (GST).

Utilizing the current Generation Skipping Transfer Tax Exemption of $1 million each, you and your spouse could fund a $2 million GST that can ensure that your estate will pass to your children, their children, and their children's children (in legal terms: this generation and any living generation plus 21 years) without being reduced by estate taxes.

When you utilize a GST, it means that the principal remains in the trust throughout the trust's duration. Since the principal is not removed from the trust, it is not subject to any estate taxes. However, each generation of heirs may receive the income that the principal produces. In this manner, you can create income-producing, estate tax free assets of $20 million for your children, grandchildren, and great-grandchildren with no additional estate taxes until after the death of the third generation.

Imagine that the Joneses have an estate worth $40 million. Their own lifestyle and future welfare is more than secure and they have already purchased adequate insurance to cover the costs of estate taxes for their children. Now their thoughts have turned to the creation of wealth for their grandchildren and posterity.

If the Jones' want to avoid gift taxes, they can use their combined $1.35 million exemption to buy insurance on themselves for their grandchildren. At average age sixty, this will net their grandchildren $13.5 million that will be available upon their deaths or in accordance with any conditions set up by the trust.

The Joneses could also use the $1.35 million to buy an insurance policy on their children for their grandchildren. Assuming their children are average age 40, the $1.35 million transfer would now net about $54 million ultimately for their grandchildren.

Using a GST, the Joneses could transfer $2 million without any gift or transfer tax. The trust would then buy insurance on the Joneses, which would produce, upon their deaths, $20 million. Because of the nature of the GST, that $20 million would not be able to be removed from the trust, however, the interest it produces would be. Even if it only earned 5% a year, $1 million annual income would be produced each and every year to be used to support the lifestyles of the Joneses' children, grandchildren and great-grandchildren. Only after approximately 100 years would there be any estate taxes.

There are several creative permutations of this plan that can extend the wealth creation even further.

If they chose to, the Joneses could have the GST use only $1 million of their $2 million transfer to buy insurance on them. The other $1 million could be used to purchase insurance on their children. In this way, the first $1 million policy would produce a $10 million benefit upon their deaths, which would provide $500,000 of additional income to their children. Then, upon the deaths of their children, the second $1 million premium would produce an additional $28 million so that their grandchildren enjoyed a combined $1.9 million of yearly interest upon the death of their parents.

Of course, an ultimate wealth creation strategy would be to use the entire $2 million to buy insurance on the Joneses' children for the grandchildren. A $2 million premium paid for a policy on the lives of the grandchildrens' parents would net $56 million, tax free, which would produce $2.8 million of annual income at 5%. In ten years, this would total $28 million; in twenty, $56 million.

In this manner, the $2 million transferred to the GST provides significant income throughout several generations without any estate tax costs.

One last note. Were the Joneses' children and grandchildren to use some of the income proceeds to purchase insurance on their children or grandchildren, and set up Generation Skipping Trusts of their own, and their children were to do the same and their children were to do the same, the legacy the Joneses created could continue virtually in perpetuity granting their family financial security forever. This is true wealth creation and truly allows the Joneses to die rich.

Using Youth to Create Tremendous Wealth

Some of the most dramatic outcomes of the use of life insurance as a wealth creation vehicle occur when policies are purchased at younger ages. Because life insurance returns are based upon mortality and health, the younger you are, the better the return you can earn. Whereas a married couple averaging age 60 can receive a 10–to–1 return on an insurance purchase, that same couple just ten years earlier at average age 50 could receive a 16–to–1 return. And, of course, if that return is properly structured within an Irrevocable Trust, it will come to the couple's heirs income and estate tax free. This makes it an effective 32–to–1 return in comparison to the appreciation from any other financial vehicle that will be subject to estate taxes.

If the couple were to put $1 million into the insurance policy, it would net a $16 million return that was the equivalent of a pretax $35.5 million return to their heirs[12]. Is there anything this couple could do with their $1 million that would return $32 million? Even if they lived to be 80 or 90 years old, it is doubtful. But what if they only lived to be 60, or 65? What if they died tomorrow? Nothing other than life insurance can produce returns like this the very next day if necessary. And unfortunately, neither this hypo-

[12] $35.5 million reduced 55% by estate taxes would leave about $16 million.

thetical couple nor any of the rest us have any guarantee that it won't be.

The potentials get even more astounding at still younger ages. At average age 40 a couple can receive up to a 28–to–1 return, income and estate tax free. That means their $1 million produces $28 million. And that $28 million can be equivalent to about $62 million pre-tax.[13] At average age 30, the returns can be as high as 50–to–1. A $1 million purchase of life insurance can produce $50 million. For the same $1 million to net the same $50 million return for the couple's heirs, it would have to grow as high as $110.5 million before taxes reduced it back down to $50 million.[14] Can a 30-year-old couple earn returns like that during their lifetimes and increase $1 million to $110.5 million? Can they know as they begin planning for their children's welfare that they will have time enough to do so? Of course not. So clearly the only wise course of action is to diversify some portion of their assets to the purchase of a life insurance policy that will produce the stated returns irrespective of time. If they get very lucky and live a very long time and have extremely good luck with their investments, the worst that will happen is that their heirs will enjoy even greater good fortune and even more financial security.

Imagine the wealth creation that can be accomplished using life insurance at younger ages.

At average age 40, both the Smiths and the Jones are able to afford to diversify $20,000 a year for their children's future.

The Smiths invest $20,000 each year in various stocks and bonds. They do not give it away to the children so they pay no gift taxes. They do well and earn a steady 10%. After 10 years, their annual $20,000 contribution has grown to $356,500. Ten years later, when the Smiths are 60, it has grown to about $1.3

[13] $62 million reduced 55% by estate taxes would leave about $28 million.

[14] $110.5 million reduced by estate taxes leaves about $50 million.

million. By the time the Smiths are 70 years old, after 10 more years of investing, they have amassed about $3.7 million from their yearly $20,000 investments and earned interest. In another ten years, by the time they are 80, the total is just over $9.7 million.

$9.7 million from a yearly invested $20,000 is certainly a substantial return. However, the Smiths had to earn 10% after tax each and every year for 40 years in order to achieve it. More importantly, they had to live to be 80, something they can't be certain they will do.

Nonetheless, let's give the Smiths the benefit of great good fortune. Let's assume they do live to their 80's earning 10% on their investments every year along the way. Now, inevitably, they die, having amassed $9.7 million for their children.

But estate taxes of $5.34 million will be due. The children will only inherit $4.36 million of that $9.7 million, about half the earned gain.

The Joneses take a different course. Using the same $20,000 a year to pay the premiums, they buy an insurance policy which, at average age 40, will produce $10 million.[15]

Assuming they also live to their 80's, the Joneses will have paid $800,000 into the policy. That $800,000 will reduce their estate and save their heirs about $400,000 in taxes making the effective cost of the policy $400,000. In return, their children will receive $10 million income and estate tax free.

More importantly, the Joneses don't have to rely on the beneficence of time or the performance of the stock market in order for their children to net this return. No matter how long they live or how well their investments perform, their children will receive the full $10 million.

[15] Based on current assumptions at the time they purchase the policy.

Life insurance beats investment potentials for wealth creation at younger ages.

THE SMITHS:		THE JONESES:	
$ 20,000	Invested Per Year	$ 20,000	Annual Premium
X 40	Years	X 40	Years*
$ 800,000	Total Invested	$ 800,000	Total Premium*
X 10%	Yearly Interest	$ 10,000,000	Insurance
$ 9,700,000	Total Amassed	– 0	Estate Tax
– 5,340,000	Estate Taxes[17]	$ 10,000,000	To Heirs
$ 4,360,000	To Heirs		

*Full benefits are available immediately upon death. 40–year premium term used only for comparison.

There's also another tremendous way to utilize the power of youth to create wealth. It allows grandparents to provide a lasting legacy of their love for their grandchildren in the form of vastly increased financial security.

I recommend this technique to couples only after they have made arrangements to provide for themselves, their children, and their estate taxes. However, assuming they have remaining resources available to be used for their grandchildren's eventual benefit, there is simply no greater leverage available than that provided by life insurance purchased on younger lives.

The Joneses are 60 years old. They have an estate worth $20 million and have enacted a thorough financial plan to ensure their own independence and well-being. They have also purchased a last-to-die life insurance policy on their lives to cover the cost of

[17] Assumes a 55% estate tax bracket on their total estate.

estate taxes for their heirs. Now, their attention has turned to their children.

The Joneses' children average age 30 at which age they can receive a 50–to–1 return on a last-to-die insurance policy. The Joneses transfer $1 million to an Irrevocable Generation Skipping Trust and the trust buys an insurance policy on their children. The Joneses pay no gift tax on the transfer as the $1 million falls within their combined exemptions. The $1 million transfer reduces the Joneses' estate from $20 million to $19 million and 'saves' their children $500,000 in estate taxes. More importantly, upon the deaths of the Joneses' children, their grandchildren receive $50 million free of income and estate taxes.

Recapture Missed Opportunities

I was having a conversation with a friend the other day about the state of the stock market. We'd been tracking its progress as it continued to rise to record-breaking levels and then adjust several hundred points back down. Though volatile, its current strength has made fortunes for numerous investors. But others, who, like my friend, are more cautious or more conservative, were hesitant to leap into the fray. They preferred to take a 'wait and see' approach, concerned about a major correction and a little leery of the maverick Internet stocks that are fueling this unprecedented rate of growth. "Now," said my friend, "I could just kick myself. I had a few opportunities to get in on the ground floor of some technology stocks but they were too speculative for me. I took a pass and now they've increased 20 times."

"What if I told you that you could recapture that opportunity?" I asked him.

He smiled and said, "Barry, you're good, but not even you can send me back in time to take advantage of a missed stock opportunity."

I smiled back and said, "Ah, but I can."

Like my friend, many older people invest their money not so much to provide for themselves, but to create an enhanced inheritance for their heirs. For these people, there is a way of using the "Die Rich" insurance techniques I've developed over the years to effectively recreate almost any lost financial opportunity.

Imagine that Mr. Smith had a chance to buy stock in Amazon.com[18] when it first came out. The initial offering was $3 a share and Mr. Smith considered buying 35,000 shares, which would have cost $105,000. But, for various reasons, he ultimately decided against the purchase. Now, Amazon.com trades near $70 a share. Which means the 35,000 shares Mr. Smith didn't buy have grown in value from $105,000 to $2.4 million and Mr. Smith lost out on one of the greatest financial opportunities of a lifetime.

Using a life insurance wealth creation technique, Mr. Smith can achieve the same amazing results for his heirs.

The $2.3 million gain Mr. Smith's Amazon.com stock would have earned would have been subject to estate taxes of $1.26 million as it passed to his heirs. They would have netted $1.03 million from his savvy investing. While this isn't bad, my "Die Rich" methods can achieve the same results more safely and retroactively.

Mr. Smith and his wife are average age 60. If he uses the same $100,000 he didn't invest in Amazon.com's IPO now to purchase a last-to-die life insurance policy on their lives, it will produce a 10–to–1 return of $1 million for his heirs which they will receive free of income and estate taxes. He matches the return he would have earned from Amazon.com's astounding growth, had he not been too cautious or too late to take advantage of the opportunity.

The markets are volatile and you just can't tell what will be up and what will be down, and when. There is no way to know if, on the day of your death, the market will be in your favor. But you do know that the insurance policy return will always be up. And your heirs won't care if their good fortune is tied to Amazon.com or an insurance company. At the bottom line, the money spends the same.

[18] Amazon.com is a registered trademark of Amazon.com, Inc. or its affiliates. As reported on the Investor Relations pages of its website, Amazon.com went public on May 15, 1997, and the IPO price was $3 (adjusted for the 3-for-1 stock split payable on January 4, 1999).

Capital Optimizer

For the most part, when talking about using life insurance to recapture opportunities, optimize assets, and create wealth, I have been suggesting the purchase of life insurance in amounts equivalent to either the amount of estate taxes or the amount that can be transferred on a gift-tax free basis. However, if you're willing or able to transfer greater sums, you can create even greater wealth.

There are limits to how much insurance any individual or couple can buy. These limits are set by the insurance industry. However, within those limits are phenomenal opportunities for wealth creation.

Let's assume that the Smiths and the Joneses are both average age 70 and both have estates worth $75 million upon which $41.25 million of estate taxes will be due.

The Smiths don't want their children to lose any of their inheritance to estate taxes so they decide to use the leverage of life insurance to recover all losses. It is their intention that their heirs inherit the entire $75 million.

Earning a 5–to–1 return, they buy an insurance policy on themselves with a death benefit of $48.5 million for a one-pay premium of $9.5 million. Gift taxes on the transfer are $5 million. Together the premium outlay and gift tax cost reduce the Smith's estate by $14.5 million to $60.5 million. After estate taxes of $34 million, their heirs are left with $26.5 million of their original $75 million estate. However with the addition of the $48.5 million tax free insurance proceeds, the heirs inherit the full $75 million. All estate and gift taxes are recovered and the Smiths are thrilled that their children will come out whole.

The Joneses, however, are after more than simply protecting their legacy from estate taxes. They want to produce wealth for their children.

The Joneses transfer $15 million to an Irrevocable Trust, which buys $76.6 million of insurance on them. They pay $8 million in gift taxes on the transfer. The total $23 million outlay reduces their estate to $52 million upon which their heirs will have to pay $28.6 million of estate taxes leaving $23.4 million. With the addition of the $76.6 million of death benefit they receive from the insurance, the heirs now inherit $100 million, tax free.

Left alone, both the Smiths' and the Joneses' estates would have been reduced from $75 million to $33.75 million by estate taxes. Using insurance simply to pay the taxes, the Smiths' heirs retain the full $75 million estate valuation. But creative capital optimization planning on the part of the Joneses creates a $100 million inheritance for their heirs—33% more than they had to begin with and three times what they would have inherited had nothing been done.

Both the Smiths and the Joneses believe in the insurance techniques and for that reason both will pass more money to their heirs than anyone who does not purchase insurance for estate protection. However, the Smiths limit their thinking to just the recovery of their estate value. The Joneses go beyond that thinking to embrace the principles of true wealth creation.

Between the insurance premiums and the gift tax, the Smiths transferred $14.5 million to accomplish their result. The Joneses transferred $23 million. The difference is $8.5 million. Yet that $8.5 million reduces the Joneses' estate and therefore their estate taxes making the effective difference only $4.5 million. With that $4.5 million they created an extra $25 million after tax. Where else can results like these be achieved by people who are 70 years old?

Of even greater drama is the fact that, in reality, the Joneses' outlay funded a result that actually compares to $220 million. A $220 million estate reduced 55% by estate taxes would net for the heirs the same $100 million that the Joneses provided using life insurance.

And all of this was accomplished using the 5–to–1 returns available to people who are 70 years old. Even at 80, when the returns are 3–to–1 the outcome far exceeds any after tax increase the same funds could possibly experience with so little time left for them to grow.

Now imagine what could be accomplished at average age 60 when the returns are twice as good. Or think about what this concept could accomplish for younger people with returns ranging from 16–to–1, to 28–to–1, and even 50–to–1.

Clearly this is the optimum, ultimate, total, and maximum expression of my "Die Rich" wealth creation techniques.

One of the best ways to die rich is to optimize your capital during your lifetime.

THE SMITHS:		THE JONESES:	
$75,000,000	Estate	$ 75,000,000	Estate
– 9,500,000	Buys Insurance	– 15,000,000	Buys Insurance
– 5,000,000	Gift Tax	– 8,000,000	Gift Tax
$60,500,000	Taxable Estate	$ 52,000,000	Taxable Estate
–34,000,000	Estate Tax	– 28,600,000	Estate Tax
$26,500,000	Net Assets	$ 23,400,000	Net Assets
+48,500,000	Insurance	+ 76,600,000	Insurance
$75,000,000	To Heirs	$100,000,000	To Heirs

Estate Preservation

Amassing wealth is only half the issue involved in leaving your heirs a legacy of financial security and safety. After spending your lifetime working and building your assets, after utilizing the plans outlined in the previous chapter, you are still faced with the impact of estate taxes that can decimate your estate by up to 55%. You are now faced with preserving your estate.

Ever since the IRS first initiated estate taxes, people have been trying to minimize their bite. Attorneys, accountants, and financial planners have created intricate shelters and strategies intended to divert funds from Uncle Sam. It is a $200 billion a year industry involving some 20,000 attorneys all trying their best to beat the government.

I have several problems with most of these strategies. To begin with, for the most part they constitute "tax avoidance"; an attempt by the wealthy to avoid paying taxes. Though tax avoidance is legal, it is also ethically questionable and can be dangerous. The IRS is not unaware of the attempts of citizens to avoid paying what has been deemed their fair share. More and more, it is examining many of the shelters and trusts established primarily to avoid taxes. I feel certain that many of the more blatant avoidance techniques will soon start to be revoked and, should this occur, the people who have been relying upon them to protect their assets will find themselves once again faced with significant tax liabilities.

Sometimes, when I share my concerns regarding these avoidance strategies with clients or at seminars the answer I receive is that they are willing to take their chances and will deal with the consequences when the time comes. But these people are closing their eyes to a very important consideration. If you are relying on some legal tax avoidance strategy to protect your estate and at some time in the future that strategy is revoked, it may be too late to effectively initiate the life insurance technique needed to save the day.

Life insurance is paid for with money but it is bought with good health. The younger and healthier you are, the better the returns you will receive. And the better the returns you receive, the more effective your planning will be. At age 60, a married couple can receive a 10–to–1 return on their last-to-die insurance purchase if they are both in good health. At age 70, even if their health hasn't deteriorated, that return is reduced by half to 5–to–1. It is still a wonderful return and it still beats hands down what almost any investment could yield, especially for people at those ages, but it could have been twice as good had the couple acted sooner.

More importantly, had their health deteriorated, their returns could suffer greatly or they could be left uninsurable. Now if the IRS revokes their tax avoidance trust, they will have no good recourse to protect their estate for their heirs.

I always suggest to people that, even if they feel a strong need for a tax avoidance shelter, they buy life insurance while they are young and healthy as well. Doing so will create a win/win situation and could prevent a terrible loss.

If the shelter works to protect their assets as they intend (and we will soon see that, even if they aren't revoked, most shelters don't work as well as life insurance under any circumstances), the insurance benefits will still be paid to their heirs, creating even greater wealth. If the shelter fails or is revoked, the insurance proceeds will be there as backup. Given this, why would anyone wait to enact the insurance solution until it might be too late?

Let's take a look at the tax avoidance strategies recommended by most tax attorneys and accountants and how they compare with life insurance under the best of circumstances. You might be extremely surprised to see the bottom line results of both tactics. You should also consult an attorney who is well versed in both the use of trusts and shelters and the uses of life insurance before deciding how to proceed.

USE YOUR EXEMPTIONS NOW OR AT DEATH

Conventional wisdom has many people holding their allowed exemptions until death as if they were something sacred. Their advisors simply deduct the amount of the exemption from the bottom line of the people's estate value, metaphorically set it aside, and then proceed with the rest of the planning.

But, by waiting until death, the asset will continue to appreciate inside the estate and, in all probability, will be substantially larger at death and therefore exceed the allowed exemption at that time. Whatever growth has occurred will be subject to taxes.

If you can afford the cash flow impairment, transferring the exemption amount out of your estate now rather than waiting until death can be a far more effective means of estate protection and preservation. By doing so, you can use the exemption funds to purchase a life insurance policy inside an Irrevocable Trust and thereby increase them 10 times at average age 60, 5 times at average age 70, and 3 times at average age 80—all still on a tax exempt basis.

REVOCABLE LIVING TRUSTS AND WILLS

These excellent trusts will provide an avoidance of any probate fees, and help protect your heirs and estate from any publicity about your personal matters. They will also act like a will relative to the disposition of your assets and determine how you wish to be treated in case of extreme life-threatening health problems. They are also an excellent method of handling any exemptions that have been retained.

But you have to be careful when establishing a Revocable Trust. The benefits listed above are pretty much *all* your living trust will do. It *does not* shelter your assets from estate taxes beyond your exemptions. Since it is revocable, meaning within your control, your assets are not considered to be out of your estate until your death(s), at which time they will be subject to the full decimation of estate taxes.

I absolutely recommend that you initiate a Revocable Trust for probate and medical determination purposes. But do not overlook the need to add life insurance to your planning mix to protect your estate from the taxes that will still be due.

IRREVOCABLE TRUSTS

As I discuss in greater detail in the chapter entitled, *The Bottom Line on Insurance*, Irrevocable Trusts are the best way to transfer assets out of your estate. These financial entities are used to hold the assets you gift to your heirs in accordance with your instructions, called indentures, at the origination of your trust. An Irrevocable Trust used to hold any life insurance policies outside your estate will assure that your death benefit proceeds will be completely estate tax free.

The same estate tax free protection is afforded your children if your assets or gifts to buy insurance are given directly to them. There is absolutely no advantage if they are held in an Irrevocable Trust other than the control of the asset you retain from the grave. The tax results are the same. You should use whichever serves your purpose better. Remember, the bottom line will prove that five unfunded Irrevocable Trusts will only provide good reading at death compared to the money provided from one in-force life insurance policy.

One mistake a lot of people make in establishing an Irrevocable Trust is to do so too soon. Trusts are not inexpensive to set up. There are legal fees, maintenance costs and tax ramifications. Unless you have another purpose or need for an Irrevocable Trust, I recommend waiting to establish it until after you have determined your insurability. In the event that it turns out that you are uninsurable, or that a surrogate insured will better accomplish your ultimate goals, you won't have wasted time and money setting up a trust that will ultimately remain unfunded.

CHARITABLE REMAINDER TRUSTS

A strategy that is quickly gaining popularity in estate planning is the use of a Charitable Remainder Trust (CRT). Among the reasons for its increased usage is the fact that a CRT is an excellent way to effectively receive a stepped up basis on an appreciated asset during your lifetime, avoid all capital gains tax, receive an increase in your income, and avoid all estate tax while having the personal satisfaction of having given a substantial gift to charity.

Charitable Remainder Trusts work by taking an appreciated asset out of your estate and gifting it to the trust. Because the beneficiary of the trust is a charity, you receive a tax benefit in making the gift. You also avoid capital gains tax on the appreciation since you have gifted it away. The trust can sell the asset and use the proceeds to produce income that they give back to you in accordance with a predetermined set of instructions based upon your anticipated need. The charity, through the trust, has been given a valuable gift and you retain income from an asset that otherwise would have been subject to capital gains or estate taxes.

But there is a drawback and it can be absolutely devastating to your heirs. Once you've given your money away to charity, your heirs do not receive even the after-tax proceeds they would have had if you just left your estate alone and let it be diminished by estate taxes. Sometimes the tax savings on the charitable donation make up a portion of this loss. Other times, the donor uses some of the income generated by the CRT to purchase a life insurance policy in an amount equal to the gifted asset's value. But this still only recovers the loss. It does not maximize the estate for the benefit of the heirs.

If you are really interested in giving to charity, increasing your income and avoiding estate taxes while still taking care of your heirs, one of my life insurance strategies can affect a much more optimized result.

This plan depends on the age of the donors. I usually find them to be in their late 70's or 80's. At those ages, you could very effectively use an approach whereby you sell your property, pay the capital gains tax and purchase an immediate annuity. In spite of the tax that has been paid, you can still receive more net income than the CRT will provide. This net excess income can be used to purchase a life insurance policy in excess of what the CRT would have produced for your heirs and you could use the remaining income to increase your own lifestyle or boost what you leave your heirs. You could even give it to a charity and they could purchase a life insurance policy on you to be paid at your deaths, accomplishing the same charitable goal as the CRT, if not more.

CHARITABLE LEAD TRUSTS

A variation on the Charitable Remainder Trust described above, the income produced by the asset gifted to a Charitable Lead Trust goes to charity for a prescribed number of years and the remainder goes to your heirs with a great discount in the taxes that must be paid. If the income on the principal transferred to the trust is not needed, this is an excellent devise for reducing taxes even if the donor is not charitable.

But be careful. Any change in your estate composition can cause a disaster. This is particularly true if this plan is offered as a specific solution to reducing estate taxes in lieu of any other. A false sense of security can develop. No further planning is arranged and other steps utilizing a life insurance approach that might have avoided this horror story are precluded.

This danger may be best illustrated by examining the case of Jacqueline Kennedy Onassis. When her estate was settled it was found that there wasn't enough money left after taxes to fund the carefully drawn estate plan that had received such accolades throughout the media and financial worlds. Her heirs ultimately wound up determining that they would be better off if they simply paid the estate taxes.

Had one simple life insurance policy been in place at the time of her death to pay the taxes, it might have made all the difference. But Jackie waited too long to realize the necessity for life insurance. She became ill and died too soon. If the plan had only been executed on a timely basis, in anticipation of her eventual death instead of as a last minute necessity, the difference to the bottom line would have been monumental.

The auction of her personal effects might not have been necessary. The costly audit and embarrassingly public review of her finances might not have been necessary. The loss of her dream for the continuing welfare of her grandchild might have remained intact and funded.

Fortunately for the rest of us, we can learn from the negative examples left us by Jackie and others like her who waited too long and relied too heavily on plans that aren't complete without the added protection only life insurance can provide.

GENERATION SKIPPING TRUSTS

The use of a Generation Skipping Trust is a method for taking great sums out of your estate before they appreciate substantially for the benefit of your grandchildren. Once transferred to such a trust, the assets can escape further estate taxes for approximately 100 years.

The government allows each taxpayer to transfer up to $1 million to a Generation Skipping Trust without the onerous 55% generation skipping tax that must otherwise be paid on such a transfer. In this manner a married couple could take advantage of both of their allowances and exemptions resulting in a $2 million generation skipping tax free transfer.

This strategy for wealth preservation is often combined with other techniques to create the maximum tax advantage. One such procedure might be to utilize a combination of a Generation Skipping Trust with a Charitable Lead Trust. Together, the two trusts could create income for your grandchildren on a highly tax advantaged basis.

But if this is such a tremendous technique for tax advantaged transfers—which it is—why would you settle for only a $1 million or $2 million transfer that is the limit of what almost all advisors recommend? The same life insurance approach that can be used to increase your exemptions can be applied here so that you can take $50 million to $100 million out of your estate on the same basis.

By buying a last-to-die policy on your children for the benefit of your grandchildren, you can, depending on their ages, effectively increase your allowed $2 million combined transfer exemptions up to 50 times or to $100 million. Instead of just transferring the money to the trust and having $2 million for your grandchildren, you combine the trust with the leverage of life insurance and the result becomes a highly optimized death benefit that can increase your grandchildren's legacy up to 50 times.

Clearly, there is no comparison. The trust on its own can not begin to produce the results that life insurance, as part of a diversified, creative plan for estate preservation, can.

GRITS, GRATS, and GRUTS

When employed by knowledgeable attorneys each of these related trusts is an excellent estate planning tool with significant value as a wealth preservation device. Yet, once again, their results when used alone can not begin to match those that are achieved when life insurance is introduced into the planning.

A GRAT is a Grantor-Retained Annuity Trust. As the grantor, you transfer assets into the trust. You retain the right to annual payments of a fixed amount of principal and interest for a prescribed number of years. Then, at the end of the period, the assets go to your beneficiary in accordance with your original intentions.

A GRUT is a Grantor-Retained Unitrust. It is similar to the GRAT described above. The only real difference is that in this case you receive a fixed percentage of the trust's assets each year rather than a predetermined annuity.

Both GRATS and GRUTS allow you to transfer assets at a significant gift tax discount. As long as you survive the term of the trust, the potentially-increasing value of the assets transferred are out of your estate and therefore avoid estate taxes when they pass to your heirs at your death.

As an example of how one of these trusts might be employed to help preserve your estate, imagine that you've received a recommendation to transfer $1 million to a GRAT in order to remove principal and future appreciation from your estate. The government assesses the value of the $1 million asset at less than $675,000 at the time of transfer, which falls within your gift and estate transfer exemption. This provides you with a 40% discount on the gift and saves you an approximate 50% tax on the $400,000, which amounts to a savings of $200,000. If the property appreciated 10% a year, it would be worth $2 million in seven years and $4 million in 14 years.

It might seem significant to transfer a $1 million asset that eventually becomes worth $4 million on a tax free basis and save $200,000 of taxes. But there are numerous other considerations to be taken into account before the true value of this technique can be measured.

While, this may be better than an outright gift of the asset we are not looking for what is better. We are looking for what is best.

To begin with, you must also consider the costs associated with this technique. They include set-up and administration expenses, attorney fees, property title costs, accounting fees, appraisal fees, and trustee's fees. Furthermore you lose potential opportunity and control of the asset. Additionally, should you die prior to the end of the term, the asset reverts to your estate and is once again exposed to the full burden of estate taxes. Since you have no guarantee that this won't happen, you take a significant risk when you employ this technique.

Interestingly, life insurance is often suggested just to offset the possibility of an early death. Yet even those advisors who understand the risk and recognize the need for insurance to protect against it, generally don't follow through far enough with their thinking.

If you used a life insurance concept in lieu of the GRAT or GRUT the results would be as follows. You could have transferred only $675,000 out of your estate on the same tax free basis as you transferred the $1 million into the GRAT. Though this would leave the additional $325,000 in your estate to eventually be exposed to estate taxes of approximately $178,750, this could easily be covered with a one-payment life insurance policy at a cost of $17,875 with an ultimate net cost of $8,937. In other words, for a net cost of only $8,937 you could cover the tax on the $325,000 left in your estate.

With the transferred $675,000, (this transfer-tax free amount will increase over the next six years to be $1 million) you can buy a life insurance policy worth $2 million to $6.75 million, depending on your ages.

If you used the entire $1 million, at a gross gift tax cost of $40,000 and a net gift tax cost of only $20,000, you could purchase a last-to-die policy with a death benefit of approximately $3 million–$10 million depending on your ages. This would be effective immediately; you wouldn't have to wait for your $1 million asset to eventually become worth $4 million—if you were lucky enough for 'eventually' to come.

One important consideration: The above approach would eliminate the income you would have received via the GRAT approach. Clearly, one size doesn't fit all and you must determine which bottom line is best for you depending on whether your objective is to save gift taxes, save estate taxes, avoid appreciation on an asset, optimize what you leave your heirs, or produce income for yourself for a limited number of years.

QUALIFIED PERSONAL RESIDENCE TRUST (QPRT)

This is a plan that has been heralded as an excellent and outstanding method of reducing smaller estates in which your home is a major asset. The house is given to your children in a QPR Trust. They agree that you can live there for a negotiated period of years after which the house belongs to them. Since they will not receive the actual gift of the house for many years, it is appraised at a great discount for the present value of the future gift. This allows a low evaluation for gift taxes and removes what may be an appreciating asset out of your estate.

While this can be an excellent plan in the right situation, it is too often written about incorrectly in the media which often quotes attorneys who have their own biases or a lack of knowledge about superior alternatives.

The disadvantages of this plan include the set-up and administration costs including attorney fees, appraisal fees, property titling costs, possibly real estate transfer tax, and trustee fees. If you die before the term of the trust is over the home will be back in your estate and your heirs will face full-value estate taxes on it. Furthermore, by setting up the QPRT, you also may have lost the opportunity to use a better alternative plan.

More importantly, you will also lose control over your home and the stepped-up basis normally available at your death.

Once again, it is imperative that you review your objectives as they pertain to your tax situation and your emotional comfort, so you can accomplish what you want, not the conventional wisdom.

A life insurance policy, purchased on a highly advantageous 3–, 5–, or 10–to–1 basis, can provide funds to pay the taxes on the home asset even it increases in value many times during your lifetime. This will allow you to retain ownership of your home without having to worry about your children's tax exposure when they inherit it. Furthermore, you will accomplish the goal of asset protection and preservation without the risk that if you die too soon, your intentions will be for naught.

In most situations, due to the leverage of the life insurance policy, the stepped-up basis and the capital gains tax that is often overlooked, a life insurance technique produces a far superior result while avoiding the worst of family discomfort and combat.

FAMILY LIMITED PARTNERSHIPS

The latest vogue in tax avoidance is the Family Limited Partnership. This is one of the avoidance strategies the IRS is not happy about and is threatening to reevaluate. Right now they are still working, though overly aggressive evaluations and discounts are being individually audited.

The main purpose of this approach is to transfer out of your estate $900,000 to $1 million at a discounted evaluation of $675,000 (or an amount equal to your current allowed exemption) thus avoiding any gift tax on the additional $325,000 transferred.

The other important purpose is to remove an appreciating asset from your estate at its current discounted value and assure your heirs that any future gains in value will escape estate taxation. This is accomplished by transferring assets to a Family Limited Partnership in return for a minority interest in the partnership. Though you retain some degree of control over the asset, it is out of your estate for estate tax purposes.

In addition to the tax advantages outlined above, there is a presumption of less exposure for the assets to creditors. It is imperative that you use an attorney who is totally conversant with every aspect of this approach as an improperly structured Family Limited Trust can result in an audit and may not achieve your full intentions.

Even when properly prepared and implemented, I have great concern with this technique. The discount sounds good, but once again, the tax savings are only based on approximately $300,000 to $400,000 that is the difference between the transferred value and the current assessed value of the assets placed into the trust. The actual gift taxes saved will really only be between $120,000 and $200,000 while the net cost to offset this 'extra tax' using a life insurance policy is only approximately $12,000 to $40,000 depending upon your ages. This may be less than the legal fees and other administration expenses, as well as any additional legal fees that will be required if your Partnership is challenged for any reason.

Planning with life insurance would produce $3 million to $10 million income and estate tax free, using the same transferred $1 million and a last-to-die life insurance policy. The return would be available immediately, if necessary; you wouldn't have to wait and hope that your $1 million transferred asset would have time to grow inside the trust to equal that return. Which do you want to use your exemption for? Immediately removing $1 million or $10 million from your estate?

INTERNAL REVENUE CODE SECTION 6166

This is the government's method of relief for those who are not liquid and can't afford to pay the estate tax within the prescribed nine months. If you qualify, you can pay off your taxes over a 14-year period. But due to the 15-year schedule of principal and interest, utilization of this "relief" effectively doubles the tax cost to your heirs. Based on a $10 million estate, with a $5 million tax, your heirs would pay a total of $10 million over the 15-year period. An accountant sometimes offers this to his client as an excellent method of paying off the estate tax instead of purchasing a life insurance policy.

If you think it through, only the most uneducated and unknowledgeable professional advisor would seriously offer this as a tax solution. If there is no other solution, under the absolute worst scenario, this may make sense. But no client, advised by a professional, should be allowed to find themselves in this position. Even if the liquidity is not available to pay for an insurance policy to cover the estate tax costs, alternatives exist that are far more favorable that this method. Among them is a technique we discussed earlier—borrowing the premium against other assets and either paying only the interest or letting the interest accrue so that there is no cost during your lifetime.

At age 60, the cost for a $5 million insurance policy would be only one payment of $500,000 based on current assumptions. This amount could be borrowed against your stock portfolio or other assets at a cost of only $35,000 per year. You could pay this interest and then, at your death when the insurance paid your heirs the $5 million death benefit, they could repay the $500,000 loan principal from the proceeds. This would still leave them $4.5 million. And the $500,000 outstanding loan would be a liability against the estate value reducing it from $10 million to $9.5 million and thereby saving your heirs $250,000 in estate taxes. In this way, the cost to your heirs of the $500,000 loan is only $250,000.

If you prefer, you could accrue the interest on the loan. If you were to live to be 80, after 20 years of interest the loan amount would total $2 million. Your heirs would be faced with $2 million of debt to be repaid out of their $5 million insurance proceeds. Yet, again, the real cost to them would be half since Uncle Sam effectively pays the other half in reduced estate taxes on your estate after the $2 million loan liability is deducted from its total value. So, for a cost of $1 million your heirs avoid the loss of $5 million in IRS Section 6166 interest.

Is there any question whatsoever about which bottom line is the most advantageous? Yet, this insanity really happens.

PRIVATE ANNUITIES

A Private Annuity is an arrangement between two parties without an insurance company. Though it is a less frequently discussed technique, it is still being used in some estate planning. It is a method of selling a business, usually to a child, grandchild or favored employee, to remove the asset from the estate and avoid gift tax and even generation skipping transfer tax. There are other applications that must be reviewed with a skilled attorney in this area and it does lend itself to highly customized situations.

The problem with a Private Annuity is that the obligation of the transferee is unsecured. For this program to work effectively, you *must* use life insurance to guarantee the transferor in case of the transferee's premature death. There may be no alternate approach.

PRIVATE FOUNDATIONS

Foundations are usually arranged not so much to avoid estate taxes as to create an institution to handle the philanthropic wishes of the creator. A foundation can be created during his lifetime or at his death, for small estates and large. It is primarily used by the more wealthy who have no heirs or only want to leave limited amounts to named beneficiaries and the rest to charity. These people gift or bequest large sums to their Foundation for it to use in charitable or non-profit endeavors. Often their children will be appointed paid trustees and receive a significant income for life from the Foundation to manage its resources.

It is extremely important that a competent attorney be consulted when creating a Private Foundation in order to assure its proper implementation. The tax implications are numerous and complex and an improperly structured Foundation can suffer terrible repercussions.

You should also remember that if you want to maximize contributions to a Foundation, life insurance policies can produce exceptionally large amounts at no additional cost to you. The leverage of using a life insurance policy can greatly increase the grantor's wishes in maximizing his gifts with "soft" dollars. The purchase of the policy can be tax deductible during the grantor's lifetime if the Foundation or charity is the owner of the policy from the inception. Or the grantor can maintain the ownership during his lifetime if he wishes to control the cash value equity until his death at which time it can be donated to the Foundation and avoid all estate taxes. The bottom line will always be enhanced when the leverage of life insurance is included.

Many of the above charitable approaches have been created and are used strictly for estate tax avoidance and tax savings. I would never recommend against charitable giving. In fact, I think we should all be doing a lot more of it. But I do not believe they should be used when charity is not your main objective and there are better techniques available to accomplish your real purpose of estate tax cost discounting and asset maximization.

There are many methods available for people who really wish to give to charity that will still provide them with tax advantages. Only then should these plans be implemented. We will look at several of them in more depth in the *Maximize Charitable Giving* section of this book.

But first, having demonstrated conclusively that all of the conventionally utilized plans for wealth preservation can be improved or surpassed by the inclusion of life insurance, we're going to review some of the concepts I have formulated to pass the greatest legacy possible to your heirs.

Again we will ask the Smiths and Joneses to help us personalize these techniques so that you might see the truth about how the best bottom line is achieved. We will follow the course of money and let simple mathematics reveal the best result.

Many of the concepts that follow are also featured on my DieRich2.com website in an interactive mode that lets you customize them to your specific situation and see how they would work to optimize your estate. You can also use the rate charts at the back of this book to calculate your own bottom line. And, of course, you can simply pro rata each example up or down by adding or subtracting zeroes as your own situation would require.

Give Away Double Your Estate Value and Avoid All Estate Taxes

This was one of the first concepts I developed for wealth preservation but I'm updating and including it in this book because it remains one of the best and most dramatic. Using this technique, you can virtually double your estate so that your heirs inherit it all and you also give it all away to charity. And you can accomplish this without paying any estate taxes.

At average age 60, The Joneses have an estate worth $9 million. They know that if they leave it unprotected, estate taxes will claim about 48% or $4.4 million, leaving their heirs a little over $4.6 million. Unsatisfied with this outcome, the Joneses transfer $900,000 to an Irrevocable Trust. They pay no gift taxes on this transfer as it falls within their combined exemptions.

The trust purchases a last-to-die policy on the Joneses' lives and receives a 10–to–1 return. The Joneses' children are named as beneficiaries.

When the Joneses die, whether it is the next day, a year later, or thirty years later, their children will receive the full $9 million death benefit income and estate tax free.

In the meantime, the Joneses have made arrangements through their will to leave their entire estate to their favorite charity. Upon their deaths, the charity receives their amassed $9 million, minus the $900,000 cost of the insurance. Because it is a charitable donation, there are no estate taxes due.

We could quibble, but I think an $8.1 million bequest to a favorite charity in addition to a $9 million inheritance for their heirs, all from the same $9 million estate, is close enough to support my earlier statement that the Joneses would be giving away their entire estate twice. Best of all, with the exception of the $900,000 transfer to the Irrevocable Trust, the Joneses did not lose a dime of their estate value during their lifetime and this plan really only cost them the "give up" of $45,000 of yearly interest, based on 5% return. Though I freeze all assets for the sake of these examples, in truth the Joneses would have had the rest of their lives to increase their estate or enjoy the lifestyle benefits available through their significant yearly interest earnings.

What bottom line on wealth preservation could be better than the one that lets you effectively double your estate and give it away twice without any estate or gift taxes?

THE JONESES:

$ 9,000,000	**Estate**
– 900,000	**Transfer To Trust Buys Life Insurance**
$ 8,100,000	**Remaining**
– 8,100,000	**To Charity At Death**
$ 0	**Remaining Estate Value**
+ 9,000,000	**Tax free Insurance Benefits**
$ 9,000,000	**To Heirs**

Avoid the Guaranteed Stock Market Crash

When I first wrote about the guaranteed stock market crash, I was referring primarily to the individual, personal crash that occurs whenever someone dies holding a significant amount of stocks in their estate portfolio. For these peoples' heirs, no matter how strong the market is at the time of their parents' deaths, and no matter how well they had chosen their investments, the market would crash as much as 55% or more the day they died. Estate taxes would claim more than half their portfolio's value. Investments held and grown for years could wind up worth less than they were originally purchased for.

But I have now expanded this concept to include the likelihood of an actual, global stock market crash. Market corrections occur. And after long periods of continued growth such as those that we have been experiencing, those corrections can hit hard. I think it is not unlikely that sometime in the next few years the markets will enter a period of correction and should this happen the losses could be severe.

Maybe it won't happen. Then again, maybe it will. And good estate planning must always take both possibilities into account. Maybe it won't happen. But what if it does?

It is exactly in response to this cautious thinking that portfolios are routinely diversified. Within an individual portfolio is a microcosm of the bigger stock market system and any single stock can "crash" at any given time. To protect against devastating losses, wise investors spread their investments around. But even the smartest investor often overlooks the one financial vehicle that, although it is not an investment, can provide the best protection for all the rest.

Life insurance, which I often refer to as The Investment Alternative, is a marvelous tool for protecting the value of investments for ones' heirs.

The Smiths and Joneses have been good friends for years. Along the way they have shared some stock tips back and forth. Mostly they have been lucky and both investors have done well. Now they are both worth about $22 million, which puts them in a 55% estate tax bracket. Both have $5 million of their estates in stocks, which represents a $1 million initial investment and $4 million of gain. The $5 million isn't needed to support either of their lifestyles and both families are intending it as a legacy for their heirs.

The Smiths are thrilled that the original $1 million they invested has grown to be worth $5 million. Even though they're aware that their children will have to pay some taxes on the gain, they are content knowing that they will still be left significantly better off than they were before.

But, when the Smiths die, their children will have to pay 55% estate taxes on the $5 million of stocks reducing them by $2.75 million to $2.25 million. Their gain has been reduced from $4 million to only $1.25 million. They have experienced a personal stock market crash and their stock values have plummeted from $5 million to $2.25 million.

The Joneses take a slightly different tact. Once they have earned some significant investment returns, they diversify their financial portfolio to include a life insurance policy. They follow a common practice in the investment world and take the original $1 million they started their investment program with out of the market. Now only gain is at risk and they have nothing of their original $1 million at risk. However, the Joneses will take the concept to the next level of intelligent planning, a step most investors aren't aware of.

They use the $1 million to buy life insurance and, being average age 70, receive a 5–to–1 return on one-pay, last-to-die policy. They have gone beyond protection against risk to true wealth creation. Now not only is their $4 million profit continuing to work for them, but they have a guaranteed return from their original $1 million for their heirs of $5 million.

At their deaths, their heirs receive only $4 million of stock, since $1 million was diverted to the purchase of the insurance. After paying estate taxes of $2.2 million on the $4 million, they are left with $1.8 million. However, they then receive the income and estate tax free insurance death benefit of $5 million, bringing their total legacy to $6.8 million. All this from a $1 million investment that would have had to go to $12.5 million in order to net the same $6.8 million after tax.

Diversify your financial portfolio to include life insurance and avoid the coming stock market crash.

THE SMITHS:		THE JONESES:	
$ 5,000,000	Stocks	$ 5,000,000	Stocks
– 2,750,000	55% Estate Tax	– 1,000,000	Buys Insurance
$ 2,250,000	To Heirs	$ 4,000,000	Stock Value
		– 2,200,000	55% Estate Tax
		$ 1,800,000	Remaining
		+ 5,000,000	Insurance Proceeds
		$ 6,800,000	To Heirs

Whether the stock market experiences a "correction" during your lifetime or not, the value of your portfolio absolutely will crash up to 55% the day you die. If any of the investing you are doing is for the eventual benefit of your heirs, your bottom line will be enhanced if you diversify some portion of your funds to the purchase of life insurance. Remember, you will still have the majority of your stake to invest as you see fit, to play the markets and hope for a big hit. But in the meantime, your legacy will be secure against the inevitable crash to come.

Protect the Full Potential of Collectibles

Collecting is fun. And often, quite profitable. My wife, Carole, turned her love of miniatures into a collection that has now became the largest museum of contemporary miniatures in the world, The Carole & Barry Kaye Museum of Miniatures[19]. While your collection may not achieve this status, it can, nonetheless, represent a significant investment of time, energy, passion, and money. Yet, like everything else you own, your collectibles are at risk from estate taxes and your heirs may be faced with a devastating choice upon your death.

To demonstrate the risk, let's imagine that you collect antiques. You love each of the pieces, you know their providence, you have researched their history, you have restored and protected them. Now, in addition to representing a significant portion of passion and pride, your collection has become worth millions.

When you die, the value of your collection will be assessed by the government and up to 55% of it will be due in estate taxes. What will your heirs do? They won't want to sell your collection off; it represents you to them. Worse, if they do have to liquidate

[19] The Carole & Barry Kaye Museum of Miniatures is located at 5900 Wilshire Boulevard, Los Angeles, CA 90036. For more information, call 323-973-MINI or 323-973-7766. Or visit the museum on the web at www.museumofminiatures.com.

some portion, they will probably lose a significant percentage of their value in a forced liquidation sale. What a tragedy. But, like so many others, it is a tragedy that can be avoided.

At average age 70, the Smiths and the Jones both have collections worth $12 million. The Smiths collect art, the Jones collect antique automobiles.

When the Smiths die, their heirs are faced with a $6.6 million estate tax bill on the $12 million value of their parents' collection. This is, of course, in addition to whatever other taxes they are faced with for the rest of their parents' estate. But this is only the beginning of the Smiths' heirs' problems. Their parents' art collection has much greater value all together than in pieces. Also, since the estate tax bill is due within nine months of the death of the last surviving parent, they don't have time to wait for a buyer willing to pay top dollar. They have to sell at distress prices in a forced liquidation. These factors combine and could devalue the art's worth by one-third.

Now the $12 million collection is reduced in value by $4 million to only $8 million. While this reduces their estate taxes from $6.6 million to $4.4 million, it also reduces their overall after tax inheritance from $5.4 million to $3.6 million. Even more devastating, they must select which of the paintings and pieces of sculpture their parents loved and cherished to put on the auction block at bargain rates.

The Joneses take a different tack. Having reached their 70's, they recognize the need for estate planning to protect the value of their antique automobile collection for their heirs. Knowing that the value of the collection faces estate taxes of $6.6 million, they get examined and find out that they can receive a 5–to–1 return on a last-to-die insurance policy. This means a policy with a death benefit of $6.6 million will cost $1.3 million on a one-pay basis.

The Joneses evaluate their collection and select those items with a combined value of $1.3 million. Doing so now spares their heirs the eventual need to try to decide which of their parents' treasures to part with. Acting now also allows them to receive the greatest sale price for the selected automobiles since it avoids a forced liquidation sale later.

They sell $1.3 million worth of cars from their $12 million collection and transfer the proceeds to an Irrevocable Trust, which purchases a life insurance policy on their lives. They pay no gift or transfer tax on the transfer as the $1.3 million is covered by their 1999 increased combined tax exemptions. Their children are named the beneficiaries of the insurance trust.

Upon the deaths of their parents, the Joneses' children will receive $6.6 million in insurance benefits that they will use to pay the estate taxes on the rest of the automobile collection which they will be able to retain intact.

Surely parting with one-twelth of a collection now in order to preserve the other eleven-twelths is a better bottom line than losing two-thirds of the collection at death. One might even say that wealth preservation of this type is a real art.

The "art" of wealth preservation helps preserve the value of your cherished collectibles for your heirs.

THE SMITHS:		THE JONESES:	
$ 12,000,000	Collection	$ 12,000,000	Collection
– 4,000,000	Loss*	– 1,300,000	Sold
$ 8,000,000	Remaining Value	$ 10,700,000	Remaining Value
– 4,400,000	Estate Taxes	– 5,885,000	Estate Tax
$ 3,600,000	Value to Heirs	+ 6,600,000	Insurance
		$ 11,415,000	Value To Heirs

*Represents losses due to forced liquidation

Upholding the truest expressions of creative financial planning, this concept can be executed in combination with one we discussed earlier for borrowing away your estate tax at no cost during your lifetime.

Avoid the Perils Of Forced Liquidation

In the previous example, we touched upon the dangers of forced liquidation. Now I want to examine in greater detail this threat to your estate value.

In any case in which a significant portion of an estate is composed of non-liquid assets, the threat of forced liquidation looms on the horizon. If not anticipated and planned for, the need to liquidate assets to pay estate taxes can increase the devaluation of an estate from the up to 55% that can be claimed by taxes to more than 75% or 80%.

Since liquid assets tend to be the least interest-producing of all, very few people of substantial wealth maintain any significant portion of their estate in cash or other liquid assets. However, if you have an estate worth more than $3 million and non-liquid assets make up more than 45% of it, when you die your heirs will be faced will the need to raise capital to pay the up to 55% estate taxes. These taxes are due in full within nine months after death. Faced with this necessity, their only choices will be to borrow the needed funds or sell off property.

If your heirs borrow the cash to pay the taxes, the interest they pay on the loan could eventually virtually double the cost of the taxes, effectively wiping out their entire inheritance.

If they sell property, they face the diminished returns earned under forced liquidation circumstances.

If the Smiths have an estate worth $18 million, their heirs will face estate taxes of $9.9 million. But the Smiths only have $5 million of liquid assets; the remaining $13 million is invested in real estate and other non-liquid vehicles.

In order to pay the tax bill as they inherit the $18 million estate upon the deaths of their parents, the Smiths' children will need to come up with $4.9 million in addition to the $5 million of liquid assets they inherited. Furthermore, if they need any liquidity for their own immediate needs, they will have to raise even more capital from the $13 million of non-liquid assets held in their parents' estate.

Assuming they decide they need $6 million—$4.9 million for taxes, $1.1 million to cover other expenses—they could borrow that $6 million against the $13 million of property. But at 7.5% interest rates, the loan will cost them $450,000 a year in interest. If they took 15 years to pay it off, they would pay $6.75 million in interest, effectively doubling the loan and, effectively, the estate tax.

It might seem better to sell off $6 million of property. Even though that would reduce the heirs' holding from $13 million to $7 million it would resolve their financial needs without the burden of loan interest. However, the $13 million valuation for their property might not represent a realistic appraisal of what they could get on the open market. Government assessments of worth for tax purposes are based upon generalized valuation information and don't necessarily correlate to the immediate sales prospects available for any given piece of real estate.

With a fixed period of time within which the sale must occur in order to produce the funds for the estate taxes, the heirs do not have the luxury to wait for a buyer willing to pay the assessed, expected value. It is not unusual in these situations for sellers to be forced into accepting significantly less than full value for their property. Should this occur, the heirs might well have to sell $9 million of their inherited property in order to realize $6 million. Now the heirs have $6.9 million left from their parents' $18 million estate—they have lost $11.1 million of their inheritance in their quest for liquidity to pay the taxes.

If the Joneses were faced with the same situation, they would be well served to follow the course laid out in the previous concept.

With their $18 million estate facing $9.9 million of estate taxes, they could avoid all need for their heirs to liquidate assets to pay estate taxes simply by using some of their existing liquidity to fund the purchase of life insurance. If the Joneses are age 60, a transfer of $990,000 to an Irrevocable Trust for the purchase of insurance will net the entire needed $9.9 million for their heirs. They will still have over $4 million in liquid assets to provide for their own needs and lifestyle and their estate taxes will be entirely provided for without any need to sell off property at their deaths. There will be no gift or transfer taxes required as the $990,000 falls within their combined exemptions.

If the Joneses are age 70, the cost for $9.9 million of insurance will be $1.9 million. Plus, they will have to pay gift taxes of $302,500 on the $550,000 of the transfer that exceeds their combined $1.35 million exemption (unless they pay part today and the rest over the years until 2006 when couples will be entitled to $2 million combined exemptions). They will still have over $3 million of liquid assets available to them plus $13 million of non-liquid assets.

Even at average age 80, when the cost of the needed $9.9 million is $3.3 million plus $1.1 million in gift taxes[20], the Joneses could afford to cover the entire estate tax for their $18 million

[20] Based on gift taxes of 55% on the $2 million of the transfer which exceeds their combined $1.35 million exemption.

estate without selling off any property. Of course, this would leave them with only $600,000 in liquid assets to support their own lifestyles so, at this point, they very well might want to sell some portion of their other holdings. However, they can do so at their leisure, without the pressure of the government deadline, and avoid the depreciation that might well otherwise devastate their worth.

Liquidity Is Not the Answer

Some people may take the previous concept to mean that having enough liquidity to cover their estate taxes is the answer to wealth preservation for their heirs. They couldn't be more wrong.

While liquidity will help avoid some of the more perilous costs of illiquidity, it is a far cry from being a sound economic plan for maximizing your heirs' inheritance. Yes, being liquid will save your heirs from the added loss that can occur due to a forced liquidation of assets. But it won't save them from the far greater loss of the cost of estate taxes.

Those people who smugly think that they have protected their prized possessions by having the cash on hand to pay estate taxes forget that their heirs will still have to hand over the cash. The better bottom line course is so simple, and yet so many people fail to grasp it: Using life insurance to discount estate tax costs can protect your estate from both the perils of illiquidity, and the perils of liquidity.

The technique for protecting against the loss of a liquid estate is no different from the basic concept of using life insurance's returns to leverage up to an effective ten times discount. Let's assume that the Smiths and Joneses each have estates worth $7 million. The Smiths, in anticipation of the tax bill, have provided for $3.3 million of liquidity for their heirs. They continue to earn interest on their $3.3 million so their plan has no negative impact on their own lifestyle and they are pleased to have protected their heirs against the need for a forced liquidation or loan upon their deaths. When the time comes, their children will pay the $3.3 million of taxes from their liquid assets and retain $3.7 million.

The Joneses take a different course. Being average age 60 and able to earn a 10–to–1 return on an insurance purchase, they divert $330,000 from their investments and properties to fund an Irrevocable Trust. The trust buys a last-to-die policy on their lives that will produce $3.3 million at their deaths for their heirs to use to pay estate taxes. The Joneses still have the use of over $6.7 million of their assets to support their lifestyle and, at their deaths, their heirs will inherit their entire estate without the loss of a single additional dime to estate taxes.

Liquidity may feel like the safe course, but without additional planning it still costs your heirs up to 55% of your total estate value.

THE SMITHS:		THE JONESES:	
$ 7,000,000	Estate	$ 7,000,000	Estate
– 3,300,000	Estate Taxes	– 330,000	Purchases Insurance
$ 3,700,000	To Heirs	$ 6,670,000	Remaining Estate
		– 3,300,000	Estate Taxes
		+ 3,300,000	Insurance Proceeds
		$ 6,670,000	To Heirs

Triple Your Heirs' Net Estate

Remembering that mathematics don't lie, I want you to follow the course of money with me to a bottom line that is effectively three times greater than it would have been had my "Die Rich" life insurance concept not been employed.

I also want you to remember the very important distinctions I showed you earlier regarding life insurance as it compares to investments. Remember, also, what I revealed about the errors in conventional thinking regarding internal rates of return and investment opportunities for the money I am telling you to outlay for insurance.

While it is true that, in today's excited market, there are stocks that are producing amazing returns, it is also true that the market is volatile and dips are as common as rises. Furthermore, it is a lot harder to predict the timing correctly to reap the big rewards than it might seem. If it weren't, everyone would be a millionaire by now. You must also remember that investment returns aren't great until they are great—and that can take some time. Time you may not have. Lastly, of course, is the reality of capital gains taxes on any assets you sell prior to your death which will then be further compounded by estate taxes. Using life insurance, you can virtually double your heirs' gross estate and triple their net estate.

The Smiths are average age 60 and have an estate worth $5 million. If they do nothing, their heirs will inherit $5 million. They will then be faced with estate taxes of $2.2 million leaving them $2.8 million.

At the same time, the Joneses, who are also age 60, take $500,000 of their $5 million estate and use it to purchase a life insurance policy on their combined lives. The purchase reduces their estate to $4.5 million. But the $500,000 diverted to the purchase of life insurance will produce an additional $5 million, which the Joneses' heirs will receive income and estate tax free. Now their total inheritance is increased to $9.5 million, virtually double the $5 million that the Smiths' children were slated to receive pre-tax.

On the $4.5 million that remains of the Joneses' original estate value, $2 million of estate taxes will be due. Their children will be left with $2.5 million plus the $5 million of insurance benefits for a total of $7.5 million. That is almost three times what the Smith children will be receiving after taxes.

Increase the net your children inherit three times!

THE SMITHS:

$ 5,000,000	**Estate**
– 2,200,000	**Estate Taxes**
$ 2,800,000	**To Heirs**

THE JONESES:

$ 5,000,000	**Estate Value**
– 500,000	**Insurance Purchase**
$ 4,500,000	**Remaining Estate**
– 2,000,000	**Estate Taxes**
$ 2,500,000	**After-tax Estate**
+ 5,000,000	**Insurance**
$ 7,500,000	**To Heirs**

For the Smiths to realize the same three times net on the after-tax value of their estate, they would have to be able to invest their entire $5 million, leaving nothing for them to support themselves with. The $5 million would then have to grow to $16.5 million, tomorrow, if necessary. That $16.5 million would then be subject to 55% estate taxes of about $9 million, leaving the same $7.5 million for their heirs that was so effortlessly and immediately produced by the life insurance concept at much less of a risk and while leaving access to the majority of the estate.

Investments have to grow by more than 300% to net the same return!

THE SMITHS:

$ 5,000,000	**Estate**
X 330%	**Return**
$16,500,000	**Value**
– 9,000,000	**Estate Taxes**
$ 7,500,000	**To Heirs**

Increase Your Exemptions

Shortly after President Clinton signed into law a schedule for increasing the amount of an estate that is exempt from estate taxes, I wrote a 24–page report detailing the effect of the increase on large estates and demonstrating how those increased exemptions could be maximized even further[21]. The text of that report has been reprinted and excerpted several times since then, yet the concept remains as fresh and important now as it was then.

We are now going into the fourth year of the nine-year exemption increase period. Individuals may now exempt the first $675,000 of their estate from estate taxes and married couples may exempt a combined $1.35 million. By 2006, individuals will be able to exempt the first $1 million and couples will be able to exempt $2 million combined between them, unless this is accelerated to a sooner date, which I believe it will be.

What does it really mean to have an exemption? Literally, it means that some portion of your assets, the exempted part, are not subject to the tax. In application, it means that your heirs inherit that portion of your estate intact. But does it really matter if the inheritance is intact because there were no taxes or whether it is intact because the taxes were replaced? I don't think so. Replacing a loss is the same, at the bottom line, as not having lost it. Replacement and exemption become interchangeable as long as

[21] To receive a free copy of Barry Kaye's special report on Clinton's Increased Exemptions, simply call 800-DIE-RICH (800-343-7424) and request one.

the net result is the same. So, while any increase is of value, what would be even more valuable would be the ability to exempt an entire estate, no matter how big, from all estate taxes. There is a way that you can, in effect, do exactly that. A perfectly legal, ethical, and demonstrable means to effectively exempt any estate worth up to $24 million from estate taxes and to 'buy' at highly discounted rates exemptions for any estate value over $24 million. The Smiths and the Joneses will show you how.

Both the Smiths and the Joneses have estates worth $24 million and are average age 60. Because the Smiths want their children to benefit from both of their $675,000 exemptions, they structure their estate so that when one of them dies their exemption goes into trust for the children. This way they avoid it becoming part of the other spouse's estate, which would defeat the purpose and make it subject to estate taxes as it passed to the heirs.

Upon the death of the second of their parents, the Smith children inherit their parents' $24 million estate. Taking into account the $1.35 million exemption, estate taxes total $13.2 million and the Smiths heirs are left with an inheritance of $10.8 million.

The Joneses are less concerned with preserving their exemptions than they are with providing the best legacy for their heirs. They transfer the $1.35 million of their combined exemptions to an Irrevocable Trust during their lifetimes. There are no gift tax consequences to the transfer because it falls within their exemptions. The trust buys a last-to-die insurance policy on the two of them and receives a 10-to-1 return.

Although the Joneses lose the use of the transferred $1.35 million during their lifetimes, they still have $22.65 million remaining to provide for their lifestyle. In fact, assuming a 5% return, their $1.35 million was only earning $67,500 a year in income. With their remaining $22.65 million earning $1.1 million, they won't suffer any negative repercussions from the transfer.

Upon the death of the second of their parents, the Joneses' children will inherit their $22.65 million estate upon which

$12.8 million of estate taxes will be due. However, they also receive $13.5 million of insurance benefits. The insurance pays the estate tax and the heirs inherit the estate virtually intact. In effect, the $1.35 million transfer to the insurance trust exempted the entire $24 million from estate taxes.

To Die Rich, simply follow this technique for exempting your entire estate from the costs of estate taxes.

THE SMITHS:		THE JONESES:	
$24,000,000	Estate	$24,000,000	Estate
–13,200,000	Estate Tax	– 1,350,000	Transfer to buy insurance
$10,800,000	To Heirs	– 12,828,750	Estate Tax
		$ 9,821,250	After-tax Estate
		+13,500,000	Insurance
		$23,321,250	To Heirs

The effectiveness of this technique is not limited to estates of $24 million or less. Although $24 million is the maximum that can be exempted in this fashion without any gift taxes, you can effectively 'buy' additional exemptions at greatly discounted rates. Think what the figures will look like when you can take advantage of two $1 million exemptions.

The logic is easy to follow. If you are worth more than $24 million, every dollar of your estate at the time it passes to your heirs will be reduced 55% by estate taxes. Yet, every dollar you divert to buy insurance will earn as much as a ten times return. Even if you have to pay gift taxes to make the transfer, you still come out way ahead by 'buying' more exemptions.

If the Joneses' estate were worth $50 million, their estate taxes would be $27.5 million. Insurance to cover the estate tax cost and exempt their estate would require a transfer of $2.75 million at average age 60. The first $1.35 million of the needed $2.75 million would be exempt from gift taxes. Gift taxes on the remaining $1.4 million would be $770,000. But as long as the Joneses lived at least 3 years after making the gift, that $770,000 would reduce their estate and therefore reduce the estate taxes. The estate tax cost savings realized by the heirs would reduce the cost from $770,000 to $346,000. So, for an effective net gift tax cost of $346,000 a transfer of $2.75 million could be made to an insurance trust. The $2.75 million transfer can not be considered a cost or expense as it is funding the highly advantaged 10-to-1 insurance return. The trust would buy $27.5 million of insurance on the Joneses, effectively exempting their entire $50 million estate from the costs of estate taxes.

Without utilizing this "Die Rich" technique, the Joneses would have saved their heirs $346,000. My way, they save them $27.5 million.

With a $75 million estate, the Joneses' heirs would be facing estate taxes of $41.25 million. It would take a $4.12 million transfer to an insurance trust to buy insurance to exempt the whole estate. Of that $4.12 million, $1.35 million would be exempt from gift taxes. The remaining $2.77 million would be subject to gift taxes of $1.53 million. In effect, $1.53 million of gift tax 'buys' the exemptions needed to protect the entire $75 million estate for the heirs. Yet, because after three years this $1.53 million reduces the Joneses' estate, it also reduces their estate taxes and saves their heirs about $841,500 making the effective net cost of the exemption $688,500.

Even if the Joneses were worth $100 million this technique would still be the far more economical way to proceed. $100 million is subject to $55 million of estate taxes. Insurance to pay the taxes and exempt the estate would cost $5.5 million, of which $4.15 would be subject to gift taxes of $2.28 million. After three years the $2.28

million reduction of the estate value would save the heirs $1.25 million of estate taxes making the effective cost of enacting this plan only $1.02 million. Is $1.02 million too much to pay to effectively exempt a $100 million estate from all estate tax costs?

At higher amounts, you can 'buy' your exemptions for the cost of the gift tax on the transfer.

Estate	**$ 50,000,000**	**$ 75,000,000**	**$100,000,000**
Tax Rate	**X 55%**	**X 55%**	**X 55%**
Estate Tax	**$ 27,500,000**	**$ 41,250,000**	**$ 55,000,000**
Discount*	**– 90%**	**– 90%**	**– 90%**
One-Pay Premium	**$ 2,750,000**	**$ 4,125,000**	**$ 5,500,000**
Exemptions	**– 1,350,000**	**– 1,350,000**	**– 1,350,000**
Gift Taxable	**$ 1,400,000**	**$ 2,775,000**	**$ 4,150,000**
Tax Rate	**X 55%**	**X 55%**	**X 55%**
Gift Tax	**$ 770,000**	**$ 1,530,000**	**$ 2,280,000**
Estate Tax Savings	**– 423,500**	**– 841,500**	**– 1,254,000**
Net Cost	**$ 346,000**	**$ 688,500**	**$ 1,026,000**

* At age 60, a one-pay, last-to-die policy provides a 10-to-1 return. Thus effectively you receive a 90% discount, based on current assumptions, and pay your taxes at only 10 cents on the dollar.

This method for increasing your exemptions will work for estates worth all the way up to $363 million. The estate taxes on $363 million are $200 million. As the maximum allowable insurance coverage for any one person is $200 million, this becomes the utmost expression of this concept.

The cost of $200 million of insurance at average age 60 is about $20 million on which gift taxes would total $11 million. This $11 million would exempt the entire $363 million from any depletion due to estate taxes. Furthermore, the $11 million outlay would reduce your estate by $11 million and therefore would reduce your estate taxes by $6 million. In effect, the net cost to accomplish this entire tax savings would be only $5 million, as opposed to $200 million of taxes.

As I said at the beginning, whether the exemption is granted by the government or provided by the insurance company, the extra money your heirs inherit spends the same.

Even at older ages, when the returns on the insurance purchase aren't as high, this plan performs better than just relying on your exemptions. Though the lower insurance return necessitates gift taxes for any estate over $7 million (average age 70) or $4 million (average age 80) the bottom line results are still inarguably better than if you do nothing. Let's compare the Joneses' $24 million estate at average age 70 and 80 versus the Smiths at any age.

Even at older ages, this "Die Rich" technique works to exempt large estates.

THE SMITHS:	THE JONESES AT AGE 70:	THE JONESES AT AGE 80:
$24,000,000 Estate	$24,000,000 Estate	$24,000,000 Estate
–13,200,000 Estate Tax	– 2,640,000 Transfer	– 4,400,000 Transfer
$10,800,000 To Heirs	– 710,000 Gift Tax*	– 1,680,000 Gift Tax*
	–12,438,250 Estate Tax	–12,438,250 Estate Tax
	$ 8,211,750 Net Estate	$ 5,481,750 Net Estate
	+13,500,000 Insurance	+13,500,000 Insurance
	$21,711,750 To Heirs	$18,981,750 To Heirs
	*Represents gift tax on $1.29 million. $1.35 million is exempt.	*Represents gift tax on $3.05 million. $1.35 million is exempt.

Less gift tax will be paid as a total $2 million exemption will be realized by 2006.

Protecting Lotteries and Structured Settlements

Sudden increases in wealth that will be paid out over time such as lottery winnings or other sweepstakes prizes, royalties, or some structured legal settlements, carry a double-edged sword of estate tax difficulties.

There is an IRS code section known as "Income In Respect Of A Decedent" that calls for estate taxes to be levied on the current value of promised income. In other words, the government figures out what the present value of the promised income is at the time of the owner's death, and assesses estate taxes based on that figure. If not properly planned for, this ruling can have financially devastating results on the family. What once seemed like a big win can quickly become a huge loss.

Suppose Mr. Jones won $12 million in his state's lottery, which was to be paid out at the rate of $600,000 a year for 20 years. Perhaps if he lives the full 20 years, Mr. Jones will spend the bulk of his winnings and estate taxes won't be a problem. But if he dies before the payment term is ended, the remainder of the payments due will become part of his estate and, unfortunately for his heirs, the government won't simply accept taxes on each yearly payment as it comes in. Instead, the IRS will determine an amount that the future payments are worth now and charge estate taxes on it. But where will Mr. Jones' family get the money to pay the taxes?

Remember, they haven't yet collected the funds that are being taxed. In all probability, the family will have to borrow the tax money against the future lottery income, greatly devaluing it.

There's a better way.

The formula by which the IRS calculates the present value of the future income is extremely complex. The amount differs based on how much has already been received and how much is outstanding. For this reason, I would simply suggest assuming that the entire $12 million is at risk, although it could be substantially less.

The estate taxes on $12 million would be about $6.2 million. The yearly cost of a $6.2 million last-to-die policy on Mr. and Mrs. Jones, assuming they are 60, would be $52,800. With an assumed $600,000 a year in newly found income, Mr. Jones could surely afford $52,800 a year to protect his winnings for his family. Then, should he die before the payment term had ended, the insurance proceeds would pay the assessed taxes for his heirs leaving them to go on collecting the remaining years of $600,000 payments that were due.

Of course, if Mr. Jones doesn't die before the end of the payout term, it is extremely likely that he and his wife will use some, if not all, of the winnings to support and enhance their lifestyles. His estate will be reduced by their spending and that will reduce his estate taxes. Should this occur, whatever portion of the $6.2 million of insurance benefits that isn't needed to pay taxes will create a "lottery winning" for his heirs as they recapture the portion of the prize their parents spent. If there are no estate tax ramifications, the $6.2 million will produce at 5% $310,000 a year in perpetuity, which could be considered a second lottery winning. In this way, everyone gets to die rich.

Maximize Charitable Giving

I have always believed that those of us who have enjoyed good fortune have an obligation to share it with others. No matter what your individual religious or spiritual beliefs may be, I think it is incontestable that we are all part of something that is bigger than we are, bigger than the reach of our extended families. The future of America and of the world is not something that will just happen. It is something that we shape today through our choices and our actions. I want a better world for my grandchildren and great-grandchildren. To that end, it is my responsibility and my joy to do what I can today to help provide a better tomorrow for them.

That is why the next three concepts are so important. They address a means to significantly increase gifts to charity without additional cost to you, which is one important part of improving life for everyone.

The proceeds from a life insurance policy can have, as the beneficiary, a charitable organization or your own foundation. If it is your intention to gift some portion of your wealth to charity, there is no better way to do so than to maximize the donation and increase it up to ten times, using life insurance.

In addition, because current tax laws favor voluntary charitable giving as a means for the private sector to help alleviate the government's attempts to improve life for all Americans, there are ways to leverage a charitable donation to benefit your family, as well. In doing so, nothing is lost to the charity. In fact, I believe that the added incentive of benefiting one's family can serve to increase the amounts given to charity.[22]

One of the best things about the concepts that follow that distinguishes them from some of the other concepts in this book is that you don't have to be rich to implement them or have them be of benefit to you. You don't have to be worth millions in order to make a difference. You don't have to be able to outlay tens of thousands of dollars to give a significant gift. In all the examples that follow, you can subtract zeroes to bring the numbers down to virtually any level and still know that you have accomplished a worthy goal.[23] Conversely, you can add zeroes if you want to give substantially beyond what is detailed on these pages.

For example, an outlay of approximately $800 a year on a last-to-die policy at average age 60 can produce $100,000 for charity while earning an up to $400 tax credit that reduces the effective cost to only $400 a year. It would take over 100 years of saving $400 a year for charity to equal the same gift.

Because of this great leverage, these charitable concepts are also more accessible to younger people who may not as yet have achieved a level of wealth that enables them to afford to outlay significant amounts. Because of the fabulous returns available at younger ages, almost anyone can afford to use these techniques to optimize their charitable inclinations.

Consider that a couple who average age 30 can purchase a life

[22] Consult your tax advisor and qualified attorney for implementation of these concepts and advice regarding their impact on your specific estate.

[23] The estate tax advantages described in the concepts that follow are not applicable to estates of less than $3 million and the impact of charitable gifting on your individual situation may be affected by your tax bracket.

insurance policy for $1,000 a year, which after their tax credit would really only be $500 a year, that could ultimately provide their charity $1 million. That's the equivalent of 2000 years of donating $500 a year.

The combination of tax credits and life insurance combine to create some of the most exciting and beneficial opportunities for charitable giving available. Occasionally when I'm talking to some parents they tell me that they don't want to use my techniques to optimize their estates for their children because they feel their children already have enough advantages. Likewise, there are some financial writers in the media who have speculated that the loss of half an estate to estate taxes isn't such a big deal because the heirs will inherit so much anyway. While I don't share these opinions, I make no judgments against those who do. But to them I say, if you don't want your kids to have more and you aren't taking anything away from the government, why would you let your fortune just evaporate into the public coffers when you could use it to do so much for so many.

There is no better way to die rich than to die rich in the knowledge that you have left behind a charitable legacy of help for others.

The More You Give Away, The More You Receive

You can just use whatever money you have slated for charitable giving, whether it is an annual gift of some percentage of your income or a one-time bequest, to greatly increase your intended donation.

Instead of gifting the money outright now, use it to purchase a life insurance policy and name the charity as the beneficiary. At your death, your charity will receive a highly optimized bequest. You can increase your donation ten times, if you and your wife purchase the insurance when you are age 60, five times if you are 70, and three times if you are 80.

The Smiths and The Joneses each decide to give $1 million to charity. The Smiths make the donation now. Because our nation favors charitable giving through tax incentives, they receive a $1 million write-off resulting in a $500,000 tax savings. In effect, their $1 million gift only cost them $500,000. The Smiths are thrilled that they can make such a generous gift and even more thrilled that they can do so in such an advantaged manner.

The Joneses also want to give $1 million to charity. But instead of giving the gift outright, they use the $1 million to buy a policy on their lives with the charity as beneficiary and owner. At average age 60, they receive a 10–to–1 return, which means that upon their deaths their donation to charity becomes $10 million instead of $1 million. They receive the same tax advantages as the Smiths did. They get the same $1 million write-off and the same resultant $500,000 tax savings for their gift but they have leveraged their $1 million gift to $10 million.

Gifts to charity can be greatly optimized using life insurance and the tax advantages of charitable giving.

THE SMITHS:		THE JONESES:	
$ 1,000,000	To Charity	$ 1,000,000	Buys Insurance
– 500,000	Charity Tax Savings	– 500,000	Charity Tax Savings
$ 500,000	Cost to Smiths	$ 500,000	Cost to Joneses
$ 1,000,000	To Charity	$ 1,000,000	Insurance
		X 10	
		$10,000,000	To Charity

If the Joneses did not execute this program until they were average age 70, their $1 million gift would increase to become a $5 million gift to their charity. Even if they wait until they are 80, they can still improve their gift's value from $1 million to $3 million.

The Joneses could further increase their gift by buying the policy on the lives of their children for the benefit of the charity. At young ages, the returns on a policy can be as much as 50 times. So, if they gift $1 million to their favorite charity or their own foundation for a policy on their children, they will gain an immediate $500,000 tax savings and, upon the ultimate death of their children, the selected charity receives $50 million.

Buying insurance on your children instead of on yourselves can optimize the charitable gift even more . . . still at no cost!

THE JONESES:

$ 1,000,000	**Buys Insurance On Their Children**
– 500,000	**Charity Tax Savings**
$ 500,000	**Cost To Jones**
$ 1,000,000	**Insurance On Children**
X 50	**Insurance Return**
$50,000,000	**To Charity**

I usually recommend to people who consult me about their charitable giving that they split the money they have slated for charity so that some is gifted immediately, some is used to buy insurance on them and some buys insurance on their children. This allows the pleasure of knowing the charity will receive an immediate gift along with the joy of substantially maximizing the entire donation.

In this way, the Joneses could take $100,000 of their $1 million intended gift and give it to the charity for current operations. Then they would take $700,000 to purchase a policy on themselves and use the remaining $200,000 to purchase a policy on their children, both for the charity. Upon their deaths, the charity will receive $7 million. Upon their children's deaths, it will receive $10 million more. Now the $1 million, one-payment outlay, which actually only cost them $500,000, will eventually produce more than $17 million for charity.

The ultimate expression of charitable giving enhanced by my "Die Rich" techniques.

THE JONESES:

$ 1,000,000	**Gift to Charity**
– 100,000	**For Current Operations**
– 700,000	**For Insurance On Them**
– 200,000	**For Insurance On Their Children**
$ 0	
$ 700,000	**For Insurance On Them**
X 10	**Insurance Return**
$ 7,000,000	**To Charity**
$ 200,000	**For Insurance On Their Children**
X 50	**Insurance Return**
$10,000,000	**To Charity**
$ 100,000	**For Current Operations**
+ 7,000,000	**Upon Their Deaths**
+10,000,000	**Upon Their Children's Deaths**
$17,100,000	**To Charity**

They could enact the exact same program using an annual payment plan as well.

Charitable giving can be one of the most delightful and fulfilling experiences there is. The pleasure that comes from knowing you have left a legacy of help for those who need it, is a very special joy. We all have something to contribute to make our world better and, using the techniques I have mentioned above, we can maximize those contributions to levels that were previously prohibitive. This is the epitome of what it means to die rich.

Use Borrowed Funds to Gift at No Cost to You

Another great way to use the incredible leverage of life insurance to maximize charitable donations is to borrow the money for the premium. This follows the basic concept I described in *Create Great Wealth for Your Heirs at Little or No Cost to You* on page 76. When we couple the tax advantages of charitable giving with the leverage of life insurance and the borrowing power of your portfolio, opportunities arise for charitable giving and family wealth creation that may seem too good to be true. But they're not. Everything contained in this concept is legal and accurate within current tax codes.

For this demonstration, let's assume that the Joneses are average age 60 and have a portfolio of $20 million in stocks and bonds. Using that portfolio as collateral, they could easily arrange to borrow $3 million at current Libor rates of 7%. The interest on the loan would be $210,000 a year, which they can pay or accrue to the principal for their heirs to pay off at their deaths on a tax deductible basis.

The Joneses donate the $3 million to charity in an insurance policy that will ultimately yield $30 million. They receive a $1.5 million tax savings for the donation, which they use to purchase $15 million of insurance for their children. This will provide their heirs with the money they need to repay both the loan principal and interest upon their parent's deaths. Now the Joneses have produced $30 million for charity with no cash outlay for them and no future cost to their heirs.

Borrow the cost of insurance to greatly enhance charitable giving.

THE JONESES:

$ 3,000,000	**Borrowed**
X 7%	**LIBOR rates**
$ 210,000	**Interest Per Year to Accrue**
$ 3,000,000	**To Insurance**
X 10	**Insurance Return**
$30,000,000	**To Charity**
$ 3,000,000	**For Charity**
X 50%	**Tax Deduction**
$ 1,500,000	**Tax Savings**
X 10	**Insurance Return**
$15,000,000	**To Heirs (pays off loan)***

* Based on life expectancy.

Simplistically the basic concept of borrowing away an insurance premium has created a highly optimized gift for charity. Creativity has then taken the tax advantages of charitable giving a step further to reimburse the cost for the heirs, or possibly even create greater wealth for them.

But there are ways to greatly enhance even this valuable outcome.

One very simple thing that the Joneses could do is to split their $3 million gift to charity into two $1.5 million one-pay premiums. One policy would be purchased on their lives and would provide $15 million for the charity. The other policy would be purchased on the lives of their children, who at average age 40 can receive a 28–to–1 return. This means that ultimately the second $1.5 million will produce $42 million in addition to the original $15 million. Nothing they have done has changed the yearly cost of the original $3 million loan or impacted their ability to recover that cost for their heirs. But now the charity receives $57 million.

Creativity enhances gifting even more!

THE JONESES:

$ 3,000,000	**Borrowed**
$ 1,500,000	**For Insurance On Them**
X 10	**Return**
$ 15,000,000	**To Charity Upon Their Deaths**
$ 1,500,000	**For Insurance On Their Children**
X 28	**Return**
$ 42,000,000	**To Charity Upon Children's Deaths**
$ 15,000,000	
+ 42,000,000	
$ 57,000,000	**Total to Charity**

In another example of innovative wealth creation, if the Joneses' children didn't need some or all of the $15 million they would receive from the policy purchased for them from the charitable donation tax credit, the Joneses could use their $1.5 million tax savings to buy insurance on their children for their grandchildren.

The Joneses could use $1.2 million of their tax savings to buy insurance on themselves for their children. This would return $12 million to their children, which would be enough to pay the loan balance after 20 years of accruing the interest. With the remaining $300,000 they could purchase a policy on their children's lives for their grandchildren. This policy could be expected to return as much as $8.4 million. Now the same borrowed $3 million, which costs the Joneses nothing, has produced $57 million for charity, $12 million for the Joneses' children, and $8.4 million for their grandchildren; $77.4 million in all.

Maybe the Joneses feel their children don't need any more money at all. They will already inherit the bulk of the Joneses' estate, which includes the $30 million in stocks, less the accrued loan principal and interest. Assuming they have already made arrangements for a policy to pay their estate taxes, and recognizing that half the outstanding loan balance is paid by the reduction in estate taxes it causes, the Joneses may well feel that their children are amply provided for. In that case, they could use the entire $1.5 million of tax savings they earn for their $3 million gift to charity to buy insurance on their children for their grandchildren. Now the grandchildren will come into approximately $42 million. This raises the amount produced to a total of $99 million; $57 million for charity and $42 million for the Joneses' grandchildren. And the Joneses never impacted their own finances or limited their access to any of the assets in any way.

It may seem confusing, but it is all true, accurate, and legal. If you don't understand each mathematical example, don't worry. What is most important is that you realize there are alternatives to conventional wisdom and that those alternatives can achieve phenomenal results for optimizing charitable giving. The specifics will depend on your individual situation. But what I most hope you take away from this is the knowledge that this is truly the absolute bottom line on maximizing and leveraging charitable giving to die rich.

Guaranteed Policies Create Opportunities for Highly Optimized Giving

I dedicated one of my *Bottom Line* columns to Ted Turner for what was, in my opinion, one of the finest acts of charity and social conscience ever up to that date. His unprecedented donation of $1 billion to the United Nations truly did, as he hoped it would, set a new standard for gallantry. The good works that can be accomplished with that money will create a lasting, living monument to the best of humanity. Ted Turner was to be congratulated. For countless people the world will truly be a better place because of what he has done.

Since that time, other marvelous acts of charity have been consummated throughout the country. The optimum to this point was $17 billion given by Bill Gates. There seems to be a new wave of understanding by older people and, more importantly, youngsters who have had tremendous success and have become billionaires.

Charitable giving is a great tradition in America. While very few people can afford to give anywhere near what Ted Turner or Bill Gates did, many give whatever they can, whenever they can. And, hopefully, many more will be inspired to undertake more charitable giving of their own.

Those who do will be well advised to utilize life insurance to enhance their gifts. With the advent of the new guaranteed policies that are overfunded to such an extent that their death benefits become greatly increased based on current assumptions, it is possible to eventually achieve a $1 billion donation for a net cost of $40 million.

Let's imagine that the Joneses have decided to emulate Ted Turner's spirit of charity. At their ages, they could purchase a guaranteed, last-to-die life insurance policy for an outlay of $80 million to produce a guaranteed $200 million. By giving the policy to charity, the $80 million becomes an immediate charitable gift and is tax deductible thereby saving them approximately $40 million in taxes and making the net cost of the policy $40 million.

The $80 million premium guarantees a $200 million return. At their ages, Mr. and Mrs. Jones could purchase $200 million of last-to-die insurance for only $20 million, however the policy would be based on current interest and mortality. By overfunding the policy, paying $80 million instead of $20 million, they guarantee the premium and death benefit.

But something almost magical happens with this type of policy. The guarantee of the death benefit and premium is based on guaranteed interest and mortality rates that are completely different from the current interest that is being earned and the mortality that is being charged. If the policy continues at current interest and mortality, then the death benefit will grow substantially since the policy has been overfunded. In this manner, the Joneses' policy will continue to grow and could eventually become worth $1 billion for their favorite charity, or their own foundation.

That would be a guaranteed $200 million and a potential $1 billion based on current assumptions for a net effective cost of only $40 million.

The same plan also works on a scaled down basis which you can envision simply by subtracting zeroes from all the stated amounts and sums. But whether your gift is $1 million, $10 million, $100 million or $1 billion, the fact you are doing good for others remains the same.

Case Studies

The previous examples have demonstrated how each of the individual "Die Rich" concepts works in a generalized manner.

However, in reality, people often have multiple marriages with children from more than one spouse. They are rarely starting from scratch and usually have some existing insurance that needs to be replaced, converted, updated, or expanded. Business interests and personal needs often mix and mingle.

On the following pages are actual cases and proposals taken from my files, with the names deleted to protect the clients' privacy. I am presenting them here to demonstrate how people like you can and have benefited from the application of my wealth creation, maximization, and preservation concepts.

Case Study #1
The Benefits of Replacing an Obsolete Policy

I want to start out with a case about replacement.

Because of the bad publicity generated by some unscrupulous insurance salespeople, replacement has become almost taboo in the industry. But there are some instances when not replacing an old policy is almost criminal. I'm going to go into this topic in more depth in the chapter entitled *The Bottom Line On Insurance*, but I think it is important to demonstrate how advantageous it can be to replace an obsolete policy with one better suited to the circumstances. The following is one such demonstration.

I had as a client a couple who several years previous to consulting me had purchased a last-to-die life insurance policy with a death benefit of $3 million for which they were paying $40,000 yearly on a life-pay basis. Since that time, the policy had accrued cash value of $129,970.

By the time they came to me, the couple felt they needed more insurance to help cover their estate taxes, which had increased since they first bought the original policy, and to leave something in excess to help create wealth for their children. They were intending to purchase a second $3 million policy. Unfortunately, the husband's age and medical condition were detrimental to an insurance purchase.

Of greater concern to me than the state of the man's health was the fact that the couple's existing policy only lasted to age 92. If one of them lived longer than that, the heirs would only receive the accrued cash value; the death benefit would no longer be available. This was a terribly precarious position to be in.

When I proposed to the couple that, rather than simply purchase a second policy we should look into replacing the first one, they were apprehensive. Like so many others, they had heard horror stories about replacement and were inclined against it. I told them I would go ahead and get the wife examined, which we had to do for the supplemental policy anyway, and then provide them with information upon which they could base their decision.

The wife's medical exam went very well and we were able to get the highest Preferred rating from a major, highly rated insurance company on her. As promised, I showed the couple the numbers just for buying a second policy as compared with replacing the old policy and buying one new one.

As it turned out, by rolling the $129,970 surrender value of the first policy into an individual new policy bought only on the wife (it would pay off whether she died first or second), we were able to secure $6.5 million of insurance for the same annual premium of $40,000 on the same life-pay basis. That was $500,000 more than they had been hoping to get from the sum of two $3 million policies with a new premium on the second $3 million policy. Furthermore, the new policy would last past age 110.

The couple almost didn't execute this plan because they were afraid to believe it was true. The idea they could pay the same annual payment and reap an additional $3.5 million of death benefit seemed too good to be true. But when we delivered the policy and everything checked out, they were overjoyed with the result.

Rather than avoid thoughts of replacement, or only review policies when new factors come up, I suggest people with older policies have them reviewed periodically.

Changes in interest, mortality, and underwriting, along with the advent of new pricing structures within the insurance industry, can create tremendous savings for people who bought during times when prices were higher, mortality lower, or underwriting more strict. More importantly, with people living longer, it is absolutely imperative that any policy that runs out previous to age 100 should, at the very least, be examined and the policy replaced if at all possible.

Case Study #2
Blending Techniques to Maximize Assets

Shortly after he attended one of my seminars, a man called my office to set up an appointment. Although he had always carried life insurance for income replacement in the event of his death, he never thought of it as a means of wealth creation. He said he was intrigued by some of my concepts and wanted to see what I might suggest for him. He wanted to maximize his assets for his children and he also hoped to be able to increase his bequests to his favorite charity.

After a thorough evaluation of his current estate status, and those of his immediate family, I proposed four means to improve the outcome for his heirs without impacting his own cash flow in any way.

I'm including his case as a demonstration of the fact that often there is no one best way to proceed with a case. By looking into various sources for premiums and applying several techniques simultaneously, we were able to virtually double this man's estate value for his heirs.

To begin with, I suggested that the man's mother borrow $1 million against her $2 million estate and have her gift the funds to his children, her grandchildren. There would be no tax consequences to the transfer, as it would fall within his mother's generation skipping exemption.

The $1 million would be used to purchase a $10 million last-to-die life insurance policy on the lives of the man and his wife. The loan would be repaid upon the mother's death out of the proceeds of her estate. During her lifetime she would maintain control of all of her assets and all of the income that those assets generate. But, at the same time, the assets would become the collateral for the $1 million loan that would produce the $10 million life insurance.

Since my client and his wife were financially secure, the loss of the $2 million they stood to inherit from his mother was no where near as significant as the ability to generate $10 million for his children. Moreover, this was an excellent method of doing estate planning for his children.

Next I looked at the man's IRA which was at risk from the double taxation that applies to IRAs at death. The man's $2 million IRA would be subject to $800,000 of income taxes and the remaining $1.2 million would be subject to over $600,000 of estate taxes, leaving only $600,000 for his children.

Assuming the IRA was appreciating 10% annually, or $200,000 a year, I recommended that he distribute the appreciation immediately since otherwise the funds would ultimately be decimated by taxation. The $200,000 would still be subject to $80,000 of income taxes each year but would leave $120,000 annually. By gifting that annual $120,000 to his children, they could purchase $16 million of life insurance on him and his wife.

In demonstrating this concept to the man I pointed out that his IRA would have to grow to be worth $60 million to net the same $16 million after income and estate taxes for his children. I also pointed out that, during his lifetime, he would still maintain control of his IRA principal in the event he wanted the funds for any reason. At death he would have the option of leaving the IRA proceeds to his children (less any taxes due) or he could opt to leave the whole amount to charity knowing that his children would receive $16 million.

As a third option for wealth creation, I suggested the man create a $16 million bequest to the charity he supported with no current cash flow impairment to him.

Since he was a wealthy man with a significant investment portfolio, I recommended he borrow $2 million against his securities to purchase a $20 million last-to-die life insurance policy on the lives of himself and his wife. Assuming a 7% yearly interest rate being accrued, the original $2 million loan would grow to $8 million over a 20-year period. However, since that $8 million outstanding loan would reduce the man's estate and therefore his estate taxes, the after-tax cost of the loan would only be $3.6 million. Upon the man's death, the $20 million would come to the trust tax free. After paying off the loan principal and interest, more than $16 million would be left to fund a foundation to make charitable contributions in the future at no cost to the man's family. In fact, his children would receive an annual trustee fee.

As my last wealth creation recommendation for this client, I offered the man a means of tripling the value of his $10 million ranch for his heirs.

At the time that he came to me, the man had been investigating creating a method of artificially reducing the value of his property. By reducing its value, he would also reduce the estate taxes due upon it. However, he might also have wound up reducing his family's ability to enjoy the property.

As an alternative, I suggested he take a $1.1 million mortgage on his ranch to purchase $11 million of life insurance. The debt service on the loan would be $77,000 per year, which is tax deductible.

I then explained to the man that, if he were to do nothing, his $10 million ranch would be worth less than $5 million to his children. Following my plan, for $34,000 after-tax annually, he could triple its value. When combined with the $5 million after tax value of the ranch, the $11 million tax free insurance brings the total value to $16 million, as opposed to only $5 million if he does nothing.

The combined effect of these four ideas was to double the value of the man's gross estate and triple the value of his net estate. All of which could be accomplished without impacting his cash flow in any way since he would be borrowing the premiums or creating them from the IRA.

This case is one of my favorite examples of the incredible results that can be achieved using a blend of methods to achieve a goal.

Case Study #3
On the Difference Underwriting Makes

I was a pioneer in getting the insurance industry to accept a single medical underwriting form for various insurance companies. This was important because previously each new application required a new exam and few people were willing to go through the process numerous times. Instead, they wound up buying all their insurance from one company to avoid multiple exams.

But part of what makes one company better than another in a certain circumstance is the underwriting. For example, together you and your spouse may receive a rating from one company that makes their policy the most cost-efficient for you. However, individually, either one of you might do better with another company that evaluates your condition differently. If you relied on the same company to provide both a last-to-die policy and a single insured policy just to avoid the one person having to take two exams you could wind up paying more than you have to or receiving less benefit.

Now, with the ability to send the same exam to several companies, we can "shop" for the best coverage, best price, and best underwriting. And that can make a significant difference in the overall outcome, as the following case study demonstrates.

When I met with this client, we discussed optimizing the excess income that he receives each year. He had several existing policies but had paid enough into them all that they no longer required additional payments. The excess income that had previously been used to pay those premiums, and gift taxes on the premiums, totaled approximately $850,000 annually. I suggested that he optimize $400,000 a year by increasing it to an ultimate $10 million.

At first the client was unsure if he believed this was the best way to go. Like so many others he was somewhat a victim of conventional wisdom. His accountant had advised him that he could invest the excess funds in municipal bonds to increase his estate for his heirs. But as I pointed out to him that it was unlikely that an annual investment of $400,000 was going to gross $10 million, he agreed it seemed improbable. As I then pointed out that the bonds would actually have to grow to be worth more than $20 million in order for them to net $10 million for his children, he agreed it was impossible and embraced the logic of my plan.

I knew that the actual final amount to be purchased would depend upon the underwriting we could obtain. After the man completed his physical exam, I sent the results to several top insurance companies and received back a wide range of ratings. However, I was able to get one company to give the man their best Preferred rating and that meant that he could get the whole $10 million. That price represented a $105,000 a year reduction in premium over the next lowest underwriting class that was being offered.

To maximize the benefit of this policy into a total "Die Rich" concept, the man then named as beneficiary of the policy a private foundation, which he created especially for this technique. With the $10 million of funding, the foundation will ultimately be able to donate a minimum of $500,000 a year to various charities, as well as provide a trustee's fee to his children of approximately $150,000–$250,000 per year. This was also equivalent to leaving his children another $10 million since, at 5%, it would take that amount of principal to produce the same $250,000 yearly in perpetuity. The foundation will last in perpetuity so that after the man and his wife are gone the family name will continue the wonderful philanthropy for which it has always been known.

I then started to analyze the man's existing policies, of which he had several.

He had one policy for $3 million that, at the time, had a cash surrender value of $980,000. It was a last-to-die policy on him and his wife but was limited in that it would only last through year 23 when he was 103 and his wife was 96. There were various options available to make the policy last longer, but they were expensive.

Instead, I submitted the underwriting to a couple of companies I know to be good for people at their ages and medical conditions. Because of favorable changes in one company's evaluation of certain health factors, I was able to create a situation in which the man was able to provide more insurance for his heirs, at better rates, with a policy that would last forever.

He transferred the $980,000 cash surrender value from the old $3 million last-to-die policy to a new one with a death benefit of $3.2 million on just his wife's life . No additional premiums were required to extend the coverage or benefit. In addition, with the policy being on the man's wife alone, if she predeceases him the death benefit will be paid out immediately; the heirs won't have to wait until the second death.

Although I usually work with last-to-die policies when two people are involved because they afford the best rates and returns, in a situation where a better rate can be achieved by insuring only one person it is preferable to go that route. That way, the payment of the death benefit may be made sooner, if the insured predeceases his/her spouse. If the insured lives longer than his/her spouse, the heirs are no more delayed than they would have been with a last-to-die policy.

The man had three additional policies. Two of them were satisfactory although one did not last as long as it should to protect his family's best interests. Even though statistically it is still rare for people to live to be 100, enough do to make it mandatory, in my opinion, for insurance policies to last at least that long, if not longer. Usually the cost to extend the coverage to age 100 is relatively minor in comparison to the overall policy cost. More importantly, it is usually quite a bit less than what the heirs have to lose should the insured outlive the policy.

In this case, I recommended that we take a "wait and see" approach with the one policy that didn't last long enough. It was my feeling that there was a good chance the policy would correct itself based on increasing interest rates over the next few years. Because the policy required no more premiums for the death benefit through the wife's age 96, based on current assumptions, were interest rates to go up and the policy to be earning more, the coverage period would wind up being extended. And since the opportunity to simply pay more into the policy to extend the coverage period would be available at any time, I recommended that the man hold off on paying anything more into the policy at this time.

The third policy was, in my opinion, severely deficient in its coverage period and I thought it unlikely that any increase in interest over the next several years would be equal to the amounts needed to sufficiently extend the coverage.

Once again I sent the medical exams to a variety of companies and once again I was able to offer my client a highly optimized solution to his dilemma.

By transferring the cash surrender value of $440,000 to a new policy, an annual premium of $15,802 would keep it in effect forever, based on current assumptions. This is in contrast to a $15,000 annual premium increase that would have been required just to extend the old policy from age 91 to age 95 and an additional $86,068 annually it would take to extend the policy beyond age 95.

The client in this case executed the programs I recommended. He now lives rich in the knowledge that when he dies, he will die richer than he otherwise would have.

Case Study #4
Planning with Multiple Marriages

This case illustrates the simple, yet dramatic, basis of my "Die Rich" principles: The use of life insurance to increase a bequest at a greatly reduced cost.

A man came to me who had had the intention of giving $1.5 million to his wife. It was his desire that the money would ultimately be distributed to her children from a previous marriage and their children together. After reading one of my books, he had realized that he could optimize the gift by using life insurance to greatly increase it.

With the aid of an attorney, the man established an Irrevocable Insurance Trust and gifted it $1 million. The remaining $500,000 was held to pay the gift tax on the transfer since he had already used up all of his exemptions and additional upcoming exemptions were already committed.

Even though his wife, on whose life the policy was purchased, was 79, she was able to receive a 3.3-to-1 return on the one-pay policy premium. The policy purchased with the $1 million is structured to last forever, based on current assumptions, and will ultimately produce $3.3 million tax free.

The same $1.5 million that the man had available to him would have had to grow to $7.4 million during his lifetime in order to net the same $3.3 million after estate taxes of $4.1 million. Clearly, it is extremely unlikely that this would occur.

Now, his wife's children will receive far more than they had ever imagined and his children will also benefit by the additional coverage that has been provided. I like this particular type of situation for the psychological effect within the family. It is a very meaningful thing to a second wife to know that her husband is concerned with taking care of her own children. It is especially valuable that this is accomplished with benefits to his children, as well, and at no additional cost to achieve the end result.

It is a very simple demonstration, yet I believe that in its simplicity lies its beauty. Without avoidance of any kind, without convoluted shelters, or complicated legal maneuvers, this man increased a $1.5 million legacy to a $3.3 million legacy. He doesn't have to wait and hope that his $1.5 million will grow to $7.4 million in time. His optimized legacy is available immediately upon his wife's death.

A slightly more than 3 times return might not seem so dramatic, particularly when returns of 10–to–1 have been routine throughout these pages and some have even gone as high as 50–to–1. But if there is anywhere else a 79-year-old woman can put $1 million and have it grow to $3.3 million even if she dies tomorrow, I have never heard of where it might be.

Case Study #5 The Municipal Bond Alternative

In the section on wealth creation techniques, I demonstrated the Municipal Bond Alternative (page 57). For that plan, I showed the advantage of selling off municipal bonds and using the principal to purchase an immediate annuity which would produce significantly more income on a tax advantaged basis.

There is another permutation of this concept that can be used to maximize wealth without having to sell off any bonds. This is a concept I developed as a demonstration for a very wealthy man who has a substantial amount of his wealth in municipal bonds.

For the example, I isolated $100 million of the man's bonds, which can be assumed to be producing $5 million of annual income. (You can customize this example to your own situation using $10 million of bonds, $1 million of bonds, or even less. Simply pro rata the numbers up or down as needed.)

Assuming that the man's purpose in holding his bonds is for safety and liquidity of principal and that he doesn't need the $5 million of yearly income to support his lifestyle or other endeavors, he could gift $3.2 million to his children or Irrevocable Trust each year. He would then pay the government $1.8 million in gift tax, thus using up the entire annual $5 million. At his and his wife's ages, $3.2 million of annual premium could purchase a life insurance policy with a death benefit of $228 million based on current assumptions.

If the man retains this isolated $100 million of bonds throughout his lifetime, at death estate taxes will claim $55 million leaving his heirs $45 million. Yet, without touching his principal and using only the 'give up' of $5 million yearly income, I have produced an additional $228 million of insurance benefit. Now his $45 million has been transformed into $273 million, income and estate tax free. This could be one of his better investments and, at the very least, an excellent means of diversification.

If the man were to live ten more years to age 80, his yearly $5 million outlay would total $50 million. Yet, had that $50 million remained in his estate it would have been subject to estate taxes of $27.5 million leaving his heirs $22.5 million. Therefore, the net cost for the insurance coverage is not $50 million but $22.5 million.

If he were to live twenty years to age to 90, the $5 million yearly becomes $100 million, which would only be worth $45 million to his heirs after estate taxes. Now it is an effective cost of $45 million that has produced the $228 million return, still a substantial growth and far more than his municipal bonds could produce. And remember, he still has the original $100 million of bonds, which, after estate taxes, will be worth approximately $45 million to his heirs. $228 million of insurance, plus $45 million of bonds equals $273 million all from the same $100 million and using income he did not otherwise need.

The man's $100 million of bonds would have to grow to be worth about $620 million in order to be worth the same $228 million to his heirs at death after estate taxes. And to plan wisely, he has to consider the reality that death can come at any time.

Which is the more sensible course—to utilize $5 million of unneeded yearly income to produce a tax free $228 million immediately upon death even if death comes tomorrow? Or, to wait and hope that time allows for $100 million of municipal bonds to grow to $620 million?

To give this plan even more potential for wealth creation, the man could isolate the income from another $10 million of his bonds—$500,000 a year—and gift $320,000 to his grandchildren in a Generation Skipping Trust.[24] He would pay approximately $180,000 a year in gift tax upon the transfer. Used to purchase an insurance policy on his children's' lives (ages 30–40), the annual $320,000 buys $200 million. Is there anywhere else that $500,000 of income a year can turn $10 million of bonds, worth $5 million at death, into $200 million for his grandchildren?

You may not have hundreds of millions of dollars to work with, but this same plan and the principles it demonstrates would work as well for you at lesser numbers as it would for the man I originally conceived it for.

[24] See chapter entitled *Build a 100-year Tax Free Dynasty* on page 96

Case Study #6
Outperforming Microsoft

As I was writing this book, a phone call came in from a man in the Northwest. He had invested $100,000 in Microsoft some time ago and at the time that he called me, after several splits, the stock was worth $650,000. In sitting down to do some estate planning the man realized he was caught somewhere in between a rock and a hard place in regards to this stock gain. If he sold the stock to reap the profit, he would be faced with capital gains taxes of 20%, which would devalue the stock by $110,000 to $540,000. But if held the stock as part of his estate for his heirs, hoping for additional gains or, at worst, that it stayed level, it would face estate taxes of 55% upon his death. His $650,000 asset would lose $357,500 to be worth only $292,500 to his children.

The man was upset at both prospects. He said it took a lot of the pleasure of having earned such a significant gain to know that so much would be forfeit to taxes.

I assured the man that there was a third option available that would not only preserve his gain but also greatly optimize it.

The man did not need the $650,000 his stock had become worth. He did not even need the $540,000 he would get from a sale of the stock after taxes. His preference was for the stock to be a legacy to his children.

I recommended that he sell the stock, which he did. He paid

$110,000 in capital gains tax and gifted the remaining $540,000 to an Irrevocable Insurance Trust. Because the $540,000 gift to the trust fell within his $675,000 exemption, he paid no gift tax on the transfer.

Using the $540,000, the trust then purchased a life insurance policy on the lives of the man and his wife who together averaged age 55. The one-pay, last-to-die policy provided a death benefit of $7 million, based on current assumptions.

This is an excellent method for maximizing an investment gain. It avoids gift tax and estate tax and turns the original gain into the funding mechanism for an even larger gain that is itself income and estate tax free if properly structured within an Irrevocable Trust. $7 million versus $292,500 from the same stock gain, a parlay from the original $100,000 invested in Microsoft to $7 million tax free for his heirs—it is a hard bottom line to argue with.

For the stock investment to net the same return for the man's heirs it would have to grow to be worth about $16 million so that after estate taxes of $8.8 million, $7.2 million would remain. Is $650,000 worth of stocks that have already grown from $100,000 going to increase in value more than 24 times more in order to be worth $16 million before tax? It is very unlikely. Is $650,000 used to buy life insurance going to produce at the deaths of the insureds $7 million that is the equivalent of $16 million before tax? Absolutely.[25] Did you ever think that life insurance could be a better investment alternative than Microsoft?

[25] Based on current assumptions. However, even if there are changes to the assumptions, the outcome will still be highly optimized as compared with the outcome if nothing is done.

Case Study #7 Cash Rich— But at What Expense

Many of the clients I deal with made their fortunes after the depression. Though they are undeniably and securely rich, they still have the fear of poverty that the children of people who lived through such a desperate time often retain. This is called a "depression mentality". Though they love their families and truly want to improve life for their posterity, they are reluctant to part with any of their money. Their security lies in being "cash rich"; a value passed on to them through their parents' experience.

One such client came to me not too long ago. He was a widower, age 72, with two children and two grandchildren.

The man had \$20 million in municipal bonds that produced \$1.25 million yearly. Alone, at his age, he lived a relatively simple lifestyle that was easily supported on \$350,000 annually. The remaining \$900,000 of yearly income he put back into more bonds.

The man agreed that he was practicing bad estate planning. He fully realized that half of everything he was putting back into the bonds for his heirs was going to be lost to estate taxes. Yet he could not get past his fear. "I'd like to protect them," he said, "and I'd like your help, but only if you can improve my children's inheritance without giving any of my money away."

I assured the man that he could still greatly improve his outcome.

Though it wouldn't be the ultimate expression of what could be accomplished, I could meet his conditions, keep him whole, and still provide an optimized estate for his heirs. The man was curious —his lawyers and accountants had always told him that without giving away a large portion of his wealth nothing could be done to avoid the losses his estate would suffer to taxes—and relieved.

I suggested to the man that he use his yearly $900,000 of "junk money" income overage to buy a life insurance policy, which, at his age, would produce $30 million for his heirs. To accommodate his conditions, his would retain ownership of the policy within his estate thereby retaining access to the cash surrender values. In effect, the policy would work much the same way as any bond, CD, or savings account, building up cash reserves against which he could borrow. Or, if he needed to at any time, he could surrender the policy for its value. His funds would still be within his control.

"How long," I asked him, "would it take your yearly $900,000 to become $30 million? More importantly, what if you die tomorrow?"

The man was thrilled. My plan achieved two goals he had previously been told were mutually exclusive and unattainable: Without giving his money away he could produce a highly optimized outcome for his children.

Of course, by arranging the purchase of the policy in this way, the proceeds would become a part of his estate upon his death and $15 million would be lost to estate taxes. However, his heirs would still come out $15 million ahead. Without this plan, they would receive only the $10 million that would remain after his $20 million of bonds were halved by estate taxes. Now they would receive that $l0 million plus $15million more.

I then presented the man with an option I was pretty sure he would be resistant to. Nonetheless, I thought it my responsibility to give him the whole picture of what could be accomplished so that he knew exactly what he was rejecting.

"How would you like the same annual $900,000 to become worth $42 million to your children?" I asked him. "It will involve giving the money away but the reality is that you can afford it, and what you will get back in terms of the joy and pleasure of leaving your children so secure is priceless. It is what I refer to as living rich and dying richer."

I told the man that if he were to gift $600,000 to an Irrevocable Insurance Trust each year and pay $300,000 in gift taxes on the transfer, the trust could purchase a life insurance policy on him that would yield $20 million for his heirs.

I then showed him how that $20 million tax free was the equivalent of $42 million before taxes. Clearly there was no way his yearly $900,000 in excess bond income was going to go to $42 million during his lifetime. If he followed this plan, I further demonstrated, his heirs would ultimately wind up with $30 million—$10 million that would remain after estate taxes were assessed on his $20 million of bonds plus $20 million of tax free life insurance. His bonds would have to grow to about $65 million to net the same inheritance for his heirs.

Once the man realized the bottom line of my suggestion, he opted to go with the plan. He told me that for an outcome like what I had just shown him, he was willing to take the risk. He then explained that in the past the legal tax avoidance plans he had been shown required him to give away large portions of his principal in order to achieve far less dramatic results for his heirs. At best they offered to minimize the taxes. Nothing else had come close to what I had just demonstrated. It was all just too much risk for too little return.

But now that he had seen my plan, which left his principal intact and used only his excess yearly income to go so far beyond tax avoidance to such significant wealth creation, he was thrilled.

I have often found it to be the case that people who are adamant about what they will and will not tolerate in regards to their estate plan are simply uninformed as to what their options actually are. Most of the time, as with this man, once they have been educated and see what can be accomplished using the leverage of life insurance, they embrace the opportunity happily.

Case Study #8
More for Less—Another Look at Replacement

Because it is such a hotbed of controversy, I want to come back to another case about replacement.

It angers me that a few bad apples who have exploited people by improperly replacing policies in order to earn the commissions have managed to create such paranoia within the public. Of course, it is wise to be cautious; there's no denying the fact that there are those unscrupulous people within every industry who will take advantage of others for their own selfish purposes. However, too many people now dismiss out of hand any question of reviewing their existing policies or replacing them with better ones because they fear churning. While I don't blame them, it saddens me to know that many people now have inadequate or antiquated coverage, or are paying too much for the coverage they have, because their policies are obsolete.

For that reason, I think it important to demonstrate again what can be accomplished when an old policy, bought during a less advantageous time, is replaced with a newer and better one.

The client in this case was 70 years old. His wife was 65. One of their many policies was a $3 million last-to-die policy that they had bought 6–7 years before for which they were paying $46,000 a year. However, because of changes in the interest since the original assumptions were made when they had bought the policy, the policy would now only last to age 95 without lowering the death benefit or increasing the premium.

I reviewed the policy, had the wife examined, and found that for the exact same $46,000 a year the couple could purchase a new policy on just the wife with a death benefit of $4 million. The new policy would last until the wife's age 110 instead of 95. Since there was $88,000 of cash value in the original policy, it could be used to pay the premium for the first two years of the new policy, thus saving $88,000.

I feel it is extremely important to demonstrate this outcome to you. Few people, approached by an insurance professional, would believe that a new policy bought on one person at age 65 could outperform an older policy bought on two people at average age 60. Yet, because of changes within the industry, the advent of new pricing and new types of policies, that is exactly the case.

Without periodic review and a willingness to consider replacement, many people are in danger from obsolete policies. At the least, they are paying too much for too little coverage. At the worst, they risk having their policy run out before they die. These outcomes are, or should be, far more objectionable than the payment of a new commission to a salesperson who diligently performs his services by identifying a potential problem and resolving it. Especially when that commission is factored into the result, paid by the insurance company, and doesn't require any further outlay on your part.

$88,000 savings, $4 million versus $3 million, the same $46,000 annual premium, coverage to age 110 versus 95, and death benefits whether the wife dies first or second. Who says it doesn't pay to replace an old policy?

I know for a fact that the client in this particular case was delighted with the outcome. Because in this case the client was me.

Case Study #9
Give to Receive

For this example, I turn to a couple in their 70's to help me demonstrate how a combination of techniques can be used to protect and optimize outcomes—the hallmarks of my wealth creation and preservation theories.

To begin with, the couple had a $6 million last-to-die policy for which they were paying $98,000 a year that was only going to last to age 95, based on the assumptions under which it was purchased.

Even though, statistically, not that many people live past age 95, statistics have no bearing on any individual person; they only apply to large groups. So while it may be statistically safe to have a policy that only lasts to age 95, no individual wants to be the one who lives to age 100 and finds their coverage gone. Especially when avoiding this situation can be accomplished at no additional cost or risk whatsoever.

In fact, in this case, we were able to not only extend the coverage to age 110, we were able to do so at a savings of $6,000 a year. We were also able to do so buying a policy only on the wife instead of using a last-to-die. That was the first step in maximizing the couple's estate. But we ultimately did so much more.

This couple had determined that they had about $240,000 a year available to use to optimize their legacy. They were looking for advice as to how to best apportion the funds to leave more for both their children and to charity.

I recommended that they take the $240,000 of available yearly funds and use it to purchase a life insurance policy with their own foundation as beneficiary. At their ages and their health, their annual $240,000 purchased $10 million of insurance for charity. And, since the $240,000 yearly premium constitutes a charitable donation and is tax deductible, they receive annual tax savings of $120,000.

I then suggested that the couple use that annual tax savings to purchase a second policy on themselves for the benefit of their children. That policy has a $5 million death benefit.

The couple was virtually speechless at the idea that the annual $240,000 they were able to divert to their plans for their posterity could reap such a remarkable outcome. They had never imagined that $240,000 a year could produce $15 million; $10 million for their charitable foundation and $5 million for their heirs.

Yet it didn't stop there.

With the children named as the trustees of the foundation, they are able to earn somewhere between $100,000–$200,000 a year in trustee fees. As I pointed out to the couple, this is the equivalent to their leaving up to $4 million additional to their children, which, at 5% interest, could create $200,000 of income in perpetuity for their heirs. Now their annual $240,000 can be said to be producing $19 million—$10 million for charity, $5 million in death proceeds to the children, and income on the equivalent of an additional $4 million for the children.

They have produced enough insurance proceeds for the children to offset any estate taxes on their remaining assets, created money for charity, and additional income to aid their children in living rich. Surely this is the ultimate bottom line on wealth creation, maximization and preservation.

Case Study #10
Creating $6 Million for $3,500 a Year

This next concept is one of the most exciting I have ever presented. I put it together for a client in California and his wife using a blend of various techniques. In the end, I was able to produce $6 million for his heirs and charity at a yearly cost to him of only $3,500.

One of the things that make this plan so exciting is the amazing return it provides for such a low effective cost. Another is the fact that it is available to virtually anyone who owns a home[26].

This client came to me as a referral. I had worked with a friend of his who had originally come to me looking only to improve an inferior policy. Ultimately the friend wound up optimizing some unneeded pension plan benefits into a significantly enhanced legacy for his children. Now he had recommended me to this new prospect to see what could be done to maximize his situation.

The new client was well versed in the uses of life insurance for estate preservation through estate tax cost discounting but was unaware of the many ways it could be used to maximize wealth. He was also unable at that time to divert any additional funds from his income to implement a plan.

I examined the man's assets to see where 'excess' funds might

[26] Some qualification is required.

be languishing, awaiting only the application of some creativity to become of real value. I found them in his house.

Like most homeowners, this man had the ability to borrow up to $100,000 against the equity in his home and receive a tax credit for loan income expense. This is the only way that you can deduct personal interest. In relatively short order I was able to show him how he could effectively turn that $100,000 equity home loan into $6 million at a net cost of only $3,500 a year, which was well within his limited budget.

I advised the man to take the $100,000 loan, which at today's 7% rates would cost $7,000 a year. However, because this loan fell within his allowable home equity loan interest tax deduction and he was in a 50% income tax bracket, he was able to deduct half the cost leaving a net expense of only $3,500 per year.

I then recommended that the man gift the $100,000 to his own charitable foundation in the form of a last-to-die insurance policy purchased on the lives of him and his wife. As the couple averaged age 50 and qualified for a 20–to–1 return, this would ultimately create up to $2 million for his charitable foundation.

In addition, I suggested the man name his children as trustees of the foundation for which they would receive approximately $50,000 a year in trustee fees. Since it would take another $1 million of principal to produce, at 5%, the same $50,000 a year income for his heirs, the $50,000 trustee fee could be seen as the equivalent of another $1 million produced from the original $100,000 loan.

Not only was this plan financially pleasing to the man, it enabled him to leave behind a lasting legacy of good works. Every year after its endowment, his foundation, under the administration of his children and in fulfillment of his desires, would gave away money to support important causes, individuals, and organizations. This thought really touched and pleased the man.

However, the benefits did not stop there.

I pointed out to the man that his $100,000 gift to charity was tax deductible and would create an additional $50,000 of tax savings. As his son and daughter-in-law averaged age 30, an insurance policy bought on their lives for the man's grandchildren would net a return of approximately $3 million.

In this way, my original statement was fulfilled. With $2 million going to the charitable foundation, trustee income from the equivalent of $1 million being produced for the man's children, and $3 million being produced for his grandchildren, a total of $6 million had been created from the $100,000 loan. And all at a net cost of only $3,500 a year.

Is there anywhere else that a 50-year-old man can put $3,500 a year and have it become worth $6 million to his heirs and favorite charities after all taxes? Is there any doubt that this is the single best bottom line that an annual $3,500 can produce?

Best of all, as I said at the beginning, this plan is available to virtually anyone with a home. There are some qualifications, but for the most part, anyone can receive a loan credit on their taxes for an up to $100,000 home equity loan. While your age, gender, marital status, and tax situation may alter your individual outcome, the leverage of life insurance coupled with the availability of charitable tax deductions, trustee fees, and loan interest tax deductions creates an opportunity for wealth creation that is the epitome of true bottom line thinking.

After creating this plan for these people, I looked into what would be the maximum optimization I could secure on this basis. I found that I could create up to $14 million for the same $3,500 a year at younger ages. Furthermore, using this technique combined with a $1 million mortgage loan, I could actually increase the total benefits for the heirs and charities up to $55 million for only $50,000 a year.

The Bottom Line on Insurance

Between 1997 and 1998, I wrote 25 articles on topics of life insurance and estate tax planning. Many of those articles appeared in the Los Angeles Times, Forbes, and other publications. In each article I looked at ways to improve your financial bottom line through the creative use of life insurance in an integrated and diversified portfolio. I also sought to explain in plain, simple terms some of the more complex and intimidating aspects of purchasing a life insurance policy. Most importantly, I tried to help people overcome the trap of conventional thinking that often kept them from utilizing these concepts.[27]

The need for these articles was, in my view, overwhelming. Even as short a time ago as 1997, many professionals and laypeople overlooked or misunderstood the value of life insurance for wealth creation and preservation. Accountants and attorneys were skeptical, mostly because they either didn't understand or, in the case of some less scrupulous practitioners, didn't profit from

[27] A full set of reprinted articles is available for your review under the section "Bottom Line Columns" at Barry Kaye's www.DieRich2.com website.

insurance sales. They passed that skepticism on to their clients, often by exaggerating the risks of life insurance or calling into question some of the aspects of how it works. Others made irrelevant comparisons that didn't take the full facts into consideration.

I am extremely pleased by the progress that has been made even in just the past two years toward overcoming these skeptics and gaining acceptance. Life insurance is becoming a much more common, if not preferred, means to protect an estate and create wealth. The professional financial planning communities, perhaps chagrined by some of the more public failures of their conventional planning, have embraced insurance and their clients are reaping the benefits.

Even so, I find that there is still a lot of misconception and misunderstanding about how insurance works and why it is so uniquely important. When I sit down with a new client, I can pretty much predict the questions he or she will ask.

For that reason, I am including here an explanation of some of the more commonly misunderstood factors that make insurance so valuable. What to consider when buying a policy. When replacement is the best course. What type of policy is best for your need. What is the truth behind the myths of conventional wisdom.

Some of what follows are reprints, in full or in part, from those articles I wrote previously. In reading them over, I find their contents to be every bit as accurate and relevant today as they were then. Other information is new. All of it goes to the bottom line benefits and realities of life insurance as an estate preservation and wealth creation tool.

Death Won't Wait

People who attend my seminar or have read my previous books are familiar with my admonition that "Death won't wait."

None of us likes to consider the realities of our own mortality. We all like to think that there's always going to be more time. And while I don't enjoy being the doomsayer, pointing out again and again that none of us has any guarantees, the truth is undeniable. Everyday we see people whose times had surely not come die anyway. We need think only of John F. Kennedy Jr. and Princess Diana to realize that death is arbitrary and capricious.

And it is not only death that is the enemy of optimized planning. When it comes to the purchase of life insurance, youth and good health are key factors in receiving the best returns for your premium dollars.

I see tragedies all the time. People who sat on the fence too long. People who died too soon. I have witnessed the pain of the families of these people as they realize the harsh truth of their situation. Because these sorts of tragedies are so needless and so avoidable, it makes them worse.

In some cases in which I've been involved, it was ultimately an attorney or accountant who delayed the process through stall tactics or bad advice. It is now beginning to happen that some of those professionals are finding themselves facing malpractice lawsuits by families whose legacies have been needlessly ravaged by taxes.

Recently, I had two clients whose plights demonstrated painfully clearly the need to act decisively as quickly as you can. I offer their stories so that others may learn from them. I do so with the consent of their families who feel, as I do, that doing so may help add meaning to their deaths by helping others avoid their mistakes.

The first case was that of a 70-year-old man I was supposed to meet with in New York just before this book went to press.

The man and I had been discussing his insurance needs for some time previous to the intended meeting. I had arranged for the man to be examined prior to my arrival and had been able to leverage one of the insurance companies I deal with into giving him an excellent rating. Now I was going to New York to discuss the specifics of the policy he was intending to buy.

When I arrived in New York, it was at the tail end of bad weather associated with a hurricane that was striking the Southern coast. The man, who lived in Long Island, didn't want to venture out in the bad weather.

We rescheduled our meeting for the following day. He never made it. This man who had just received an excellent insurance rating died overnight leaving his widow and children without the insurance protection he desired for them. And, while we ultimately went ahead and purchased coverage on the wife for the protection of the heirs against estate tax costs, it was not as advantageous a return as we would have received had we been able to buy a last-to-die policy on both the man and his wife.

On that very same trip, I was to meet with a man who was sick with Parkinson's disease. We had communicated about his insurance needs through his attorney back and forth from my office and had a plan in place to buy coverage on his wife. Now that I was in New York, we were going to meet and consummate the purchase.

It's a funny thing but sometime in the course of my various conversations with his attorney it had come up that this man had a liking for a particular kind of cookie frequently called "black and whites." So, in preparation for our meeting, I'd had a platter of these cookies set out for him.

I'm sure by now you know what's coming. Though he was in the advanced stages of Parkinsons, the man had been told by his physicians that he had another seven years of life to look forward to. He came to my hotel and we met to discuss the insurance policy. Then he left, taking the policy with him for review and also taking, as a gift from me, the cookies he was so fond of. He died the next day. The cookies went uneaten and the policy went unsigned.

Ultimately we were still able to go ahead and insure the wife for the benefit of their children. But this self-made man, to whom family was so important, never got to see for himself the consummation of his desires for them.

No one knows what life, or death, has in store for them. This man was told by top doctors in the field that he had seven years left to live. The rest of us live our lives in expectation of statistical probabilities. But while mathematics may be able to determine that premature death will only occur to one out of every so many of us, it can't tell us which one.

Life insurance is the only financial tool whose returns are not determined by time. Had the man in my first example made it into the city to sign the insurance contract the day we had planned to meet and then gone ahead and died that night, his heirs would have received every single dime of death benefit he had desired for them.

There are enough unavoidable tragedies out there, waiting to strike. Don't let your family become victims of an avoidable one. Death won't wait for you to be ready to face the truth. Death comes at its own schedule, not yours. Is avoiding confronting the reality of mortality really worth the risk of leaving your family unprotected?

Life Insurance Spends Just the Same as "Real" Money

It seems that there has always been an unreasoned dislike of life insurance. I have speculated in my other books, at my seminars, and in discussions on the subject about where the dislike may come from. I have thought it might have to do with the fear of mortality and a desire to avoid thinking about the fact of our eventual deaths. I have thought it might have come from bad experiences with pushy salespeople. Furthermore I have suggested that the whole topic might just seem too "ghoulish" for many people.

Professionals outside the insurance industry have also maligned and disregarded life insurance. I have always supposed they were simply unknowledgeable or were seeking to protect their own billables. Stockbrokers put insurance down until they needed new profit centers and found insurance to be a wonderful means of additional income. Now, after 40 years, they discuss insurance. Even attorneys and accountants who are allowed in many states to be licensed to sell insurance now advocate its advantages. Even banks now sell life insurance.

For years, people rebelled when I told them that the means for accomplishing the highly optimized ends of my wealth creation and preservation techniques was life insurance. I could see in their faces the transformation from excitement to disappointment. More than one prospect ultimately decided not to execute the plan he had been so anxious to put in place simply to avoid buying a life insurance policy.

Life insurance, as I utilize it on behalf of my clients, becomes a funding mechanism which, as an alternative to any investment, can effectively increase your estate tax exemptions up to $363 million, turn any tax into an asset, protect the value of your investment portfolio, recapture a financial loss, double the proceeds from the sale of a business, optimize your municipal bond yields up to 25%, increase your IRA or pension 10–to–20 times.

That the vehicle that accomplishes these valuable financial feats is life insurance is irrelevant to the benefits my clients reap. Life insurance is a method, a concept, an approach, a vehicle, a design, an idea, a formula, a system, a program, a technique. It is a means to an end, an end that nothing else can achieve in the same way with the same results.

Estate planning for wealth creation and preservation is not a legal happening. It is an economic event. Estate taxes are a dollars and cents proposition. Mathematics and simple arithmetic producing a clear bottom line will indicate whether a complicated, convoluted estate plan is necessary to reduce and pay taxes or whether the use of a life insurance policy is the more efficient and the least expensive method. No rhetoric from any attorney, adviser or insurance man is necessary. Just the bottom line.

As always, I include one caution that I can not emphasize enough. As part of a diversified portfolio, the life insurance policies I recommend are an invaluable tool. However, you should not utilize any financial vehicle if doing so will negatively impact your lifestyle. Use only funds that you do not require to support your current comfort level. Or reallocate existing funds from current investments that you have already determined as being available. Your well-being must always come first in any plan that you undertake.

As unbearable as it is to contemplate chemotherapy or radiation as treatments for cancer, you would not hesitate, were the need to exist, to overcome your distaste for the subject and embrace the only means available to cure you. Well, as chemotherapy cures your health, life insurance can cure the ravages against your wealth. Whether or not you believe in life insurance, whether you like it or not, the terms and words don't matter; only the result does. If chemotherapy will cure your cancer and let you live longer and healthier, you'll find a way to accept and ultimately be grateful for it. That life insurance can cure the decay of your estate is, similarly, something you should also learn to embrace and appreciate.

Once you have provided for yourself and have funds available to use to grow and protect your estate, don't let the words "life insurance" dissuade you from following the best route to an optimized bottom line. Whether the check comes from your stock, real estate, munis, CDs, T-Bills, business interest, or insurance, once cashed it all spends the same.

Life Insurance Is Not an Expense

You are over 60 years old. You are worth $2 million or more. You want to buy life insurance to discount your estate taxes or just to optimize your assets. You want to increase manyfold what you leave to your children, grandchildren, other heirs, favorite charity, or foundation. You want to die rich. But—you do not want to impair your own cash flow. You do not want to pay now. You want to buy now and pay later.

You would like to make any later payments at your death and you would like to make the principal and interest tax deductible. You don't want the expense of life insurance. What do you do?

Conventional wisdom says you can pay for your life insurance on a monthly, annual, limited, or one-pay basis. The shorter the pay period, the lower the overall cost but the greater the short-term cash flow impairment. If you pay annually over your lifetime there will be a higher total cost but the least annual cash flow impairment allowing you to buy even more insurance. Also, paying the lower annual premium can be the cheapest method depending on when you die. Remember that any premiums paid would have only been worth one half had the money been left in your estate after taxes. Then compare that to the millions this method creates.

More importantly, is there really any cost? Why is life insurance at this age and with the above stated assets considered an expense? If you put $1 million into real estate or stocks with the promise that it would produce $10 million tax free at your death, would that be considered an expense? Of course not.

Then how can you consider the same $1 million put into life insurance that produces $10 million as an expense? It is funny how common sense and logic are rarely applied to life insurance particularly when you realize stock or real estate may not be worth $10 million whenever you die but insurance always will be (based on current assumptions.) I have demonstrated in individual concepts throughout this book various means of buying and funding life insurance that by now should have made it clear that life insurance is not an expense. Summarized together those points should lead you directly to the best bottom line thinking.

The answer to not paying premiums is simple: Borrow the premium.

Just like you financed your receivables and mortgaged your real estate to build your fortune, you can borrow the funds to finance your insurance and then either pay the interest yearly or accrue it until your death. Since the loan, both principal and interest, is considered a liability it will reduce your gross estate thus reducing your estate tax.

As I demonstrated earlier, Uncle Sam will have paid 55% of your debt at your death thus effectively making the entire loan tax deductible.

You can do this with your margin account at your stockbroker or your bank with low cost Libor rates. There is also a way to do it with an insurance company but it may not provide the lowest cost.

There are also other creative methods of buying insurance without impairing your cash flow.

You can use your pension or IRA money if you do not need a part or all of it for your retirement. Since it will be worth less than thirty cents on the dollar at your death after taxes it doesn't make sense to accumulate money here for your heirs. You don't even have to touch the principal if you freeze your IRA and just use the yearly appreciation to pay for the insurance. This can effectively increase your IRA up to 20 times after tax as I showed you in the concept entitled *Pension and/or IRA Maximizer* on page 53.

If you are older you can increase your income substantially from Muni's, CD's and T-Bills by purchasing an immediate annuity and using the increased income to pay for the insurance. It can be even more interesting if you borrow the money to buy the immediate annuity. The greater return will not only pay for the life insurance but can also be enough to pay the interest on the loan.

You can possibly increase your insurance at no cost by reviewing your existing insurance. In many instances older policies have become antiquated and should be replaced if you are more concerned with the ultimate death benefit rather than the cash value. Using the current premium, the existing cash value and a different type policy will usually make a huge difference.

Also, consider converting an existing annuity into a life insurance policy if you no longer need the ultimate proceeds for yourself and wish to leave it to your heirs. This can increase the annuity proceeds up to 10 times on a tax free basis with no additional outlay on your part.

The additional five ideas that follow can use either your own money or borrowed money to fund the policy purchase. However these techniques represent the optimum method of leveraging your assets for giving to charity at no cost or for your heirs.

You are allowed to gift $10,000 yearly tax free to each of your children. Insurance can leverage that $10,000 up to $1 million. You can also gift $675,000 increasing to $1 million by 2006 without any gift or transfer tax liability. Using life insurance, you can leverage that figure up to $20 million tax free cash or effectively increase your exemptions up to $40 million. (See the concept entitled *Maximize Gifts and Exemptions* on page 67.)

I also showed you how you can turn any tax into an asset for your heirs. Instead of paying $1.1 million tax on a $3 million estate and receiving nothing back, give the $1.1 million to an insurance company before you die and your heirs will receive up to $11 million tax free. This will pay the tax and leave up to $10 million for your children and grandchildren. If your estate is $10 million with a $5 million tax due, the same $5 million paid to an insurance company will pay the tax and leave up to $35 million to your heirs. This can also be paid for on an annual basis. (See the concept entitled *How a Tax Can Become an Asset* on page 73.)

Finally, there is the exciting concept for those interested in giving substantial money to charity at no cost. (See the concept entitled *Using Borrowed Funds to Gift at No Cost to You* on page 163.)

Borrow against your portfolio of stocks and bonds, donate money to your own charitable foundation or favorite charity to buy a life insurance policy with a death benefit of up to 10 times the amount of your loan. Take the tax deduction savings and buy a large policy on your lives for your children to offset the loan at your death. They will have money left over, your charity will profit handsomely.

You will have paid no money out of your pocket whatsoever and there will be no cost to your heirs. You will have bought life insurance and never paid a penny for it. Good estate planning should pay the tax for you, optimize your assets and never hurt any other American. The "Die Rich" concepts presented in this book will do all of that. And more.

Hopefully you now can see the magnitude of the opportunities available. If you gave someone a dime and he gave you back a dollar, would you worry about the loss of the dime? Of course not. At the bottom line the outlay for insurance can be as little as the dime, the return as much as the dollar. So what are you worried about?

The Truth About "Based on Current Assumptions"

It is inarguable that life insurance, performing as a means of wealth creation and preservation, is the single most reliable and effective estate planning tool for people who want to optimize their assets and discount their estate tax cost.

Yet many people still resist life insurance because of the phrase "Based on Current Assumptions," which disclaims all the quotes and proposals they receive. The caveat carries with it doom-and-gloom ideas of exploding premiums and vanishing benefits. However the real tragedy occurs when someone is dissuaded from buying needed insurance because they do not fully understand the truth of those four fear-provoking words. And it is made worse by attorneys and accountants who are not knowledgeable on the subject and who manipulate people's fears to convince them not to buy. Even some unscrupulous insurance agents will intentionally misrepresent the facts about the impact of "Based on Current Assumptions" on a competitor's proposal just to steal the business.

What exactly does "Based on Current Assumptions" mean? How does it impact a policy's cost and return? These are important things to know and understand before buying a life insurance policy.

The return on a life insurance policy is calculated by the insurance company based on your expected mortality (how long you can be statistically assumed to live given your age and current health) and the interest rates they are currently earning on the money you pay them. It is how those earnings go to their bottom line of expenses that dictates their profit.

When you apply for a policy, you are quoted a price that will yield a quoted return "Based on Current Assumptions."

As long as the mortality assumptions made about the group you fall into and the interest rates the insurance company is earning on your money hold to current levels, you will receive the death benefit that was presented to you for the cost that was quoted. Even given the limits implied by the caveat, this is still far more of a certainty than you could expect from virtually any investment.

Let's look at the factors upon which "Based on Current Assumptions" rests. First, mortality. The longer you live, the more premiums the insurance company collects and earns returns on. Therefore, the less your policy costs.

It is not changes in your mortality expectations that can effect the cost of an insurance policy. It is changes in the mortality assumptions of the whole pool of potential insureds, basically the population of America, in most cases. And those mortality assumptions have improved for many years.

The insurance company must show the maximum mortality charge possible as a major part of the guaranteed column of your policy proposal in accordance with legal requirements. However, the potential of mortality assumptions reversing and going to their maximum (the inclusion of which is used to protect the client by putting in a ceiling) are remote.

The other major aspect of the assumptions is based on interest earnings. Remember, the more interest the insurance company can be expected to earn with your money, the less the cost for your desired return. If interest rates go up, allowing the insurance company to realize higher yields on their investments, the cost of the return you want goes down. If interest rates go down, causing the insurance company to earn less with the same money, the premium needed to produce the originally determined amount of death benefit goes up.

But you must remember that the horror stories you've heard of hugely ballooning premiums were caused by policies sold 7 to 10 years ago when interest was 10% to 12%. Right now we are living in a world of approximately 6% to 7% interest. The guarantee in almost all policies is no less than 4%. From 11% to 4% was a huge drop that necessitated large premium increases. But from the current 6% to 7% the worst potential scenario doesn't make such a big difference. Let's take an honest look at what could happen.

Based on current assumptions, the yearly cost for a $1 million last-to-die policy purchased at average age 60 on a life-pay basis is approximately $7,551. If interest assumptions go down 1% and stay there the yearly cost rises to $8,691.

Clearly, the increased cost is minimal and, when measured against the return, its tax free nature and the fact of its immediate availability at death, almost negligible in relationship to the resulting death benefit.

Now, let's look at it the other way. What if interest rates go up as I think they are much more likely to do.

The same policy currently costing $7,551 annually would only cost $6,288 a year if interest rates go up 1% and stay there. The difference can be used to fund additional premiums or can save yearly cash outlay. In either event, the policy still produces the same $1 million.

When you really think about it, you will realize that all your investments, with the exception of some very conservative, safe but low-yielding bonds, are interest sensitive and based on current assumptions. Our whole economy is. There is nothing so different or so fearful about the investment alternative of life insurance.

Your stocks offer you no guarantee at all. Your real estate offers you no guarantee at all. Your CD's and savings account are completely dependent upon the current interest rates exactly as a life insurance policy is.

Yet, none of them can perform as well as a life insurance policy can for the ultimate good of your family whether their need of it comes tomorrow, in one year, or twenty years from now.

Even with the caveat of current assumptions, interest is guaranteed never to be lower than 4% depending on the individual company. And if interest or mortality changes, you can always pay more, reduce the death benefit or do nothing if you stilll think the policy will last longer than you will. And now, with many companies offering a "catch-up provision" as part of their policies, you can pay the minimum rates and add more later without additional interest.

Furthermore, many companies have now introduced guaranteed policies. You pay more for the security of never having your premiums change but for some people it is worth it. Personally, I recommend going in at the lowest rate possible. You can always make up the guarantee and interest later if the need arises. However, if your peace of mind is enhanced by a guaranteed premium rate, there can be one additional benefit to using this type of policy, as I demonstrated in detail in the concept entitled *Guaranteed Returns Create Enormous Potentials*, on page 87.

It has been said that life insurance is of maximum value only if you die. That the longer you live, the less value it has. There might be some statistical truth in that opinion, but there is absolutely no relevance to reality since statistics don't apply to individuals and there is no way you can know how long you will live. But now with the advent of these guaranteed policies and the remarkable growth they experience the whole issue is moot. Clearly insurance can become a source of ever-increasing value the longer you live.

The more you pay, the more the guarantee. The more the guarantee, the more the overpayment. The more the overpayment, the more the potential growth of the death benefit. The more the death benefit, the more tax free money out of your estate for the same gift tax!

The bottom line is nowhere near as baffling as it may have seemed before. Given the interest and mortality assumptions being utilized to determine policy returns today, it is my opinion that there is no better time for consumers to benefit from the many financial opportunities afforded by a properly structured life insurance policy used as part of a diversified financial portfolio to help them die rich.

The Internal Rate of Return Myth

The internal rate of return is a non-scientific unit of measurement used to compare the value of investments. Theoretically the net return is measured against the factor of the time it took for the investment to earn the return and a basis of comparison exists by which one investment's performance can be measured against another. All of which would be fine and good if it had any relevance at all to real life which, unfortunately, it does not.

But no one knows how much time is left to them. Illness, accident, and tragedy is all around us. If you are investing some portion of your estate in order to leave your heirs better off, how can you justify making only investments that require time you may not have in order to fully mature and reach their greatest potential? If you die tomorrow will the stock you bought with the anticipated growth potential have achieved even a fraction of that growth? Almost assuredly, it will not. While, equally assuredly, the life insurance policy that you purchased will.

You raise this point to your financial advisor and he or she replies by telling you that the stocks are now part of your estate and your heirs will inherit them so they can continue to grow and earn that great internal rate of return within your heirs' estates. But remember, as they come to your heirs they will be subject to estate taxes of up to 55%. Right away, those stocks have lost as much as half their value. And, given the possibility of forced liquidation, the true loss could be substantially more. Now the stock needs to increase by 100% just to stay even! To reach the net return you had hoped for, the stock now needs to increase even more.

Even bonds, T-Bills and Munis, vehicles that do offer a promised amount of income, are subject to taxation that makes them worth less than half to your heirs. Point this out to your financial advisor the next time your are reviewing your portfolio. Ask that they provide the same guarantees that life insurance does: that they promise the amount of return available; that they promise to make it available in full the very next day, if needed; that they promise the return will gross enough to net the desired amount after taxes are paid, and see what they say. Ask them to promise that you will die rich. Then ask them again why they haven't advised you to include life insurance, the one financial vehicle that can make all those claims, in your portfolio.

The Real Truth About Replacement

You have probably read some recent newspaper accounts of an unethical technique unfortunately utilized by some insurance salespeople to sell more product. The scandal revolves around the topic of replacement policies. The unscrupulous salesperson pushes a client to buy a new policy to replace an old one despite the fact that doing so is costly and can result in a significant loss to the client. This is called "churning" to replace old policies and earn new commissions.

It is a terrible thing when a so-called professional puts his own interests above those of his client. But even more terrible is the fact that, after hearing these stories in the news, people become so determined not to be taken advantage of in this way that they may not listen to or believe the legitimate salesperson when he tells them that replacing an existing policy is in their best interest.

As in any system, the fact that there is opportunity for abuse does not necessarily mean that the system itself is flawed. The truth is that in many cases replacing an old policy with a new one is in your best interest. I am going to examine some of the circumstances in which that might be the case to help people better evaluate for themselves when they are being given valuable, legitimate advice and when they are being taken advantage of.

For years the conventional wisdom from the insurance industry was that you never dropped an old insurance policy. You could supplement it with additional, new policies but you never abandoned an existing policy.

I have never understood the thinking behind this rule. It seems ridiculous to hold onto something that is obsolete when new products and pricing structures offer so much more for so much less. But, as with many instances of conventional wisdom, few people really look at or question the basis of the rule. Both consumers and industry professionals have been content to accept it at face value. This has allowed many unknowledgeable attorneys and financial advisors to give bad advice.

But a closer examination of the "no replacement" rule reveals it to be simple dogma without any real basis in fact in many instances. In truth, the exact opposite can often be the case. Changes in the insurance industry can make changes in your old insurance policies the smartest, most effective way to proceed.

There are four major reasons given why replacement is not a good thing. Let's look at each one and you'll see why they simply don't hold up across the board.

The first belief has been that since you had bought the policy when you were younger, your premiums couldn't be improved or duplicated now that you were older. Given that insurance rates are based on your age and expected mortality this may seem to make sense. But it doesn't take into account new pricing structures offered by insurance companies.

For example, if you bought a policy before the advent of the last-to-die policies which base their return on two separate lives, your rates could be considerably higher than what is available on a last-to-die basis. In other cases, the competitiveness of the insurance industry has simply caused the prices to drop or the existing cash value could be used to lower your outlay.

It is important of course, when comparing the quote given you on a new policy versus what you are paying for an old one, that you make sure you are comparing apples to apples. Check that the recommended new policy lasts as long, or longer, than the old one and that you aren't being quoted an extremely favorable initial rate that is going to blow up after a few years or vanish early. I recommend you only look at policies that extend to at least age 100.

But if the policy you are being shown does meet these criteria and is cheaper than the one you have, why wouldn't you replace the one with the other? Are the people who coined the conventional wisdom going to pay your insurance premiums for you? Would you retain a stock that no longer had its original potential?

The second reason given for the 'no replacement' rule has to do with the contestability of a policy. Most policies become incontestable after two years. This period protects the carrier against the possibility that the insured lied about his or her health when purchasing the product. During the contestability period if you die and it is discovered that you lied, the insurance carrier can challenge the payment of the benefits.

For this reason, people have been told not to replace an old policy that is past the contestability period. The prevailing opinion is that a new policy would require a new contestability period and conceivably put your benefit at risk for another two years. But this is only the case if you plan to lie on your application.

If your application is legitimate so is your claim to your benefits and your proceeds are not at risk. There is simply no reason to hold onto a policy because its incontestability period has passed, particularly if you are about to save a large amount of money on a new policy, as long as it is your intention to be truthful about your health.

The third often-quoted reason for not replacing a policy is the suicide clause. Many people erroneously believe from watching dramatic television programs that suicide negates the paying of insurance benefits. This is generally not true. In most instances there is a clause in the policy that states that the benefits will not be paid if the insured commits suicide within the first two years of having bought the policy. What most consumers don't realize is that if you commit suicide after that two-year period, carriers will pay the benefits. This is based on psychologists' reports that if you really wanted to commit suicide, you couldn't wait two years to do so.

Industry pundits who argue against replacing old policies might suggest that if you start a new policy, you'll have to endure the suicide clause all over again. That's a fine argument—if you're contemplating taking your own life. But if you're not, is it any kind of reason to forego the tremendous savings available by replacing obsolete policies?

Lastly, you might be told not to consider replacing an antiquated policy with a new one because doing so will earn your salesperson a new commission and you will have to pay a new acquisition cost. What's wrong with that?

If your salesperson is doing his job, finding areas that can be improved in your policy, saving you money, why shouldn't he be entitled to additional commission? Every day people buy and sell stocks, bonds, commodities, futures, and options and quietly factor in the broker's commission to determine their profit and loss position. Why is that any different with life insurance? Only the end result is important.

Insurance isn't an investment, but if replacing one policy with another benefits your overall position why should the fact that the salesperson makes a commission along the way be so onerous that you would actually consider not taking the step most advantageous to you just to thwart him?

When removed from the aspect of myth and bad publicity and looked at from the standpoint of reason and sound judgement, the objections to policy replacement become trivial and meaningless. The truth is much simpler.

You Can Buy Insurance Even if You're Uninsurable

It is a tragedy I encounter all too often and one that never fails to sadden and upset me. Far too many people only begin thinking about their estate planning and family legacies after they have become too old or too ill to be insurable.

It is human nature, I guess, to put off thinking about mortality and death until the topic is virtually unavoidable.

But unfortunately, by that point, it is usually too late and you may be uninsurable. Your options and opportunities become limited, your heirs face the dual loss of the parents they love and the up to 55% decimation of all you had worked so hard for.

Many people despair when the truth of this becomes known to them. Suddenly they see all too clearly what they often would not look at before: That the legacy of their lifetimes faces decimation and their heirs will not derive the benefits they had worked so hard and so long to provide. It is a sad realization, indeed. But despair is not necessary. There are still ways to accomplish the asset management goals of the uninsurable.

The very first thing you need to do is verify that you are indeed uninsurable. It can sometimes happen that what one insurance company turns down another will approve. It could be just as simple as using a different agent.

Furthermore, advances in medicine may make a condition that

five years ago caused you to be labeled "uninsurable" insurable now.

But even if you get the same dire "uninsurable" prognosis, there are still options available to you.

My firm has always tried to take one exam and send it to five or ten companies. This not only gives a greater possibility of securing coverage but it also pits one company against the other for the maximum leverage and it also provides diversification.

Even so, there are those cases for which insurance is just not possible. Yet even then, there are still options and it is extremely important that, if you find yourself in this situation, you are aware of what those options are.

Many insurance agents and most of the financial advisors who don't specialize in insurance products are unfortunately unaware of the techniques which can be employed to secure the benefits of insurance in estate planning for people who are uninsurable. They just throw up their hands, tell you they're sorry, and recommend whatever less effective stopgap measures, as they can understand.

Don't fall too easily into their gloom; there are still ways to go. And one of them is to use a surrogate insured on who the policy is purchased. Borrow someone else's life.

Obviously, if one partner in a marriage is uninsurable the first place to look would be to the other. You could no longer benefit from the lower pricing of a last-to-die policy, but at least coverage would be available that would meet your asset management goals.

If both partners are uninsurable, you should then look around at the other members of your extended family.

Perhaps you have younger siblings who are still insurable and a policy could be purchased on them. Now, when you die, your children would suffer the depletion of your estate from estate taxes but, when their Uncle and Aunt died, they would regain it. This means that they could still expect to recoup the loss within the same generation.

In all other regards, the plan works the same as any other. The funds for the policy are transferred from your estate into an Irrevocable Trust and any gift taxes owed as a result of the transfer are paid. The trust then purchases a policy on the lives of the Aunt and Uncle, or whomever is available to serve as a surrogate whether it is aunt, uncle or both; cousin, godparent, or godparents.

Of course, the selection of the surrogate should take into consideration the return the selection will earn and the time it might take for the heirs to recoup the loss.

For example, a last-to-die policy on the heirs' 60-year-old Aunt and Uncle would pay a better return than a male only policy on their 70-year-old Godfather. But, in all likelihood, they will have to wait longer to receive that return.

The options and impacts will have to be fully considered in order for you to make an informed decision that best fulfills your goals. Using a surrogate insured, the losses suffered can be fully recovered within the same generation and your heirs can ultimately receive your entire estate.

Even if there is no one to use as a surrogate, the losses suffered by your estate can still be recovered. However, you may now have to skip one generation to do so.

If you are uninsurable, it is pretty safe to assume that your children are not. Using the same techniques as previously discussed, you can transfer funds to an Irrevocable Trust, paying any necessary gift taxes, and the trust can now use the funds to purchase insurance on your children for your grandchildren.

One great benefit of doing this is that the children, at their younger ages, will receive a huge return for the insurance purchase. Now the portion of the estate lost to taxes is recovered for the grandchildren at significantly less cost.

Whereas a policy on the 60-year-old Aunt and Uncle, had they been available, would have netted an approximate 10-to-1 return, a policy on the children for the benefit of the grandchildren can net as much as a 16–to–1 to 50–to–1 return!

So, if you needed to recoup $3 million that was going to be lost to estate taxes for your heirs, it would cost $300,000 using a last-to-die, one-pay policy on the Aunt and Uncle based on current assumptions but only $60,000 to $100,000 if using a last-to-die, one-pay policy on the lives of your son and daughter-in-law.

If your children will still inherit enough, despite the tax loss, to support them nicely throughout their lifetimes, you might want to consider utilizing this generation skipping method even if a surrogate is available just to take advantage of the great returns available at younger ages.

Moreover, if you could afford the entire $300,000 premium that would have been needed to purchase the $3 million on the lives of the Aunt and Uncle, you might want to consider applying that same amount to a policy taken out on the lives of your children if they qualify.

At a 30–to–1 return, the $300,000 would net $9 million. At a 40–to–1 return it would net $12 million. And, at a 50–to–1 return it would provide a highly optimized $15 million! Now you have not simply recouped a $3 million tax loss, you have truly employed the power of life insurance to create great wealth for your grandchildren and posterity.

From the dismay of being uninsurable, you would have reached the heights of financial optimization and diversification.

Thinking creatively, with a deep comprehension of the opportunities and alternatives available, there is almost no financial situation that can not be enhanced and resolved by the inclusion of life insurance in a diversified financial portfolio.

Don't give up too easily. Be sure you have secured all the information and pursued every option. Very rarely do I encounter a situation in which the label "uninsurable" really applies. Anyone who lived rich, can die rich.

Making Life Insurance Proceeds Estate Tax Free

Another aspect of the plans discussed in the concepts in this book has to do with the use of an Irrevocable Trust. This is a crucial part of the structuring of these concepts but is often misunderstood.

One of the key elements of the value of my methods has to do with the fact of the possible estate tax free nature of life insurance. Congress has also passed laws that protect life insurance proceeds from income taxes. This makes them unique and uniquely valuable in asset management and estate planning.

To make the benefits estate tax free, however, the policy must exist outside the estate of the person who is insured. If it resides within their estate, the proceeds will be subject to estate taxes as they pass from the owner to the beneficiaries. For that reason, we utilize an Irrevocable Trust or your heirs can own the policy. The only important point is that you must not own the policy.

An Irrevocable Trust is a legal entity separate from the person who establishes it. Property put into the trust is no longer owned by the grantor, it exists outside the estate and is therefore not subject to estate taxes as it passes on to its trustees and beneficiaries.

By utilizing an Irrevocable Trust to purchase the life insurance policy, the proceeds from that policy will come to the heirs both income and estate tax free. The way it works is that the person or couple seeking to purchase the insurance consults a good estate planning attorney who sets up the trust. They then gift the money for the insurance premium to the trust. If the amount of money needed to fund the premium exceeds the individual lifetime tax free gift exemption of $675,000 or the combined amount for a couple of $1.35 million[28] or the annual allowable $10,000 per person who is named as a beneficiary within the Irrevocable Trust, gift taxes will be assessed on the amounts in excess. However, in almost all cases, it can be shown that the gift taxes will still be way less than the eventual estate taxes would be if the plan were not undertaken.

Once the money has been gifted to the trust, the trust purchases the life insurance policy on the lives of the couple or individual naming the trust as beneficiary. In this way, the insurance proceeds are protected and the heirs receive them income and estate tax free.

One drawback of the Irrevocable Trust is that property placed into it can not be removed from it. This is why it is called an Irrevocable Trust; it cannot be revoked. Your estate planning attorney will be able to explain all the ramifications of this concept. It is for this reason that I caution people not to undertake these plans with anything but excess, extra, unneeded funds. If there is any concern that the money might be needed during your lifetime, you should not undertake these plans. However, you could, in that instance, simply gift the policy to the children and that way, if the money is needed during your lifetime, you can work it out with them.

People sometimes erroneously think that a Revocable Trust, or what is popularly called a Living Trust, will accomplish the same goal as an Irrevocable Trust. But this is simply not the case. The primary purpose of a Living Trust is to avoid probate costs and publicity, a wholly different matter from estate tax costs, and to arrange to shelter the $675,000 tax exemption that each spouse in

[28] $675,000 per individual and $1.35 million per couple represents the current tax exemptions as of 2000. Those amounts will increase to $1 million per individual and $2 million per couple over the next 6 years or possibly sooner.

a marriage is allowed in 1999. If a spouse dies and his/her $675,000 exemption goes directly to the surviving spouse, it becomes part of the remaining spouse's estate. Now when the surviving spouse dies, only one $675,000 can pass on the heirs tax free. If, however, the original $675,000 went to an Irrevocable Trust or to the children directly, instead of into the remaining spouse's estate, it would remain tax free when it inevitably passed on to the heirs.

The differences between a Revocable Trust and Irrevocable Trust are significant. Most importantly, a Revocable Trust is revocable and the government does not view the assets placed within it to have been removed from your estate. A Revocable Trust can only shelter up to the $1.35 million of current combined tax exemptions from estate taxes. No matter how much more of a person's or couple's assets are placed into the trust, it won't protect more than $675,000 – $1.35 million. Everything in excess of the $1.35 million will be subject to the exact same estate taxes as if it were not placed into the Revocable Trust! This is an extremely critical fact to know when undertaking your asset and estate planning!

An Irrevocable Trust removes property from your estate and allows it to pass to your heirs estate tax free.

Now you are likely, and rightly, thinking that you could place any asset into an Irrevocable Trust for the benefit of your heirs and avoid the estate taxes on that asset's value. Some lawyers look at their clients at this point and say, "Well, if you want to avoid paying estate taxes, we can place your stocks or real estate into an Irrevocable Trust and you will derive the same benefit as you would from the life insurance. In this way, they too can pass to your heirs estate tax free."

Your lawyer is right, you can put your stocks or bonds or real estate into an Irrevocable Trust and therefore remove it from your estate. He is wrong though, and, in my opinion, almost to a point of malpractice, to let you think that the same end will be accomplished. It will not.

If you put shares of a stock worth $1 million dollars into an Irrevocable Trust for the good of your heirs, you will indeed have transferred $1 million out of your estate. You may or may not have to pay gift taxes to do this, but that is irrelevant to this discussion as you would or would not have had to pay the same gift taxes on a cash transfer of $1 million to the trust for the purchase of life insurance.

At your death, the $1 million worth of stock would indeed come to your heirs estate tax free. However, at whatever point that your heirs sell that stock, if it has gained in value, there will be capital gains taxes to pay. The cost basis is the cost that was paid by the original owner. If the asset had been transferred at death it would have received a stepped-up basis and there would be no capital gains tax but there will be estate tax. The $1 million transfer only avoids the estate taxes; some gift taxes are paid or the exemptions are used. However, at whatever point that your heirs sell that stock, if it has gained in value, there will be capital gains taxes to pay. If the asset had been transferred at death it would have received a stepped-up basis and there would be no capital gains tax but there will be estate tax. Either way, there's a price to pay for success. The only way to avoid this is to have a stock, bond, or piece of property that doesn't increase in value, which actually defeats the purpose of transferring the asset out of your estate.

Unless you know how to die rich using life insurance that can optimize the $1 million transfer three, five, or ten times in accordance with your age.

Remember it is imperative that the policy is owned by your intended heirs or an Irrevocable Trust in order to make the proceeds estate tax free.

About Cash Values

I want to take a brief look at the manner in which cash values increase in an insurance policy and the impact they have upon you. This is not a highly critical area of concern in most of the plans I recommend for my clients. For the purposes of using life insurance as an alternative to investing, I generally do not structure policies to accrue the largest cash values. However, it is a factor of insurance policies that people know just enough about to have it be of concern. Also, in the new 'fully guaranteed' policies and concepts I am presenting, the build up of cash values plays a hugely significant role in providing unprecedented returns.

All life insurance policies used for the purposes described in this book have an equity. This is called cash value. There are usually two columns on your initial proposal. Most of the times they are called accumulated value and cash value or surrender value.

The difference between the two columns is the initial administrative costs including commissions charged against the cash value of the policy. These expenses are usually amortized over a 10–20 year period depending on the individual insurance company. You will notice from that point on, after the amortization is complete that both columns are the same for the rest of the life of the policy.

In the case of a one-pay policy, the cash value will usually equal and exceed the initial premium by the fourth to tenth year depending on the company.

In the past, insurance agents told you that this cash value could be used in case of emergency, to put your children through school, or even for your own retirement by utilizing a loan against the policy. This is why you paid larger premiums to create larger cash values as described previously under the section on fat/thin policies.

My purpose now is to use these policies to optimize the death benefit and minimize the cash value. This is why I have recommended thin policies, saving up to 30%, with the lowest premiums possible since the cash value is not important for this purpose.

I am only interested in maximizing the death benefit at the lowest cost possible.

Cash values are available and can be used in a variety of ways, including loans, however it is not recommended in the overall concepts included in this book since any loan against the policy would deplete the death benefit.

Naturally, if you pay a greater premium this will create larger cash values thus providing extra margin that can be used to absorb any negative change of the original assumptions. If there is excess cash value and it grows because of positive impacts on the original assumptions then the death benefit may ultimately grow as well.

As a general rule, I do not recommend that my clients purchase policies that carry excessive cash values. Doing so only needlessly drives up the price and I believe most people would rather pay less and retain their funds, even knowing that they might have to come back at a later day and pay more into the policy if the assumptions change to their detriment.

Nonetheless, you should be aware of how cash values work in a policy before making any decision about which premium option to utilize in making your purchase of a life insurance policy.

Types of Policies

WHO TO INSURE

The outcome of your usage of a life insurance policy as an alternative to investing is also dependent upon the type of policy that you select. Throughout most of the examples I have used in this book, I have shown the results based upon using a last-to-die policy. I do this for two reasons. One because last-to-die policies offer the best return. And two, because last-to-die policies are most appropriate for the type of tax cost discounting and wealth creation and maximization that we have been discussing.

But there are other types of available policies and each has their usefulness in different situations. As in any field of financial planning, an informed decision is the best decision. Let's take a brief look at the three basic choices for the insured—male, female and last-to-die—to examine how to select which might be best for your specific situation.

A policy based on the life of a man only is perhaps the most traditional and familiar of policy types. In the history of the insurance industry, policies were sold to serve as protection in the event of the unforeseen and tragic death of the household breadwinner, who, for the most part in those days, was the man of the house. Insurance proceeds were intended to provide the widow with the means to continue providing for herself and her family.

Ironically, of the three choices for who to insure, the male only policy receives the lowest return. There are two basic reasons for this. To begin with, statistically men do not live as long as women. As we just learned, this lower mortality assumption makes the cost of the policy go up. Secondly, in most marriages the man is older than the woman so, at the time that they begin to consider the purchase of a life insurance policy, he can be presumed to have already lived a higher percentage of his full expectancy.

Of course, if the purchase of life insurance is being undertaken for the reasons it was traditionally sold, to protect a widow left without resources, a policy on the life of the man is the only way to go. But unfortunately, all too often that same approach is inappropriately carried over onto the use of life insurance as an alternative to investing for estate management and planning and couples wind up paying far more than they should to achieve their goals.

Insuring the woman alone makes a little more sense than insuring the man alone since, as was just stated above, she has a greater life expectancy and is probably younger. Therefore, it is fair to presume that she will receive a better return then he will. Keep in mind, an estate may pass from one partner to the other in a marriage without any death taxes being levied. Estate taxes only come into play when the estate passes out of the marital situation. Since it is assumed that the woman will live longer, it can make sense for estate planning purposes to insure her life. But, as I have reiterated many times throughout this book, there are no guarantees when it comes to death except that it will happen sooner or later to all of us. Should the woman be insured and die first, the heirs will come into the insurance benefits but not the estate, which would most likely remain in the possession of her widower. The proceeds can be structured to remain in a trust in order to ensure they are still around to pay the taxes at the time of his death, but then what was the point of having the coverage be on her only?

Of course, there are some situations and conditions that will necessitate making a choice that is not solely based on age and life expectancies and rates. Instances where the decision about whether to insure the man or the woman will be determined by the circumstances of the couple's lives. Perhaps it is a second marriage for one or both of them and there are children from the previous marriage to be considered in the estate planning. If the woman's children are to be provided for separate from the man's, it stands to reason separate policies would be needed.

Or, perhaps one of the two is uninsurable. In that event, there would be no choice but to insure only the other.

However, in most instances of estate planning, I recommend what is commonly called a last-to-die, survivorship, or second-to-die policy.

A last-to-die policy basically combines the ages of the man and woman and arrives at an "average age" for the life expectancy of the two of them. Since the expected combined survivorship of the two people is greater than that for either one of them, the insurance company will have longer to collect premiums and earn interest. That means the premium for the policy can be less for the same amount of benefit than a comparable male only or female only policy. As we are not concerned with earning returns for a surviving spouse in these situations but instead have as a focus the protection of the estate as it passes to the heirs, the last-to-die type policies offer by far the most optimized returns. The second death that creates the need to pay the taxes also creates the proceeds with which to pay the taxes.

To see illustrations of how the cost and return are impacted by your choice of policy type, study the charts included at the back of this book. They will provide a comprehensive comparison and allow you to best assess your own needs.

HOW TO PAY

The other major factor that will affect the cost and performance of your policy is the manner in which you elect to pay for it. Policies can be paid for in full, or financed and paid for over time. They can even be structured to be paid over your entire lifetime. But, as with any financed purchase, there is an increased cost involved. In the examples I use in this book, I have usually utilized a one-pay method in order to best demonstrate the incredible benefit of life insurance as an alternative to investing. But I have also shown several concepts where we use financing in order to demonstrate the fact that, even with financing costs included, life insurance still offers a uniquely beneficial opportunity for wealth creation and preservation. I have also shown you how to have your policy absorb the cost of the financing, how Uncle Sam actually pays half of it, and how to recoup the cost of financing for your family. Now, let's make a slightly closer examination of how these different policies are structured and how those differences impact your decision.

There are three basic types of payment options: one-pay, limited-pay and life-pay.

A one-pay policy is the most cost efficient in the long run. Because it receives the full cost of your desired coverage up-front, the insurance company has the funds on hand longer and will therefore earn a longer period of time worth of interest. Because they make more, they are able to charge you less. Of course, the cost of a one-pay policy is still based upon the current assumptions that determined your rate to begin with and so even this type of policy can see some changes in its cost that might require subsequent, additional payments. Although it is just as possible, especially in light of today's assumptions, that changes in those assumptions could work in your favor to build up higher cash values or to increase the ultimate death benefit. Meanwhile, the cost of the single payment plus any additions that might be needed because of changes in the original assumptions would still almost assuredly be considerably less than paying for the policy on a limited-pay or life-pay basis. Remember, the one-pay rate is significantly less to begin with and any increases that might impact the limited-pay or life-pay will also affect a one-pay policy.

There is only one major drawback to consider in a one-pay policy. Because you have paid for the entire policy from the beginning, should the coin toss of life go against you and death to occur sooner rather than later, you would have paid more than was necessary. With a limited-pay or life-pay policy, you have only paid for coverage through a certain period. In a manner of speaking, each new payment continues the coverage, extending it as through the next portion of your life. If you die before you have paid the whole amount, it is the insurance company's loss, not yours. They will pay the whole stated return without having collected the full premium cost.

This is where it is up to you to make the decision. If you select the limited- or life-pay to avoid overpaying in the beginning and wind up living through the terms of the policy, you will have paid, in total, more than if you had made one payment. But if you opt for the one-pay plan and die too soon after having purchased it, you will have significantly overpaid for the return you receive.

The limited- and life-payment options are versions of the same thing. You extend the payments of your policy premium over time. With a limited-pay plan, there are a fixed number of payments to be made and those are usually made yearly for the defined period of time; generally limited-pay policies are structured to be paid within five, seven, or ten years although almost any plan you prefer can be accommodated.

With a life-pay you very simply pay a premium every year for the rest of your life. It is the same as a limited-pay except that it is structured so that the premium continues to age 100 or until you die, whichever comes first.

Of course, all premium quotations are still based on the current assumptions at the time of the purchase. Yet, no matter which option you choose, the product still produces its incredible return.

As discussed above, the limited-pay and life-pay options both have advantages and disadvantages. By spreading your payments out over time, you incur what is basically, for the sake of this model, a finance charge and so the total cost of your coverage is higher than that for a one-pay plan yielding the same result. And the longer the time over which you spread your payments, the higher the total for the policy will be. However, by paying over a larger period instead of in one lump sum, you can positively impact your cash flow possibly allowing you to afford much greater coverage than if you had to pay for the whole thing at once. Furthermore, remember that, if you elect a limited-pay or life-pay option and die early on in the policy's life the insurance company will still provide the full return you had purchased even though you had only paid a small portion of the total stated cost of the policy. However, please do keep in mind that changes in the assumptions which were current at the time that you purchased your policy will impact its performance no matter whether you elected a one-pay, limited-pay, or life-pay plan. I prefer a life-pay to a limited-pay because you can buy more for the same yearly outlay. I call it 'option' insurance. You can always cut back but usually people want more insurance when they get older and they are pleased that they bought more at the lower price when they were younger and possibility healthier.

There is another objection you might hear raised about insurance and the structuring of policies. Sometimes it happens, that a policy is structured in such a way that the coverage only extends through years 80, 85, or 90 of a person's life. This usually happens when an insurance salesperson is trying to get the premium down to a level that satisfies or entices the client. By structuring the policy in such a way that the coverage ends at age 80, 85, or 90 the cost can be reduced because there is an added element of chance in the insurance company's favor. Should the insured live past 80, 85, or 90 years, the insurance company would not have to pay any death benefit even though they had collected the premiums for all those years. This can leave a person fortunate enough to live longer exposed to the reality of death without any coverage or with a huge premium needed to keep the policy in force.

We only use and recommend policies that cover through age 100 or even beyond. Yet, even so, some detractors from life insurance in general will use the fact of its age-based limitation to suggest it is not a valuable, viable form of economic protection. We all hope to live forever, but, of course, none of us will. Will you really live to be 100? I certainly hope so. Be truthful, how likely is it? Only a handful of people out of the billions who inhabit earth have ever done so.

Maybe you will beat the odds. Or maybe you will achieve the average. Then again, there is always the possibility that you will be the one who does not achieve the average. It is hard to contemplate but avoidance won't change fate. Insurance, however, can greatly improve your economic fate.

Is the likelihood that you will live past 100 greater than the likelihood that you won't? More importantly, is the likelihood that you will live past 100 great enough to void the incredible benefits available through an Investment Alternative insurance technique? Particularly since you can arrange it to go to 115 and beyond.

It may well be that all these choices and options are what concern people about using life insurance as an alternative to investments to protect and optimize their estates. It can all seem so very complicated and uncertain. There is something to be said for the simplicity of selecting a stock, buying it, and waiting for it to achieve your hoped-for result. No caveats. No payment options. Yet you must keep in mind that along with the loss of caveats and options you are losing some other extremely important benefits as well. Those caveats are protecting a predetermined return that no stock can ever offer you. Those options help to make it possible for the return you need the policy to return to be available the very first day after you buy it. No stock can ever make that claim under any circumstances.

Life insurance operates differently than any investment because it is different. And it is those differences that make it so uniquely valuable to you. There is simply not another financial vehicle that can perform as life insurance does. Nothing else that can predetermine its return under any terms or caveats. Nothing else that can make its full return available from the first day. Nothing else that can come to your family both income and estate tax free for its full promised amount.

Having seen the true impact of the caveats and the real considerations of the payment options, you should by now have realized that the horrible dangers your advisors may have warned you about are simply not true. A properly bought and structured insurance policy is not an open-ended document that an insurance company can change overnight to massively inflate its costs and deflate its returns. It is a tightly devised and well-regulated financial vehicle that very clearly and very specifically states it possibilities and potentials for your review. There are some risks involved in terms of changes to the current assumptions, but then again I know of absolutely no risk-free investments and absolutely no other vehicles whose risks are balanced by such a wealth of benefits and potentials. Now, having the facts to replace the fearful insinuations you may have been exposed to, you can decide for yourself.

HOW TO BUY

I stated above that it was understandable that the purchase of life insurance, with its payment options and terms, could seem so much more complicated than a purchase of a stock that you simply select, buy, own, and then sell when it, hopefully, achieves its potential. But, in fact, don't you occasionally buy your stocks on margin?

In several of the sample concepts which appear earlier, I showed you how to borrow the cost of your insurance policy using the margin available from your existing stock portfolio or the loan power of your asset base. In this way, you can still purchase your policy on a one-pay basis, thereby getting the absolute best rate, without having to be out of pocket for the full purchase price.

You may now be wondering why it would be advantageous to borrow the money from another source rather than simply use a limited-pay or life-pay plan. The answer is rather simple. When you finance the money for the insurance premium by selecting a limited-pay or life-pay option from the insurance company, the cost of that financing is built into the payments that you make. But when you borrow the money for the premium from an outside source, many options become available for its ultimate repayment. Though we examined those options in the concepts presented earlier, let's review them again.

To begin with, you can pay cash for your policy, reallocating funds from existing stocks, CD's, T-Bills, municipal bonds or your IRA or pension fund. Remember how much more advantageous we revealed a life insurance policy could be for your family's welfare than your IRA or pension fund due to the tax free nature of the insurance proceeds. While there might initially be some taxes or penalties to be paid in liquidating those accounts, the benefits will still greatly out-weigh them. I can not more strongly recommend that you consider this reallocation of your available funds to diversify your assets and include life insurance. Not for what it is, but for what it does in your overall financial plan. Its unique benefits add an element of valuable security to your plans that no other financial vehicle can match in terms of rate of return, tax advantages, and certainty. It is my belief that no effective, efficient estate planning can occur until or before life insurance has been looked into.

However, even if you do not want to reallocate existing funds or are not in position to be able to do so, you can still take advantage of the marvelous opportunities presented by life insurance at almost no cost to you whatsoever while still receiving the best rate from the insurance company. You do this by using the leverage of your existing portfolio to borrow the funds for a one-pay policy. By buying a one-pay policy, you get the best rate available for your coverage, thereby protecting your family's future for the least cost available and earning the best return. More importantly, you can do so at a mere fraction of the cost of the policy or at virtually no cash flow impairment to you whatsoever!

Consider this. Your broker call rates or Libor rates are probably about 7.5% right now. So you could borrow the cost of your one-pay insurance premium for a 7.5% annual interest cost. Assuming you have a substantial enough portfolio to even require estate planning at this level, your brokerage firm would surely be more than accommodating of any loan you wished to make and would almost as certainly not be concerned with repayment of the principal loan amount. Clearly, with your portfolio as collateral, they know they are covered. This means that if you have purchased an insurance policy for a $500,000 premium in order for your heirs to receive a $5 million death benefit, you are really paying only $37,500 of interest a year for it. Is there any investment of which you are aware that can perform like that? That will net $5 million tax free at your death for a cost of only $37,500 a year and will do so even if you have only paid one year's worth of the interest cost? If cash and CD's and T-Bills and munis are considered liquid assets to be used during your lifetime, or by your heirs at death, how can you not have the most liquid asset at your death of them all, with the built-in optimizer, ready to go to work at the moment's notice that might well be all you get just before dying? You could also borrow the annual premium on a life-pay basis if you thought it was only necessary for a few years before you have the money to pay the payments.

This is the point where some people bring up the question of the principal loan amount. They question my numbers, saying that I am 'gilding the lily' by failing to take into account that expense. But consider this. You need never pay back the principal loan amount during your lifetime. If cash flow is a concern in your financial planning, you can simply allow that principal loan amount to remain in place until such time as your estate passes on to your heirs. At the time of your death, the loan can be repaid by your heirs as they inherit your estate.

Let's assume that you needed the $5 million of coverage because your $10 million estate was going to be faced with $5 million in estate taxes. The one-pay cost for a $5 million policy, assuming you and your spouse average age 60, would be about $500,000 which you are borrowing at the rate of $37,500 a year. Those yearly $37,500 payments are funding a return, based on current assumptions, of $5 million. Without the insurance, your heirs will inherit only $5 million of your $10 million estate. With the insurance, they will inherit the full $10 million minus the $500,000 that will go towards repaying the principal loan amount. $9.5 million for $37,500 a year, or $5 million—the choice is yours but it seems clear to me.

Furthermore, consider this: Had you not paid the $37,500 per year in interest costs, it would have remained in your estate and been subject to estate taxes. And since every dollar which remains in your estate at the time of your death is subject to the up to 55% estate tax, each is worth only half to your heirs. That means that the $37,500 yearly payments really only cost $18,000 and the $500,000 principal loan repayment only costs your heirs half. In effect, Uncle Sam has repaid the other half of your loan. Now, effectively, $18,000 net annually is funding a net return of $5 million. It is all in the math and it is indisputable. You have created

$5 million at a net cost of $250,000 plus net interest. Can you get the same return anywhere else? If you think you can, I'd like to know where and I want to be first in line to buy.

As a further point to consider, you need not even make the loan payments in the financing model described above. Rather than pay the $37,500 annual payments, you could simply let them accrue. Your brokerage firm, holding as security your millions of dollars worth of stocks and bonds, will allow you to borrow up to the margin regulations maximum. They would simply add the unpaid yearly interest fees to the original principal loan amount of $500,000 and would be repaid the enire amount at the time that your estate passed onto your heirs. Suppose you live twenty years beyond the date on which you took out the loan. For the couple featured in this example, that would put them into their 80's. Accruing for twenty years, the unpaid, compounding $37,500 annual interest payments and principal would total about $2 million. The net cost to their heirs would be $1 million to fund a $5 million return, based on current assumptions. Will any of your stocks increase more than four times over their current value in the next 20 years? More importantly, will they increase the more than eight times over their current value they would have to before estate taxes cut them in half in order for them to net the same four times return? Your heirs could receive $5 million from your $10 million estate if you do nothing but follow the course you are already on. Or they could receive $9 million even after repaying the principal loan amount and the accrued interest. Your current portfolio would have to increase from its present value of $10 million to more than $19 million to net the same $9 million for your heirs. In this model, $1 million buys $5 million effectively without it ever costing you a single dollar during your lifetime.

The options available for you to utilize in designing a purchase plan that best fits your situation and desires are virtually endless. Policies can be structured to accommodate any estate, marital, and financial situation. The only thing that does not change from situation to situation is the fact that nothing works as an alternative to investing like life insurance does. Nothing can match the tax free yields and the immediate availability of the full promised return. No diversified portfolio intended to provide a secure legacy for your family can possibly be said to be effectively or efficiently designed if it does not include life insurance to optimize and maximize your assets and recoup the losses of estate taxes.

When this is fully realized and completely accepted, life insurance will become a part of every portfolio and not being recommended by advisors will be tantamount to malpractice. Most important is diversification. You are only using a small part of your assets to accomplish this. Or, in the case of many of my concepts, including utilizing loans, no cash flow whatsoever.

UNIVERSAL LIFE VS. WHOLE LIFE

There is much misinformation on this subject. If you speak to an agent who is associated with a company that sells whole life, they will tell you their policy is best. If you listen to an agent who sells universal policies they will tell you that it is best. The bottom line will show you the truth. It is simple; just look at the prices. You don't want to pay more than you have to. All insurance companies pay when you die, so why overpay when you can save the money or buy more for the same price.

The real facts are that the universal life premiums were substantially lower than whole life when they were first released in the late 70's. This caused an immediate barrage of false and misleading propaganda about universal life in order to protect the turf and status quo of the long existing whole life and, more importantly, to protect the commissions, since the new universal life paid much lower commissions to the agents in most cases, based on much lower premiums for the buyer.

This propaganda has remained with many attorneys who first

heard this years ago. I can't tell you how many times an attorney has insisted on whole life to the detriment of the client because of this predetermined mindset. I recommend to my client whichever policy is best, usually based on price, if both policies are really equal. This is where the misinformation works to the disadvantage of the client. The client is told the whole life policy is guaranteed. It usually is not. Only the premium is guaranteed. The dividends are based on current assumptions as is universal life, and can and do change. This will change the end result of the whole life policy in the same manner as universal life.

The universal life premium is flexible, allowing the premium to be higher, lower or skipped in accordance with the contract without a loan. Whole life policies were almost always more expensive than universal life so it wasn't long before they simply could not compete on a price basis. Many mutual whole life companies started subsidiary companies in order to sell universal life policies on a more competitive basis. Most whole life dividend companies created new term riders that brought the premium and the commissions down so they could compete with universal life. The term element removed whatever guarantee was left completely from the whole life policy.

Agents were now selling various combinations of 50% whole life/50% term. This has proliferated to 40%/60%, 30%/70% and even 10%/90% combinations thus completely diluting the whole life policy and its guarantees. However most advisers are not really familiar with this and many agents overlook stating anything beyond the original guarantee. If term is not introduced to the whole life policy it just won't be competitive.

Universal life is easier to understand, less complicated, more flexible, and almost always less expensive. It is interesting to observe that you can always make a universal life policy into a whole life policy by over-funding the premium and paying too much but you can never make a whole life policy into a universal life policy. My clients are usually sophisticated and want to bring the premiums down to the lowest possible price and this is accomplished by funding for a minimal cash value at age 100. There are now a number of companies that guarantee that if you have any cash value at age 100 the policy goes to age 110 and beyond without any additional premium. Since you do not want, need, or get back the cash value when you die, why would you possibly fund for a more expensive cash value equal to the whole life policy death benefit at age 100? It is not complicated to figure out using a $1 million policy that the premium will be lower on a universal life policy that requires $1 of cash value to continue past age 100 than on a whole life policy that requires up to $1 million of cash value at age 100 to continue.

A strange situation has also developed recently. Many of the previously highly rated Mutual whole life insurance companies have had their ratings reduced while some of the companies offering universal life policies are now among the highest rated companies in the industry.

Stop listening to everyone's opinion and preconceptions. Go to the bottom line. That's where the savings are.

FAT/THIN POLICIES

I believe in giving insurance companies the least amount of money for the most amount of insurance. Years ago some insurance man probably explained the uses for your policy's cash values in an emergency. He probably further stated that you could borrow against the cash value to put your children through school or for your own retirement.

I buy policies for my clients strictly for death purposes. The cash value is of little importance other than to keep the policy in force. The insurance company will not give you back the cash value at your death so it is meaningless. Therefore I try to squeeze all the cash value out of the policy which results in a lower premium. I call this a thin policy versus a fat policy with a larger unnecessary cash value. In this manner, using a thin policy, you can save up to 60% on your premium or increase the death benefit up to 300% for the same premium.

Supporting America in the New Millennium

As the 21st century dawns, opportunity in America has reached new levels. Computer technologies and e-commerce have helped to create sustained economic growth. Unemployment is down, inflation is low, and seemingly everyday new fortunes are made.

The freedom to pursue these opportunities and the infrastructure that supports them are afforded us all by the ideologies and policies of America. And if I sound like an over-the-top patriot, it is because I am. Our country remains the greatest that has ever been and we should each, in my opinion, feel grateful and privileged to be citizens.

Yet there are those people who are surprised to find out how much of a zealot I am on this subject. They think that because I seek to help people avoid the disastrous effects of estate taxes that I must be anti-government. That wanting to preserve wealth for my clients means that I resent the policies that are so taxing.

They could not be more wrong.

Estate taxes were first initiated in an attempt to prevent the dynastization of America. The government was seeking a means to redistribute wealth in order to prevent a single small group of wealthy families from gaining control of the economy. They wanted to preserve democracy by avoiding having an unfair amount of power and clout residing in only a few hands. And they also felt it fair that those who had profited the most from the business climate and attendant opportunities provided citizens should contribute the most to maintaining it.

Whether or not their policies were fair or effective is a debate for another forum. But as someone who has risen from nothing to great success, I place great value on the freedoms afforded me to pursue my ambitions. I do feel that it is right for all of us to give something back.

None of the concepts I employ takes anything away from the government. In fact, quite to the contrary, using life insurance to discount estate tax costs in order to create and preserve wealth actually benefits the country. With the insurance company effectively paying the taxes, the government gets its money in total more quickly and with less legal ramifications and unnecessary expense. Costly reviews of crafty shelters, delays in paying, and payment schedules that stretch over 15 years all take money out of the government's pocket. My "Die Rich" techniques put money in.

At the same time, these strategies also leave more money in the hands of private people and industry. More money remains in circulation, funding more investments and developing new businesses. More people work, and therefore more people pay income taxes. More people have money to spend, and therefore more people pay sales taxes. More people have money to give to charity, and therefore the government's need to support various causes is lessened. With more people spending more money on consumer goods, manufacturers sell more and then make more. With more goods being manufactured, more people are needed to work and the whole cycle begins anew bringing more wealth to our nation.

And at every step of the way, the benefits enjoyed by Americans are generating more and more revenues for the government.

Unlike legal tax avoidance strategies, the life insurance proceeds used to fund these concepts serve an important dual role in maintaining the economic health of our country. They benefit the government immediately through the timely payment of estate taxes and they help to sustain a vital economy for years to come.

As we ride a wave of sustained growth and prosperity into the new millennium, it may seem that the days of hardship are behind us for good. But history shows us that economies are always in flux; reversals happen. And, while our government's coffers now boast a surplus, we are still faced with immense, and immensely expensive, challenges to better our society. Too many people are still homeless and hungry, too many people lack adequate medical care, too many children receive a sub-standard education, social security remains at risk, as does our environment. Meanwhile, as our world grows smaller, our responsibility to other, less fortunate countries grows bigger.

All of these things require funding. Funding that is only available through the taxes that we pay. To support America in the coming millennium, we can not afford the selfish practices of tax avoidance. Especially when they are not necessary. We have the means to better life for ourselves, for our children, and for our country. Life insurance employed in the ways I have described here is that means. The means to live rich, die rich, and leave a richer legacy behind.

Rate Charts

As I did in my last book, *The Investment Alternative,* I am including on the pages that follow a set of charts and tables that will give you information relative to your own mortality and federal estate tax brackets. More importantly, you will find charts that will help you customize the concepts you have read about to your own financial and estate situation. Of course, if you prefer, you can visit my website at *www.DieRich2.com* and utilize the interactive chart feature to simply input your data and see the concept resolve for your situation. Or you can call my office at 1-800-DIE-RICH (800-343-7424) for a personalized, no-obligation, confidential proposal. However, if you prefer, you can consult the pages that follow to determine an estimate for coverage based on your age and marital status. Remember that these estimates do not constitute a quotation. Although they represent accurate rates from real insurance companies, there are too many variables that affect insurance costs to include them all here. However, there is no reason for you to pay more than the lowest prices from the highest rated insurance companies since all policies pay off the same.

Using the information that follows you should be able to begin formulating the best approach to suit your needs. The policy premium charts should be extremely helpful in showing you your costs at any age from 30 through 90, in giving you a further understanding of how a policy actually works, and helping to demonstrate the true effect of "based on current assumptions."

Each rate chart shows you the current rates, based on current assumptions. It then shows you what the effect on your premiums would be if interest rates went down 1% or up 1%. In the next column you'll see the rates for a guaranteed policy, one that guarantees its rates won't go up or benefits go down irrespective of market conditions, mortality statistics, or current assumptions. (These guaranteed policies are described in detail in the concept entitled *Guaranteed Returns Create Enormous Potentials* on page 87.) In the boxed column at the far right of the page, you'll find what the death benefit would be on a policy bought at guaranteed rates should the current assumptions remain as they are.

I have further broken the charts down to include rates for male, female, and last-to-die policies on a one-pay and life-pay basis.

All premiums listed are based on a $1 million death benefit. You can pro rata up or down to the amount you wish to buy to determine the approximate premium.

I have used some of the lowest priced, highest rated insurance companies to give you an approximate idea of the premiums. However, all insurance companies' stated rates are subject to change at any time. To keep you up to date and make sure you are able to customize these concepts to your situation accurately, and secure the lowest rates available, please feel free to call my office at 1-800-DIE RICH (800-343-7424).

From this information, you should be able to customize your understanding of how a policy would work to achieve the "Die Rich" concepts included in this book.

One Payment Premium for $1,000,000 Death Benefit Based on

Male Age 30

Insurance Company	Current Mortality Current Interest	Current Mortality Current Interest +1%	Current Mortality Current Interest -1%	Guaranteed Mortality Guaranteed Interest	Death Benefit at age 100 based on guaranteed premium at current interest and mortality
E	40,513	30,525	56,105	200,714	19,894,838
A	45,227	35,486	59,612	401,522	19,929,372
D	53,916	41,507	72,811	231,651	11,745,985

Male Age 35

Insurance Company	Current Mortality Current Interest	Current Mortality Current Interest +1%	Current Mortality Current Interest -1%	Guaranteed Mortality Guaranteed Interest	Death Benefit at age 100 based on guaranteed premium at current interest and mortality
E	52,167	39,749	70,890	237,180	16,899,472
A	58,647	46,446	76,171	439,615	17,199,759
B	63,290	50,558	93,448	144,562	10,412,717
D	68,413	53,488	90,389	272,649	10,233,326

One Payment Premium for $1,000,000 Death Benefit Based on

Male Age 40

Insurance Company	Current Mortality Current Interest	Current Mortality Current Interest +1%	Current Mortality Current Interest -1%	Guaranteed Mortality Guaranteed Interest	Death Benefit at age 100 based on guaranteed premium at current interest and mortality
E	68,610	53,347	90,823	280,301	14,313,990
A	78,687	63,505	99,841	521,700	14,495,957
B	84,233	68,361	119,926	182,667	9,243,567
D	91,507	73,502	117,010	321,356	8,775,488

Male Age 45

Insurance Company	Current Mortality Current Interest	Current Mortality Current Interest +1%	Current Mortality Current Interest -1%	Guaranteed Mortality Guaranteed Interest	Death Benefit at age 100 based on guaranteed premium at current interest and mortality
E	90,048	71,625	115,954	330,236	12,078,643
A	102,985	84,490	128,029	545,371	12,642,664
D	104,501	84,773	131,696	498,863	8,984,994
B	112,759	93,295	154,277	230,686	8,169,688

One Payment Premium for $1,000,000 Death Benefit Based on

Male Age 50

Insurance Company	Current Mortality Current Interest	Current Mortality Current Interest +1%	Current Mortality Current Interest -1%	Guaranteed Mortality Guaranteed Interest	Death Benefit at age 100 based on guaranteed premium at current interest and mortality
E	117,749	95,940	147,395	387,301	10,142,291
A	133,122	111,043	162,194	595,186	10,745,727
D	134,337	119,910	164,302	581,057	7,835,394
B	149,019	125,659	196,294	289,831	7,216,815

Male Age 55

Insurance Company	Current Mortality Current Interest	Current Mortality Current Interest +1%	Current Mortality Current Interest -1%	Guaranteed Mortality Guaranteed Interest	Death Benefit at age 100 based on guaranteed premium at current interest and mortality
E	152,507	127,258	185,707	451,405	8,474,736
A	170,501	144,714	203,524	694,499	7,914,675
D	170,506	145,490	202,795	676,289	6,845,428
B	201,745	174,425	253,993	362,293	6,227,090

One Payment Premium for $1,000,000 Death Benefit Based on

Male Age 60

Insurance Company	Current Mortality Current Interest	Current Mortality Current Interest +1%	Current Mortality Current Interest -1%	Guaranteed Mortality Guaranteed Interest	Death Benefit at age 100 based on guaranteed premium at current interest and mortality
E	193,422	165,130	229,481	520,978	7,022,650
A	214,251	185,092	250,637	719,641	7,914,675
D	217,206	189,956	251,056	793,208	5,986,043
C	224,367	192,719	264,517	532,836	5,036,816
B	260,371	229,500	316,392	446,974	5,399,600

Male Age 65

Insurance Company	Current Mortality Current Interest	Current Mortality Current Interest +1%	Current Mortality Current Interest -1%	Guaranteed Mortality Guaranteed Interest	Death Benefit at age 100 based on guaranteed premium at current interest and mortality
E	243,315	212,794	281,053	594,131	5,751,500
D	266,197	238,098	300,162	921,000	5,255,073
A	267,331	235,492	306,060	799,191	6,500,693
C	276,343	242,642	317,800	592,119	4,349,293
B	325,908	295,224	386,805	541,945	4,606,719

One Payment Premium for $1,000,000 Death Benefit Based on

Male Age 70

Insurance Company	Current Mortality Current Interest	Current Mortality Current Interest +1%	Current Mortality Current Interest -1%	Guaranteed Mortality Guaranteed Interest	Death Benefit at age 100 based on guaranteed premium at current interest and mortality
E	313,343	281,828	351,039	667,278	4,623,099
D	326,133	298,555	358,592	1,083,587	4,641,562
A	332,813	299,415	372,387	850,683	5,252,886
C	340,771	306,310	381,855	751,949	3,986,609
B	420,106	385,080	476,703	646,193	3,796,367

Male Age 75

Insurance Company	Current Mortality Current Interest	Current Mortality Current Interest +1%	Current Mortality Current Interest -1%	Guaranteed Mortality Guaranteed Interest	Death Benefit at age 100 based on guaranteed premium at current interest and mortality
A	404,897	371,680	443,234	942,153	4,298,651
E	405,169	373,478	441,746	736,780	3,644,100
C	417,399	384,201	455,782	957,447	3,646,565
D	433,500	433,500	441,849	1,248,366	3,906,522
B	499,628	465,966	550,669	729,080	3,059,128

One Payment Premium for $1,000,000 Death Benefit Based on

Male Age 80

Insurance Company	Current Mortality Current Interest	Current Mortality Current Interest +1%	Current Mortality Current Interest -1%	Guaranteed Mortality Guaranteed Interest	Death Benefit at age 100 based on guaranteed premium at current interest and mortality
A	464,817	434,020	499,474	991,404	3,404,553
E	545,161	512,244	581,883	797,204	2,790,160
B	573,469	543,819	615,180	802,817	2,411,182
C	587,365	552,879	625,524	990,291	2,912,126
D	736,900	736,900	736,900	1,253,533	2,788,461

Male Age 85

Insurance Company	Current Mortality Current Interest	Current Mortality Current Interest +1%	Current Mortality Current Interest -1%	Guaranteed Mortality Guaranteed Interest	Death Benefit at age 100 based on guaranteed premium at current interest and mortality
C	667,945	636,530	702,119	887,084	2,090,381

Life Payment Premium for $1,000,000 Death Benefit Based on

Male Age 30

Insurance Company	Current Mortality Current Interest	Current Mortality Current Interest +1%	Current Mortality Current Interest -1%	Guaranteed Mortality Guaranteed Interest	Death Benefit at age 100 based on guaranteed premium at current interest and mortality
E	3,060	3,060	3,383	9,554	13,779,712
A	3,123	2,691	3,708	9,664	13,638,899
G	3,382	3,360	4,005	9,370	16,417,778
B	3,410	2,675	4,142	10,306	16,514,794
H	3,437	2,890	4,196	9,955	11,769,752
D	3,488	3,007	4,147	9,676	7,953,133
C	3,492	2,958	4,221	10,482	10,295,650

Male Age 35

Insurance Company	Current Mortality Current Interest	Current Mortality Current Interest +1%	Current Mortality Current Interest -1%	Guaranteed Mortality Guaranteed Interest	Death Benefit at age 100 based on guaranteed premium at current interest and mortality
E	3,620	3,085	4,336	11,804	12,194,004
A	4,092	3,558	4,793	11,936	11,302,729
B	4,143	3,585	5,376	12,724	14,338,950
G	4,262	3,840	5,030	11,736	14,587,924
H	4,435	3,765	5,331	12,312	10,578,192
C	4,490	3,857	5,326	12,961	9,422,148
D	4,495	3,920	5,252	11,927	7,242,370

Life Payment Premium for $1,000,000 Death Benefit Based on

Male Age 40

Insurance Company	Current Mortality Current Interest	Current Mortality Current Interest +1%	Current Mortality Current Interest -1%	Guaranteed Mortality Guaranteed Interest	Death Benefit at age 100 based on guaranteed premium at current interest and mortality
E	4,834	4,260	5,668	14,743	10,827,043
B	5,454	4,967	7,086	15,944	12,486,996
A	5,557	4,905	6,389	14,905	9,742,606
G	5,668	5,160	6,589	14,892	12,891,310
C	5,857	5,122	6,799	16,196	8,669,385
H	5,938	5,142	6,968	15,396	9,477,586
D	6,163	5,496	7,012	14,886	6,541,102

Male Age 45

Insurance Company	Current Mortality Current Interest	Current Mortality Current Interest +1%	Current Mortality Current Interest -1%	Guaranteed Mortality Guaranteed Interest	Death Benefit at age 100 based on guaranteed premium at current interest and mortality
E	6,480	6,060	7,440	18,594	9,674,128
G	7,355	6,482	8,444	19,063	11,586,407
D	7,407	6,610	8,384	18,756	5,788,299
A	7,534	6,751	8,506	18,794	8,301,963
C	7,716	6,879	8,759	20,441	8,019,873
H	7,722	6,792	8,892	19,442	8,647,891
B	7,779	6,962	9,407	20,216	10,944,449

Life Payment Premium for $1,000,000 Death Benefit Based on

Male Age 50

Insurance Company	Current Mortality Current Interest	Current Mortality Current Interest +1%	Current Mortality Current Interest -1%	Guaranteed Mortality Guaranteed Interest	Death Benefit at age 100 based on guaranteed premium at current interest and mortality
E	8,734	8,559	9,809	23,718	8,713,657
D	9,865	8,984	10,918	23,897	5,469,295
G	9,903	8,862	11,166	24,720	10,408,458
A	9,931	9,006	11,051	23,969	7,657,578
C	10,166	9,230	11,304	26,105	7,499,096
H	10,319	9,267	11,609	24,839	7,879,073
B	10,634	9,688	12,451	25,943	9,728,078

Male Age 55

Insurance Company	Current Mortality Current Interest	Current Mortality Current Interest +1%	Current Mortality Current Interest -1%	Guaranteed Mortality Guaranteed Interest	Death Benefit at age 100 based on guaranteed premium at current interest and mortality
E	11,775	11,360	12,958	30,662	7,938,389
D	13,076	12,127	14,182	30,594	5,179,669
A	13,149	12,065	14,426	30,981	6,812,369
H	13,406	12,255	14,792	32,177	7,287,407
C	13,434	12,409	14,651	33,804	7,087,909
G	13,720	12,506	15,153	32,486	9,391,813
B	15,520	14,152	17,057	33,835	8,596,754

Life Payment Premium for $1,000,000 Death Benefit Based on

Male Age 60

Insurance Company	Current Mortality Current Interest	Current Mortality Current Interest +1%	Current Mortality Current Interest -1%	Guaranteed Mortality Guaranteed Interest	Death Benefit at age 100 based on guaranteed premium at current interest and mortality
E	15,710	15,560	16,975	40,146	7,293,481
H	17,343	16,131	18,779	42,252	6,765,650
A	17,502	16,251	18,942	40,557	6,037,806
D	17,667	16,679	18,789	39,333	4,877,796
C	17,796	16,698	19,068	24.270	2,749,503
G	19,115	17,731	20,708	43,275	8,550,848
B	23,470	19,623	22,622	44,740	7,818,073

Male Age 65

Insurance Company	Current Mortality Current Interest	Current Mortality Current Interest +1%	Current Mortality Current Interest -1%	Guaranteed Mortality Guaranteed Interest	Death Benefit at age 100 based on guaranteed premium at current interest and mortality
E	22,059	22,059	22,419	53,324	6,714,600
H	22,903	22,836	24,285	56,357	6,286,995
D	23,155	22,207	24,214	50,437	4,551,394
A	23,595	22,192	25,175	53,859	5,767,636
C	23,630	22,488	24,924	31,320	2,476,590
G	28,909	24,392	27,609	58,494	7,887,226
B	32,430	27,500	29,960	59,996	7,189,941

Life Payment Premium for $1,000,000 Death Benefit Based on

Male Age 70

Insurance Company	Current Mortality Current Interest	Current Mortality Current Interest +1%	Current Mortality Current Interest -1%	Guaranteed Mortality Guaranteed Interest	Death Benefit at age 100 based on guaranteed premium at current interest and mortality
D	30,978	30,184	31,858	65,304	4,164,211
A	32,294	30,789	33,959	72,404	5,055,407
C	32,440	32,440	33,541	41,730	2,238,399
E	33,060	33,060	33,060	71,705	6,096,849
H	34,375	34,375	35,053	76,267	5,800,585
G	35,423	33,896	37,111	80,205	7,325,100
B	52,780	35,374	39,172	81,782	6,514,366

Male Age 75

Insurance Company	Current Mortality Current Interest	Current Mortality Current Interest +1%	Current Mortality Current Interest -1%	Guaranteed Mortality Guaranteed Interest	Death Benefit at age 100 based on guaranteed premium at current interest and mortality
D	44,670	44,094	45,298	85,174	3,629,717
A	45,013	43,456	46,711	98,500	4,789,826
E	48,060	48,060	48,819	97,483	5,494,252
C	49,220	49,220	49,220	57,710	2,026,399
G	51,113	49,729	52,620	111,936	6,666,232
H	52,542	52,542	52,542	104,698	5,390,341
B	76,550	46,128	49,868	109,447	5,771,664

Life Payment Premium for $1,000,000 Death Benefit Based on

Male Age 80

Insurance Company	Current Mortality Current Interest	Current Mortality Current Interest +1%	Current Mortality Current Interest -1%	Guaranteed Mortality Guaranteed Interest	Death Benefit at age 100 based on guaranteed premium at current interest and mortality
I	60,000	60,000	60,000	60,000	1,000,000
A	63,422	61,992	65,170	133,597	4,892,434
D	73,690	73,690	73,690	111,556	2,861,948
G	73,846	72,685	75,101	128,494	5,019,513
E	77,588	76,277	78,984	132,219	4,722,606
C	90,580	90,580	90,580	90,940	1,125,406
B	110,450	56,941	60,544	146,268	4,915,395

Male Age 85

Insurance Company	Current Mortality Current Interest	Current Mortality Current Interest +1%	Current Mortality Current Interest -1%	Guaranteed Mortality Guaranteed Interest	Death Benefit at age 100 based on guaranteed premium at current interest and mortality
I	78,600	78,600	78,600	78,600	1,000,000
D	112,040	112,040	112,040	164,611	2,677,265
C	125,230	125,230	125,230	125,230	1,189,854

Male Age 90

Insurance Company	Current Mortality Current Interest	Current Mortality Current Interest +1%	Current Mortality Current Interest -1%	Guaranteed Mortality Guaranteed Interest	Death Benefit at age 100 based on guaranteed premium at current interest and mortality
D	90,000	90,000	90,000	90,000	1,000,000

One Payment Premium for $1,000,000 Death Benefit Based on

Female Age 30

Insurance Company	Current Mortality Current Interest	Current Mortality Current Interest +1%	Current Mortality Current Interest -1%	Guaranteed Mortality Guaranteed Interest	Death Benefit at age 100 based on guaranteed premium at current interest and mortality
A	31,760	24,977	42,027	373,301	18,254,571
E	31,992	24,165	44,826	179,046	18,175,498
B	42,197	34,027	62,758	266,579	16,747,572
D	46,138	35,416	62,706	201,166	10,447,594

Female Age 35

Insurance Company	Current Mortality Current Interest	Current Mortality Current Interest +1%	Current Mortality Current Interest -1%	Guaranteed Mortality Guaranteed Interest	Death Benefit at age 100 based on guaranteed premium at current interest and mortality
E	40,960	30,916	56,420	211,514	15,415,199
A	41,209	32,650	53,825	410,080	15,664,093
B	54,324	44,036	79,025	326,422	14,383,371
D	58,860	45,902	78,229	236,698	9,073,603

One Payment Premium for $1,000,000 Death Benefit Based on

Female Age 40

Insurance Company	Current Mortality Current Interest	Current Mortality Current Interest +1%	Current Mortality Current Interest -1%	Guaranteed Mortality Guaranteed Interest	Death Benefit at age 100 based on guaranteed premium at current interest and mortality
A	53,767	43,054	69,127	485,044	13,204,893
E	54,457	42,009	72,942	249,707	12,993,178
B	69,286	56,521	98,571	399,599	12,385,357
D	77,870	62,176	100,465	278,308	7,778,595

Female Age 45

Insurance Company	Current Mortality Current Interest	Current Mortality Current Interest +1%	Current Mortality Current Interest -1%	Guaranteed Mortality Guaranteed Interest	Death Benefit at age 100 based on guaranteed premium at current interest and mortality
A	68,770	55,548	87,215	525,594	11,305,463
E	73,021	57,757	94,870	293,456	10,878,470
D	78,501	64,055	98,790	424,615	8,515,606
B	92,513	76,795	126,778	492,228	10,554,811

One Payment Premium for $1,000,000 Death Benefit Based on

Female Age 50

Insurance Company	Current Mortality Current Interest	Current Mortality Current Interest +1%	Current Mortality Current Interest -1%	Guaranteed Mortality Guaranteed Interest	Death Benefit at age 100 based on guaranteed premium at current interest and mortality
A	88,249	72,120	110,115	538,542	9,711,693
E	96,680	78,301	122,062	343,502	9,084,496
D	98,800	82,090	121,272	490,852	7,396,934
B	122,806	103,792	162,164	604,287	8,959,437

Female Age 55

Insurance Company	Current Mortality Current Interest	Current Mortality Current Interest +1%	Current Mortality Current Interest -1%	Guaranteed Mortality Guaranteed Interest	Death Benefit at age 100 based on guaranteed premium at current interest and mortality
A	114,532	95,147	140,033	600,856	8,193,240
E	123,981	102,377	152,827	400,197	7,590,061
D	124,843	106,018	149,315	577,438	6,527,454
B	163,677	141,075	207,977	741,567	7,576,627

One Payment Premium for $1,000,000 Death Benefit Based on

Female Age 60

Insurance Company	Current Mortality Current Interest	Current Mortality Current Interest +1%	Current Mortality Current Interest -1%	Guaranteed Mortality Guaranteed Interest	Death Benefit at age 100 based on guaranteed premium at current interest and mortality
A	149,417	126,607	178,508	693,171	6,926,126
E	159,218	134,429	191,213	463,839	6,305,498
D	160,107	139,371	186,207	692,762	5,823,037
C	180,180	151,272	217,591	369,402	3,684,759
B	209,869	183,792	258,335	898,507	6,431,638

Female Age 65

Insurance Company	Current Mortality Current Interest	Current Mortality Current Interest +1%	Current Mortality Current Interest -1%	Guaranteed Mortality Guaranteed Interest	Death Benefit at age 100 based on guaranteed premium at current interest and mortality
A	191,437	165,526	223,504	753,126	5,846,332
E	197,978	170,617	232,194	535,044	5,234,280
D	198,900	177,080	225,570	826,644	5,201,864
C	225,228	193,598	264,809	451,425	3,390,422
B	264,187	235,022	315,556	1,985,628	5,458,811

One Payment Premium for $1,000,000 Death Benefit Based on

Female Age 70

Insurance Company	Current Mortality Current Interest	Current Mortality Current Interest +1%	Current Mortality Current Interest -1%	Guaranteed Mortality Guaranteed Interest	Death Benefit at age 100 based on guaranteed premium at current interest and mortality
A	239,901	211,841	273,639	840,066	4,921,122
D	242,386	220,367	268,540	987,033	4,646,027
E	248,292	219,403	283,265	610,470	4,284,807
C	282,699	249,354	323,020	605,243	3,369,446
B	345,079	313,795	396,705	1,308,101	4,504,066

Female Age 75

Insurance Company	Current Mortality Current Interest	Current Mortality Current Interest +1%	Current Mortality Current Interest -1%	Guaranteed Mortality Guaranteed Interest	Death Benefit at age 100 based on guaranteed premium at current interest and mortality
D	295,488	274,071	320,174	1,130,612	3,955,274
A	302,173	273,413	335,726	906,771	4,027,102
E	338,137	308,497	372,653	689,000	3,434,766
C	357,642	324,567	396,299	739,893	3,014,184

One Payment Premium for $1,000,000 Death Benefit Based on

Female Age 80

Insurance Company	Current Mortality Current Interest	Current Mortality Current Interest +1%	Current Mortality Current Interest -1%	Guaranteed Mortality Guaranteed Interest	Death Benefit at age 100 based on guaranteed premium at current interest and mortality
A	358,585	331,486	389,301	903,161	3,169,921
E	464,986	433,249	500,680	762,211	2,705,271
D	490,000	490,000	490,000	1,143,190	2,836,793
B	512,325	483,986	525,545	1,698,508	2,897,606
C	539,196	503,371	579,130	959,019	2,794,249

Female Age 85

Insurance Company	Current Mortality Current Interest	Current Mortality Current Interest +1%	Current Mortality Current Interest -1%	Guaranteed Mortality Guaranteed Interest	Death Benefit at age 100 based on guaranteed premium at current interest and mortality
C	638,360	605,264	674,508	1,003,232	2,289,614
D	809,200	809,200	809,200	1,032,086	1,893,301

Life Payment Premium for $1,000,000 Death Benefit Based on

Female Age 30

Insurance Company	Current Mortality Current Interest	Current Mortality Current Interest +1%	Current Mortality Current Interest -1%	Guaranteed Mortality Guaranteed Interest	Death Benefit at age 100 based on guaranteed premium at current interest and mortality
A	2,225	2,112	2,661	8,407	14,266,228
E	2,660	2,660	2,683	8,309	12,240,458
H	2,684	2,627	3,284	8,651	10,460,424
C	2,941	2,459	3,539	9,105	9,020,707
D	2,965	2,553	3,540	8,419	7,066,612
G	3,120	3,120	3,120	8,056	14,821,812
B	3,340	2,259	3,395	9,006	14,433,864

Female Age 35

Insurance Company	Current Mortality Current Interest	Current Mortality Current Interest +1%	Current Mortality Current Interest -1%	Guaranteed Mortality Guaranteed Interest	Death Benefit at age 100 based on guaranteed premium at current interest and mortality
E	2,820	2,660	3,415	10,201	10,758,203
A	2,878	2,486	3,413	10,319	33,746,435
G	3,240	3,240	3,645	10,037	12,971,683
H	3,457	3,389	4,169	10,633	9,300,576
C	3,740	3,179	4,440	11,188	8,190,699
D	3,835	3,342	4,496	10,314	6,364,299
B	3,980	3,022	4,397	11,050	12,386,585

Life Payment Premium for $1,000,000 Death Benefit Based on

Female Age 40

Insurance Company	Current Mortality Current Interest	Current Mortality Current Interest +1%	Current Mortality Current Interest -1%	Guaranteed Mortality Guaranteed Interest	Death Benefit at age 100 based on guaranteed premium at current interest and mortality
E	3,795	3,560	4,488	12,627	9,406,995
A	3,826	3,334	4,476	12,770	10,901,829
G	4,080	4,080	4,668	12,621	11,436,022
H	4,578	4,527	5,401	13,175	8,256,686
B	4,710	4,020	5,669	13,656	10,748,585
C	4,820	4,180	5,628	12,860	7,462,758
D	5,179	4,603	5,928	12,739	5,692,370

Female Age 45

Insurance Company	Current Mortality Current Interest	Current Mortality Current Interest +1%	Current Mortality Current Interest -1%	Guaranteed Mortality Guaranteed Interest	Death Benefit at age 100 based on guaranteed premium at current interest and mortality
A	5,046	4,431	5,833	15,887	9,254,214
E	5,183	4,562	5,981	15,712	8,222,868
G	5,417	5,280	6,236	15,932	9,930,179
D	5,447	4,904	6,123	15,997	5,423,130
H	5,927	5,875	6,873	16,412	7,414,647
C	6,238	5,515	7,163	17,267	6,823,607
B	6,260	5,541	7,445	17,110	9,264,579

Life Payment Premium for $1,000,000 Death Benefit Based on

Female Age 50

Insurance Company	Current Mortality Current Interest	Current Mortality Current Interest +1%	Current Mortality Current Interest -1%	Guaranteed Mortality Guaranteed Interest	Death Benefit at age 100 based on guaranteed premium at current interest and mortality
A	6,787	6,028	7,729	19,934	7,881,269
D	7,033	6,419	7,776	20,085	5,056,873
E	7,038	6,314	7,943	19,718	7,243,417
G	7,097	6,840	8,042	20,283	8,759,862
H	7,788	7,735	8,855	20,624	6,672,695
C	8,065	7,232	9,099	21,694	6,296,255
B	8,430	7,655	9,808	21,639	8,044,482

Female Age 55

Insurance Company	Current Mortality Current Interest	Current Mortality Current Interest +1%	Current Mortality Current Interest -1%	Guaranteed Mortality Guaranteed Interest	Death Benefit at age 100 based on guaranteed premium at current interest and mortality
D	9,195	8,532	9,975	25,756	4,778,975
A	9,224	8,296	10,340	25,286	6,764,419
E	9,322	8,480	10,341	25,016	6,494,035
G	9,812	9,000	10,899	26,145	7,720,028
H	10,069	9,974	11,251	26,209	6,071,301
C	10,425	9,472	11,574	27,557	5,863,529
B	11,850	10,704	13,062	27,751	7,026,839

Life Payment Premium for $1,000,000 Death Benefit Based on

Female Age 60

Insurance Company	Current Mortality Current Interest	Current Mortality Current Interest +1%	Current Mortality Current Interest -1%	Guaranteed Mortality Guaranteed Interest	Death Benefit at age 100 based on guaranteed premium at current interest and mortality
D	12,366	11,689	13,145	33,642	4,541,566
E	12,513	11,561	13,631	32,212	5,859,238
A	12,787	11,667	14,095	32,557	5,842,404
C	13,599	12,524	14,857	19,210	2,290,045
G	14,059	12,974	15,309	34,237	6,878,798
H	14,298	14,298	14,298	33,821	2,820,702
B	16,190	14,622	17,170	35,967	6,282,043

Female Age 65

Insurance Company	Current Mortality Current Interest	Current Mortality Current Interest +1%	Current Mortality Current Interest -1%	Guaranteed Mortality Guaranteed Interest	Death Benefit at age 100 based on guaranteed premium at current interest and mortality
D	16,277	15,628	17,011	44,022	4,295,848
E	16,422	15,379	17,617	42,428	5,405,543
A	17,794	16,470	19,301	42,878	5,573,331
C	18,128	16,958	19,461	24,740	2,056,050
G	18,730	17,448	20,160	45,893	6,376,824
H	20,678	20,678	20,678	44,682	5,142,583
B	23,210	19,608	22,291	47,837	5,783,286

Life Payment Premium for $1,000,000 Death Benefit Based on

Female Age 70

Insurance Company	Current Mortality Current Interest	Current Mortality Current Interest +1%	Current Mortality Current Interest -1%	Guaranteed Mortality Guaranteed Interest	Death Benefit at age 100 based on guaranteed premium at current interest and mortality
D	21,341	20,762	21,986	57,367	3,976,672
E	22,255	22,059	23,439	56,978	4,973,412
G	24,169	22,920	25,618	63,017	5,905,064
A	24,662	23,135	26,359	57,578	4,936,097
C	24,887	23,674	26,237	32,910	1,849,574
H	31,265	31,265	31,265	60,276	4,679,694
B	35,870	62,516	29,784	65,344	5,240,585

Female Age 75

Insurance Company	Current Mortality Current Interest	Current Mortality Current Interest +1%	Current Mortality Current Interest -1%	Guaranteed Mortality Guaranteed Interest	Death Benefit at age 100 based on guaranteed premium at current interest and mortality
D	28,744	28,265	29,269	73,373	3,485,366
E	34,953	34,059	36,000	78,870	4,482,948
H	47,831	47,831	47,831	84,040	4,406,143
G	35,277	34,061	36,583	89,405	5,432,359
A	35,283	33,950	37,133	79,696	4,805,353
C	38,170	38,170	38,170	46,070	1,664,234
B	59,950	40,147	37,024	89,574	4,722,109

Life Payment Premium for $1,000,000 Death Benefit Based on

Female Age 80

Insurance Company	Current Mortality Current Interest	Current Mortality Current Interest +1%	Current Mortality Current Interest -1%	Guaranteed Mortality Guaranteed Interest	Death Benefit at age 100 based on guaranteed premium at current interest and mortality
I	41,729	40,780	42,727	128,493	5,092,235
G	45,600	45,600	45,600	45,600	1,000,000
H	47,831	47,831	47,831	84,040	4,406,143
D	49,000	49,000	49,000	94,896	2,752,310
A	51,299	49,752	53,279	111,930	4,182,687
E	59,037	57,825	60,326	110,772	4,037,369
C	76,590	76,590	76,590	76,950	1,000,000
B	90,720	51,602	48,505	123,737	4,135,441

Female Age 85

Insurance Company	Current Mortality Current Interest	Current Mortality Current Interest +1%	Current Mortality Current Interest -1%	Guaranteed Mortality Guaranteed Interest	Death Benefit at age 100 based on guaranteed premium at current interest and mortality
I	62,160	62,160	62,160	62,160	1,000,000
D	80,920	80,920	80,920	143,033	2,554,761
C	112,200	112,200	112,200	112,200	1,146,400

Female Age 90

Insurance Company	Current Mortality Current Interest	Current Mortality Current Interest +1%	Current Mortality Current Interest -1%	Guaranteed Mortality Guaranteed Interest	Death Benefit at age 100 based on guaranteed premium at current interest and mortality
D	93,000	93,000	93,000	93,000	1,000,000

One Payment Premium for $1,000,000 Death Benefit Based on

Last To Die Age 30

Insurance Company	Current Mortality Current Interest	Current Mortality Current Interest +1%	Current Mortality Current Interest -1%	Guaranteed Mortality Guaranteed Interest	Death Benefit at age 100 based on guaranteed premium at current interest and mortality
A	16,397	11,568	24,418	141,440	40,376,938
B	19,506	14,268	27,749	158,397	12,992,850
D	20,140	12,940	32,106	224,651	12,884,782

Last To Die Age 35

Insurance Company	Current Mortality Current Interest	Current Mortality Current Interest +1%	Current Mortality Current Interest -1%	Guaranteed Mortality Guaranteed Interest	Death Benefit at age 100 based on guaranteed premium at current interest and mortality
A	22,772	16,380	32,987	171,604	33,746,435
D	26,923	17,945	41,243	270,025	11,359,593
B	27,058	20,164	37,511	201,855	11,164,679
E	27,470	19,226	40,326	166,281	12,153,893
C	30,284	20,711	46,047	328,698	8,267,968

One Payment Premium for $1,000,000 Death Benefit Based on

Last To Die Age 40

Insurance Company	Current Mortality Current Interest	Current Mortality Current Interest +1%	Current Mortality Current Interest -1%	Guaranteed Mortality Guaranteed Interest	Death Benefit at age 100 based on guaranteed premium at current interest and mortality
A	30,532	22,185	43,387	206,260	28,068,952
E	35,552	25,410	50,782	199,864	10,460,807
D	35,836	24,778	52,780	323,756	10,009,862
B	37,746	28,761	50,866	258,672	9,746,329
C	39,338	27,783	57,684	371,711	7,786,834

Last To Die Age 45

Insurance Company	Current Mortality Current Interest	Current Mortality Current Interest +1%	Current Mortality Current Interest -1%	Guaranteed Mortality Guaranteed Interest	Death Benefit at age 100 based on guaranteed premium at current interest and mortality
A	41,514	30,695	57,559	247,670	23,305,709
E	47,052	34,631	65,832	240,494	8,983,900
D	49,900	35,918	70,454	386,659	8,620,236
C	52,093	38,073	73,440	531,963	7,088,513
B	52,636	41,104	68,858	330,778	8,466,806

One Payment Premium for $1,000,000 Death Benefit Based on

Last To Die Age 50

Insurance Company	Current Mortality Current Interest	Current Mortality Current Interest +1%	Current Mortality Current Interest -1%	Guaranteed Mortality Guaranteed Interest	Death Benefit at age 100 based on guaranteed premium at current interest and mortality
A	57,526	43,609	77,357	297,523	19,315,405
E	62,593	47,133	85,771	288,498	7,696,125
D	66,415	49,682	90,141	459,266	7,532,194
C	70,198	52,415	96,236	595,381	6,612,269
B	73,031	58,540	92,694	421,970	7,318,799

Last To Die Age 55

Insurance Company	Current Mortality Current Interest	Current Mortality Current Interest +1%	Current Mortality Current Interest -1%	Guaranteed Mortality Guaranteed Interest	Death Benefit at age 100 based on guaranteed premium at current interest and mortality
F	78,764	60,008	104,862	n/a	n/a
A	79,541	61,960	103,634	355,917	15,957,602
E	84,593	64,983	111,825	345,530	6,573,555
D	87,754	67,997	114,621	541,098	6,546,073
C	89,032	68,449	118,155	982,469	6,720,149
B	101,105	83,268	124,450	536,735	6,284,409

One Payment Premium for $1,000,000 Death Benefit Based on

Last To Die Age 60

Insurance Company	Current Mortality Current Interest	Current Mortality Current Interest +1%	Current Mortality Current Interest -1%	Guaranteed Mortality Guaranteed Interest	Death Benefit at age 100 based on guaranteed premium at current interest and mortality
F	109,586	86,574	140,299	n/a	n/a
A	109,635	87,914	138,274	422,764	13,105,874
E	114,400	90,892	145,765	412,072	5,585,154
D	114,897	92,246	114,564	630,491	5,645,960
C	118,853	94,657	151,749	463,111	3,465,740
B	132,148	111,669	158,322	679,886	4,044,723

Last To Die Age 65

Insurance Company	Current Mortality Current Interest	Current Mortality Current Interest +1%	Current Mortality Current Interest -1%	Guaranteed Mortality Guaranteed Interest	Death Benefit at age 100 based on guaranteed premium at current interest and mortality
D	148,742	123,614	180,464	723,122	4,813,748
E	150,467	123,188	185,519	488,013	4,716,177
A	151,429	125,219	184,688	499,293	10,691,195
C	153,191	125,607	189,304	298,894	2,604,811
B	176,230	153,341	204,407	854,635	4,605,444

One Payment Premium for $1,000,000 Death Benefit Based on

Last To Die Age 70

Insurance Company	Current Mortality Current Interest	Current Mortality Current Interest +1%	Current Mortality Current Interest -1%	Guaranteed Mortality Guaranteed Interest	Death Benefit at age 100 based on guaranteed premium at current interest and mortality
F	177,893	209,541	248,553	n/a	n/a
D	191,039	164,244	223,661	806,689	3,999,998
C	198,567	168,089	236,824	368,764	2,252,583
E	200,903	170,289	238,782	574,395	3,931,610
A	205,308	174,852	242,586	583,200	8,650,342
B	211,608	188,501	239,225	475,745	3,124,744

Last To Die Age 75

Insurance Company	Current Mortality Current Interest	Current Mortality Current Interest +1%	Current Mortality Current Interest -1%	Guaranteed Mortality Guaranteed Interest	Death Benefit at age 100 based on guaranteed premium at current interest and mortality
D	237,152	210,616	268,384	862,638	3,230,427
C	257,666	225,320	296,794	484,820	2,230,997
E	264,254	231,545	303,256	666,719	3,232,416
A	288,512	252,351	331,281	668,103	6,738,871
B	315,946	287,176	349,184	1,292,767	3,246,086

One Payment Premium for $1,000,000 Death Benefit Based on

Last To Die Age 80

Insurance Company	Current Mortality Current Interest	Current Mortality Current Interest +1%	Current Mortality Current Interest -1%	Guaranteed Mortality Guaranteed Interest	Death Benefit at age 100 based on guaranteed premium at current interest and mortality
D	280,306	257,255	306,936	867,498	2,472,736
E	347,193	314,069	385,250	757,574	2,601,355
C	402,842	371,602	438,472	786,360	2,212,615
A	407,844	366,062	455,607	743,816	5,006,572
B	438,989	470,454	474,270	1,540,098	2,637,962

Last To Die Age 85

Insurance Company	Current Mortality Current Interest	Current Mortality Current Interest +1%	Current Mortality Current Interest -1%	Guaranteed Mortality Guaranteed Interest	Death Benefit at age 100 based on guaranteed premium at current interest and mortality
D	360,884	338,229	385,963	786,691	1,672,185

Life Payment Premium for $1,000,000 Death Benefit Based on

Last To Die Age 30

Insurance Company	Current Mortality Current Interest	Current Mortality Current Interest +1%	Current Mortality Current Interest -1%	Guaranteed Mortality Guaranteed Interest	Death Benefit at age 100 based on guaranteed premium at current interest and mortality
F	981	370	1,598	n/a	n/a
A	1,138	949	1,498	6,175	11,915,801
D	1,267	950	1,767	8,358	7,885,601
B	1,297	1,061	1,632	5,425	11,059,992
C	1,387	1,039	1,094	6,866	8,035,584
H	1,525	1,126	2,096	7,267	8,172,039
G	1,880	1,880	1,927	5,718	10,920,856

Last To Die Age 35

Insurance Company	Current Mortality Current Interest	Current Mortality Current Interest +1%	Current Mortality Current Interest -1%	Guaranteed Mortality Guaranteed Interest	Death Benefit at age 100 based on guaranteed premium at current interest and mortality
F	1,266	683	1,973	n/a	n/a
A	1,588	1,355	2,038	7,724	10,247,184
D	1,709	1,290	2,296	10,039	6,950,930
B	1,812	1,508	2,227	6,889	9,565,632
C	1,902	1,471	2,518	8,699	7,463,747
H	2,042	1,542	2,714	8,809	7,300,150
G	2,400	2,400	2,622	7,248	9,507,192
E	3,090	3,090	3,090	7,534	8,101,298

Life Payment Premium for $1,000,000 Death Benefit Based on

Last To Die Age 40

Insurance Company	Current Mortality Current Interest	Current Mortality Current Interest +1%	Current Mortality Current Interest -1%	Guaranteed Mortality Guaranteed Interest	Death Benefit at age 100 based on guaranteed premium at current interest and mortality
F	1,807	1,178	2,622	n/a	n/a
A	2,145	1,858	2,709	9,642	8,860,432
D	2,330	1,784	2,987	12,054	6,126,521
C	2,492	1,985	3,193	10,617	7,077,518
B	2,554	2,168	3,060	8,805	8,301,464
H	2,727	2,126	3,528	10,889	6,551,206
G	2,840	2,840	3,571	9,212	8,323,334
E	3,090	3,090	3,090	9,405	7,229,952

Last To Die Age 45

Insurance Company	Current Mortality Current Interest	Current Mortality Current Interest +1%	Current Mortality Current Interest -1%	Guaranteed Mortality Guaranteed Interest	Death Benefit at age 100 based on guaranteed premium at current interest and mortality
F	2,629	1,824	3,472	n/a	n/a
A	2,948	2,609	3,645	12,135	7,704,226
D	3,262	2,619	4,082	14,471	5,298,671
C	3,344	2,746	4,139	13,636	6,656,624
E	3,489	3,489	4,045	11,861	6,469,093
B	3,610	3,132	4,214	11,332	7,227,870
H	3,642	3,126	4,573	13,527	5,914,960
G	3,963	3,320	4,854	11,773	7,524,451

Life Payment Premium for $1,000,000 Death Benefit Based on

Last To Die Age 50

Insurance Company	Current Mortality Current Interest	Current Mortality Current Interest +1%	Current Mortality Current Interest -1%	Guaranteed Mortality Guaranteed Interest	Death Benefit at age 100 based on guaranteed premium at current interest and mortality
F	3,742	2,817	4,648	n/a	n/a
A	4,147	3,771	4,998	15,457	6,744,247
E	4,414	4,089	5,370	15,087	5,822,281
D	4,439	3,680	5,375	17,405	4,655,531
C	4,587	3,831	5,555	17,507	6,273,007
H	4,792	4,792	5,864	17,048	5,401,905
B	5,101	4,526	5,801	14,714	6,320,269
G	5,314	4,433	6,404	15,164	6,548,872

Last To Die Age 55

Insurance Company	Current Mortality Current Interest	Current Mortality Current Interest +1%	Current Mortality Current Interest -1%	Guaranteed Mortality Guaranteed Interest	Death Benefit at age 100 based on guaranteed premium at current interest and mortality
F	5,185	4,075	6,194	n/a	n/a
A	5,862	5,485	6,883	19,894	5,953,460
C	5,930	5,078	6,990	21,829	6,058,112
E	6,090	5,589	7,204	19,448	5,278,488
D	6,112	5,164	7,096	21,120	4,109,904
H	6,715	6,715	7,554	21,832	4,971,751
G	7,152	6,079	8,439	19,776	5,911,397
B	7,215	6,553	7,994	19,316	5,549,722

Life Payment Premium for $1,000,000 Death Benefit Based on

Last To Die Age 60

Insurance Company	Current Mortality Current Interest	Current Mortality Current Interest +1%	Current Mortality Current Interest -1%	Guaranteed Mortality Guaranteed Interest	Death Benefit at age 100 based on guaranteed premium at current interest and mortality
F	7,551	6,288	8,691	n/a	n/a
C	8,165	7,200	9,328	28,977	5,810,616
D	8,239	7,241	9,398	26,043	3,667,526
A	8,344	8,042	9,549	25,895	5,294,809
E	8,794	8,090	9,762	25,437	4,816,964
H	9,566	9,566	10,014	28,324	4,599,787
B	9,746	9,050	10,540	25,708	4,971,364
G	9,902	8,610	11,405	26,174	5,346,827

Last To Die Age 65

Insurance Company	Current Mortality Current Interest	Current Mortality Current Interest +1%	Current Mortality Current Interest -1%	Guaranteed Mortality Guaranteed Interest	Death Benefit at age 100 based on guaranteed premium at current interest and mortality
F	10,890	9,478	12,263	n/a	n/a
C	10,967	9,889	12,229	15,690	1,716,061
D	11,259	10,159	12,503	33,347	3,377,716
E	11,652	11,090	13,082	33,850	4,463,789
A	12,076	11,986	13,474	34,297	4,747,245
H	12,387	12,387	13,469	37,437	4,278,594
B	13,719	13,021	14,492	34,811	4,463,597
G	13,903	12,560	15,603	35,358	4,855,604

Life Payment Premium for $1,000,000 Death Benefit Based on

Last To Die Age 70

Insurance Company	Current Mortality Current Interest	Current Mortality Current Interest +1%	Current Mortality Current Interest -1%	Guaranteed Mortality Guaranteed Interest	Death Benefit at age 100 based on guaranteed premium at current interest and mortality
C	15,490	15,490	16,578	20,730	1,392,336
D	16,139	14,399	16,868	44,762	3,221,827
H	17,032	15,580	18,806	49,896	3,982,919
B	17,404	16,789	18,071	48,086	4,175,745
A	17,843	17,843	19,064	46,197	4,287,045
E	18,090	18,090	18,090	46,089	4,140,633
G	19,757	18,560	21,608	48,501	4,421,092

Last To Die Age 75

Insurance Company	Current Mortality Current Interest	Current Mortality Current Interest +1%	Current Mortality Current Interest -1%	Guaranteed Mortality Guaranteed Interest	Death Benefit at age 100 based on guaranteed premium at current interest and mortality
D	21,311	20,149	22,570	60,745	3,062,355
H	24,275	22,492	26,216	67,692	3,721,421
G	26,661	24,880	28,586	67,448	4,086,092
E	27,090	27,090	27,090	64,126	3,844,490
B	29,448	28,629	30,310	67,431	3,774,286

Life Payment Premium for $1,000,000 Death Benefit Based on

Last To Die Age 80

Insurance Company	Current Mortality Current Interest	Current Mortality Current Interest +1%	Current Mortality Current Interest -1%	Guaranteed Mortality Guaranteed Interest	Death Benefit at age 100 based on guaranteed premium at current interest and mortality
D	28,691	27,689	29,760	81,850	2,794,676
G	34,087	32,501	35,769	96,209	3,711,951
H	35,563	33,607	37,651	93,250	3,420,628
E	38,090	38,090	38,090	90,417	3,491,912
A	44,543	41,823	47,144	88,039	3,268,625
B	48,439	47,456	49,450	96,039	3,366,705
C	56,160	56,160	56,160	61,740	1,540,029

Last To Die Age 85

Insurance Company	Current Mortality Current Interest	Current Mortality Current Interest +1%	Current Mortality Current Interest -1%	Guaranteed Mortality Guaranteed Interest	Death Benefit at age 100 based on guaranteed premium at current interest and mortality
D	45,085	43,801	46,425	103,243	2,200,605
H	52,150	50,075	54,331	129,327	3,030,006

SPIA $1,000,000 Annuity–Life

Male

Age	Annual Annuity Income	Tax Exclusion Ratio	Non Taxable Income	After 40% Federal Income Tax	Net Return
70	$110,093	58.6%	$ 64,510	$ 91,861	9.1%
75	131,783	63.2	83,287	112,384	11.2
80	163,754	67.9	111,189	142,728	14.2
85	209,859	74.5	156,345	188,454	18.8
89	259,611	80.2	208,208	239,050	23.9

Female

Age	Annual Annuity Income	Tax Exclusion Ratio	Non Taxable Income	After 40% Federal Income Tax	Net Return
70	$ 96,284	67.0%	$ 64,510	$ 83,575	8.3%
75	113,625	73.3	83,287	101,490	10.1
80	140,743	78.9	111,046	128,865	12.8
85	183,586	85.1	156,232	172,644	17.2
89	233,674	89.2	208,437	223,579	22.3

Joint (100% To Survivor)

Age	Annual Annuity Income	Tax Exclusion Ratio	Non Taxable Income	After 40% Federal Income Tax	Net Return
70	$ 84,510	58.9%	$49,776	$70,616	7.0%
75	96,692	64.6	62,463	83,000	8.3
80	115,184	70.6	81,320	101,639	10.1
85	143,034	76.8	109,850	129,761	12.9
89	174,178	82.0	142,826	161,637	16.1

Net returns based on life expectancy.

Call 1-800-343-7424 for current rates.

Federal Estate Tax Based on new exemptions

Assets	2000-2002	2002-2003	2004	2005	2006
$ 1,000,000	$ 125,250	$ 116,000	$ 58,500	$ 19,500	$ -
$ 1,100,000	$ 166,250	$ 157,000	$ 99,500	$ 60,500	$ 41,000
$ 1,200,000	$ 207,250	$ 198,000	$ 140,500	$ 101,500	$ 82,000
$ 1,300,000	$ 249,250	$ 240,000	$ 182,500	$ 143,500	$ 124,000
$ 1,400,000	$ 292,250	$ 283,000	$ 225,500	$ 186,500	$ 167,000
$ 1,500,000	$ 335,250	$ 326,000	$ 268,500	$ 229,500	$ 210,000
$ 1,600,000	$ 380,250	$ 371,000	$ 313,500	$ 274,500	$ 255,000
$ 1,700,000	$ 425,250	$ 416,000	$ 358,500	$ 319,500	$ 300,000
$ 1,800,000	$ 470,250	$ 461,000	$ 403,500	$ 364,500	$ 345,000
$ 1,900,000	$ 515,250	$ 506,000	$ 448,500	$ 409,500	$ 390,000
$ 2,000,000	$ 560,250	$ 551,000	$ 493,500	$ 454,500	$ 435,000
$ 2,100,000	$ 609,250	$ 600,000	$ 542,500	$ 503,500	$ 484,000
$ 2,200,000	$ 658,250	$ 649,000	$ 591,500	$ 552,500	$ 533,000
$ 2,300,000	$ 707,250	$ 698,000	$ 640,500	$ 601,500	$ 582,000
$ 2,400,000	$ 756,250	$ 747,000	$ 689,500	$ 650,500	$ 631,000
$ 2,500,000	$ 805,250	$ 796,000	$ 738,500	$ 699,500	$ 680,000
$ 2,600,000	$ 858,250	$ 849,000	$ 791,500	$ 752,500	$ 733,000
$ 2,700,000	$ 911,250	$ 902,000	$ 844,500	$ 805,500	$ 786,000
$ 2,800,000	$ 964,250	$ 955,000	$ 897,500	$ 858,500	$ 839,000
$ 2,900,000	$ 1,017,250	$ 1,008,000	$ 950,500	$ 911,500	$ 892,000
$ 3,000,000	$ 1,070,250	$ 1,061,000	$ 1,003,500	$ 964,500	$ 945,000
$ 3,100,000	$ 1,125,250	$ 1,116,000	$ 1,058,500	$ 1,019,500	$ 1,000,000
$ 3,200,000	$ 1,180,250	$ 1,171,000	$ 1,113,500	$ 1,074,500	$ 1,055,000
$ 3,300,000	$ 1,235,250	$ 1,226,000	$ 1,168,500	$ 1,129,500	$ 1,110,000
$ 3,400,000	$ 1,290,250	$ 1,281,000	$ 1,223,500	$ 1,184,500	$ 1,165,000
$ 3,500,000	$ 1,345,250	$ 1,336,000	$ 1,278,500	$ 1,239,500	$ 1,220,000
$ 3,600,000	$ 1,400,250	$ 1,391,000	$ 1,333,500	$ 1,294,500	$ 1,275,000
$ 3,700,000	$ 1,455,250	$ 1,446,000	$ 1,388,500	$ 1,349,500	$ 1,330,000
$ 3,800,000	$ 1,510,250	$ 1,501,000	$ 1,443,500	$ 1,404,500	$ 1,385,000
$ 3,900,000	$ 1,565,250	$ 1,556,000	$ 1,498,500	$ 1,459,500	$ 1,440,000
$ 4,000,000	$ 1,620,250	$ 1,611,000	$ 1,553,500	$ 1,514,500	$ 1,495,000
$ 4,500,000	$ 1,895,250	$ 1,886,000	$ 1,828,500	$ 1,789,500	$ 1,770,000
$ 5,000,000	$ 2,170,250	$ 2,161,000	$ 2,103,500	$ 2,064,500	$ 2,045,000
$ 5,500,000	$ 2,445,250	$ 2,436,000	$ 2,378,500	$ 2,339,500	$ 2,320,000

$ 6,000,000	$ 2,720,250	$ 2,711,000	$ 2,653,500	$ 2,614,500	$ 2,595,000
$ 6,500,000	$ 2,995,250	$ 2,986,000	$ 2,928,500	$ 2,889,500	$ 2,870,000
$ 7,000,000	$ 3,270,250	$ 3,261,000	$ 3,203,500	$ 3,164,500	$ 3,145,000
$ 7,500,000	$ 3,545,250	$ 3,536,000	$ 3,478,500	$ 3,439,500	$ 3,420,000
$ 8,000,000	$ 3,820,250	$ 3,811,000	$ 3,753,500	$ 3,714,500	$ 3,695,000
$ 8,500,000	$ 4,095,250	$ 4,086,000	$ 4,028,500	$ 3,989,500	$ 3,970,000
$ 9,000,000	$ 4,370,250	$ 4,361,000	$ 4,303,500	$ 4,264,500	$ 4,245,000
$ 9,500,000	$ 4,645,250	$ 4,636,000	$ 4,578,500	$ 4,539,500	$ 4,520,000
$ 10,000,000	$ 4,920,250	$ 4,911,000	$ 4,853,500	$ 4,814,500	$ 4,795,000
$ 11,000,000	$ 5,452,250	$ 5,443,000	$ 5,385,500	$ 5,346,500	$ 5,327,000
$ 12,000,000	$ 6,120,250	$ 6,111,000	$ 6,053,500	$ 6,014,500	$ 5,995,000
$ 13,000,000	$ 6,720,250	$ 6,711,000	$ 6,653,500	$ 6,614,500	$ 6,595,000
$ 14,000,000	$ 7,320,250	$ 7,311,000	$ 7,253,500	$ 7,214,500	$ 7,195,000
$ 15,000,000	$ 7,920,250	$ 7,911,000	$ 7,853,500	$ 7,814,500	$ 7,795,000
$ 16,000,000	$ 8,520,250	$ 8,511,000	$ 8,453,500	$ 8,414,500	$ 8,395,000
$ 17,000,000	$ 9,120,250	$ 9,111,000	$ 9,053,500	$ 9,014,500	$ 8,995,000
$ 18,000,000	$ 9,720,250	$ 9,711,000	$ 9,653,500	$ 9,614,500	$ 9,595,000
$ 19,000,000	$ 10,320,250	$ 10,311,000	$ 10,253,500	$ 10,214,500	$ 10,195,000
$ 20,000,000	$ 10,920,250	$ 10,911,000	$ 10,853,500	$ 10,814,500	$ 10,795,000
$ 25,000,000	$ 13,750,000	$ 13,750,000	$ 13,750,000	$ 13,750,000	$ 13,750,000
$ 30,000,000	$ 16,500,000	$ 16,500,000	$ 16,500,000	$ 16,500,000	$ 16,500,000
$ 35,000,000	$ 19,250,000	$ 19,250,000	$ 19,250,000	$ 19,250,000	$ 19,250,000
$ 40,000,000	$ 22,000,000	$ 22,000,000	$ 22,000,000	$ 22,000,000	$ 22,000,000
$ 45,000,000	$ 24,750,000	$ 24,750,000	$ 24,750,000	$ 24,750,000	$ 24,750,000
$ 50,000,000	$ 27,500,000	$ 27,500,000	$ 27,500,000	$ 27,500,000	$ 27,500,000
$ 55,000,000	$ 30,250,000	$ 30,250,000	$ 30,250,000	$ 30,250,000	$ 30,250,000
$ 60,000,000	$ 33,000,000	$ 33,000,000	$ 33,000,000	$ 33,000,000	$ 33,000,000
$ 65,000,000	$ 35,750,000	$ 35,750,000	$ 35,750,000	$ 35,750,000	$ 35,750,000
$ 70,000,000	$ 38,500,000	$ 38,500,000	$ 38,500,000	$ 38,500,000	$ 38,500,000
$ 75,000,000	$ 41,250,000	$ 41,250,000	$ 41,250,000	$ 41,250,000	$ 41,250,000
$ 80,000,000	$ 44,000,000	$ 44,000,000	$ 44,000,000	$ 44,000,000	$ 44,000,000
$ 85,000,000	$ 46,750,000	$ 46,750,000	$ 46,750,000	$ 46,750,000	$ 46,750,000
$ 90,000,000	$ 49,500,000	$ 49,500,000	$ 49,500,000	$ 49,500,000	$ 49,500,000
$ 95,000,000	$ 52,250,000	$ 52,250,000	$ 52,250,000	$ 52,250,000	$ 52,250,000
$ 100,000,000	$ 55,000,000	$ 55,000,000	$ 55,000,000	$ 55,000,000	$ 55,000,000

1980 Commissioners Standard Ordinary Mortality Table

Life Expectancy in Years

Age	Male	Female	Age	Male	Female	Age	Male	Female
0	70.83	75.83	**34**	39.54	43.91	**67**	12.76	15.83
1	70.13	75.04	**35**	38.61	42.98	**68**	12.14	15.10
2	69.20	74.11	**36**	37.69	42.05	**69**	11.54	14.38
3	68.27	73.17	**37**	36.78	41.12	**70**	10.96	13.67
4	67.34	72.23	**38**	35.87	40.20	**71**	10.39	12.97
5	66.40	71.28	**39**	34.96	39.28	**72**	9.84	12.26
6	65.46	70.34	**40**	34.05	38.36	**73**	9.30	11.60
7	64.52	69.39	**41**	33.16	37.46	**74**	8.79	10.95
8	63.57	68.44	**42**	32.26	36.55	**75**	8.31	0.32
9	62.62	67.48	**43**	31.38	35.66	**76**	7.84	9.71
10	61.66	66.53	**44**	30.50	34.77	**77**	7.40	9.12
11	60.71	65.58	**45**	29.62	33.88	**78**	6.97	8.55
12	58.75	64.62	**46**	28.76	33.00	**79**	6.57	8.01
13	58.80	63.67	**47**	27.90	32.12	**80**	6.18	7.48
14	57.86	62.71	**48**	27.04	31.25	**81**	5.80	6.98
15	56.93	61.76	**49**	26.20	30.39	**82**	5.44	6.49
16	56.00	60.82	**50**	25.36	29.53	**83**	5.09	6.03
17	55.09	59.87	**51**	24.52	28.67	**84**	4.77	5.59
18	54.18	58.93	**52**	23.70	27.82	**85**	4.46	5.18
19	53.27	57.98	**53**	22.89	26.98	**86**	4.18	4.80
20	52.37	57.04	**54**	22.08	26.14	**87**	3.91	4.43
21	51.47	56.10	**55**	21.29	25.31	**88**	3.66	4.09
22	50.57	55.16	**56**	20.51	24.49	**89**	3.41	3.77
23	49.66	54.22	**57**	19.74	23.67	**90**	3.18	3.45
24	48.75	53.28	**58**	18.99	22.86	**91**	2.94	3.15
25	47.84	52.34	**59**	18.24	22.05	**92**	2.70	2.85
26	46.93	51.40	**60**	17.51	21.25	**93**	2.44	2.55
27	46.01	50.46	**61**	16.79	20.44	**94**	2.17	2.24
28	45.09	49.52	**62**	16.08	19.65	**95**	1.87	1.91
29	44.16	48.59	**63**	15.38	18.86	**96**	1.54	1.56
30	43.24	47.65	**64**	14.70	18.08	**97**	1.20	1.21
31	42.31	46.71	**65**	14.04	17.32	**98**	0.84	0.84
32	41.38	45.78	**66**	13.39	16.57	**99**	0.50	0.50
33	40.46	44.84						

Deaths Per Thousand At Various Ages

1980 Commissioners Standard Ordinary Mortality Table

Number Expected to Die Each Year

Age	Males Per 1,000	Females Per 1,000	Age	Males Per 1,000	Females Per 1,000	Age	Males Per 1,000	Females Per 1,000
0	4.18	2.89	**34**	2.00	1.58	**67**	30.44	17.43
1	1.07	.87	**35**	2.11	1.65	**68**	33.19	18.84
2	.99	.81	**36**	2.24	1.76	**69**	36.17	20.36
3	.98	.79	**37**	2.40	1.89	**70**	39.51	22.11
4	.95	.77	**38**	2.58	2.04	**71**	43.30	24.23
5	.90	.76	**39**	2.79	2.22	**72**	47.65	26.87
6	.85	.73	**40**	3.02	2.42	**73**	52.64	30.11
7	.80	.72	**41**	3.29	2.64	**74**	58.19	33.93
8	.76	.70	**42**	3.56	2.87	**75**	64.19	38.24
9	.74	.69	**43**	3.87	3.09	**76**	70.53	42.97
10	.73	.68	**44**	4.96	3.32	**77**	77.12	48.04
11	.77	.69	**45**	4.55	3.56	**78**	83.90	53.45
12	.85	.72	**46**	4.92	3.80	**79**	91.05	59.35
13	.99	.75	**47**	5.32	4.05	**80**	98.84	65.99
14	1.15	.80	**48**	5.74	4.33	**81**	107.48	73.60
15	1.33	.85	**49**	6.21	4.63	**82**	117.25	82.40
16	1.51	.90	**50**	6.71	4.96	**83**	128.26	92.53
17	1.67	.95	**51**	7.30	5.31	**84**	140.25	103.81
18	1.78	.98	**52**	7.96	5.70	**85**	152.95	116.10
19	1.86	1.02	**53**	8.71	6.15	**86**	166.09	129.29
20	1.90	1.05	**54**	9.56	6.61	**87**	179.55	143.32
21	1.91	1.07	**55**	10.47	7.09	**88**	193.27	158.18
22	1.89	1.09	**56**	11.46	7.57	**89**	207.29	173.94
23	1.86	1.11	**57**	12.49	8.03	**90**	221.77	190.75
24	1.82	1.14	**58**	13.59	8.47	**91**	236.98	208.87
25	1.77	1.16	**59**	14.77	8.94	**92**	253.45	228.81
26	1.73	1.19	**60**	16.08	9.47	**93**	272.11	251.51
27	1.71	1.22	**61**	17.54	10.13	**94**	295.90	279.31
28	1.70	1.26	**62**	19.19	10.96	**95**	329.96	317.32
29	1.71	1.30	**63**	21.06	12.02	**96**	384.55	375.74
30	1.73	1.35	**64**	23.14	13.25	**97**	480.20	474.97
31	1.78	1.40	**65**	25.42	14.59	**98**	657.98	655.85
32	1.83	1.45	**66**	27.85	16.00	**99**	1000.00	1000.00
33	1.91	1.50						

The Chance Of Dying Before Age 65[1]

From a group of 1,000 persons your age, the chart below illustrates the number who will still be alive at age 65. The third column indicates the probability that you will not be alive at age 65.

From 1,000 Males			From 1,000 Females		
Age at Last Birthday	**Number Still Alive at 65**	**Chance of Not Being Alive**	**Age at Last Birthday**	**Number Still Alive at 65**	**Chance of Not Being Alive**
30	755	25%	**30**	832	17%
31	757	24%	**31**	833	17%
32	759	24%	**32**	834	17%
33	761	24%	**33**	835	17%
34	763	24%:	**34**	836	16%
35	764	24%	**35**	837	16%
36	766	23%	**36**	834	16%
37	767	23%	**37**	841	16%
38	769	23%	**38**	843	16%
39	772	23%	**39**	845	16%
40	773	23%	**40**	847	15%
41	775	23%	**41**	850	15%
42	778	22%	**42**	853	15%
43	780	22%	**43**	855	15%
44	784	22%	**44**	858	14%
45	787	21%	**45**	860	14%
46	791	21%	**46**	863	14%
47	795	21%	**47**	867	13%
48	800	20%	**48**	871	13%
49	805	20%	**49**	875	13%
50	810	19%	**50**	879	12%
51	816	18%	**51**	882	12%
52	823	18%	**52**	886	11%
53	829	17%	**53**	892	11%
54	835	17%	**54**	898	10%
55	843	16%	**55**	904	10%
56	854	15%	**56**	911	9%
57	864	14%	**57**	918	8%
58	876	12%	**58**	926	7%
59	888	11%	**59**	935	7%
60	903	10%	**60**	944	6%
61	918	8%	**61**	953	5%
62	935	7%	**62**	963	4%
63	954	5%	**63**	973	3%
64	976	2%	**64**	986	1%

1 **Based on Commissioners 1980 Standard Ordinary Mortality Table.**

1986 Life Expectancy Table

Life Expectancy in Years[1]

Age	Male	Female	Age	Male	Female	Age	Male	Female
0	71.3	78.3	**30**	43.7	49.7	**60**	18.0	22.5
1	71.1	78.0	**31**	42.7	48.8	**61**	17.3	21.7
2	70.2	77.0	**32**	41.8	47.8	**62**	16.7	20.9
3	69.2	76.1	**33**	40.9	46.8	**63**	16.0	20.1
4	68.2	75.1	**34**	40.0	45.9	**64**	15.3	19.4
5	67.3	74.1	**35**	39.1	44.9	**65**	14.7	18.6
6	66.3	73.1	**36**	38.2	44.0	**66**	14.1	17.9
7	65.3	72.2	**37**	37.3	43.0	**67**	13.4	17.1
8	64.3	71.2	**38**	36.4	42.1	**68**	12.8	16.4
9	63.3	70.2	**39**	35.5	41.1	**69**	12.2	15.7
10	62.4	69.2	**40**	34.5	40.2	**70**	11.7	15.0
11	61.4	68.2	**41**	33.6	39.2	**71**	11.1	14.3
12	60.4	67.2	**42**	32.8	38.3	**72**	10.6	13.7
13	59.4	66.2	**43**	31.9	37.3	**73**	10.1	13.0
14	59.4	65.2	**44**	31.0	36.4	**74**	9.6	12.4
15	57.5	64.3	**45**	30.1	35.5	**75**	9.1	11.7
16	56.5	63.3	**46**	29.2	34.6	**76**	8.6	11.1
17	55.6	62.3	**47**	28.4	33.7	**77**	8.2	10.5
18	54.6	61.3	**48**	27.5	32.8	**78**	7.7	9.9
19	53.7	60.4	**49**	26.6	31.8	**79**	7.3	9.4
20	52.8	59.4	**50**	25.8	31.0	**80**	6.9	8.8
21	51.9	58.4	**51**	25.0	30.1	**81**	6.5	8.3
22	51.0	57.5	**52**	24.1	29.2	**82**	6.1	7.8
23	50.1	56.5	**53**	23.3	28.3	**83**	5.8	7.3
24	49.2	55.5	**54**	22.5	27.5	**84**	5.5	6.8
25	48.2	54.6	**55**	21.8	26.6	**85**	5.2	6.4
26	47.3	53.6	**56**	21.0	25.8			
27	46.4	52.6	**57**	20.2	24.9			
28	45.5	51.7	**58**	19.5	24.1			
29	44.6	50.7	**59**	18.8	23.3			

1 **Latest table available in 1990 from Department of Health and Human Services. Based on expectancies during 1986**

Bank vs. Insurance Policy

The Power of Compound Interest and The Investment Alternative

Age 60	Bank	Insurance			
		Plan 1*		Plan 2†	
Year	Life or Death at 5% Tax Free	In Life Cash Value	At Death Policy Pays	In Life Cash Value	At Death Policy Pays
1	1,050,000	801,322	6,850,000	735,288	8,748,212
2	1,102,500	882,554	6,850,000	820,213	8,748,212
3	1,157,625	959,930	6,850,000	898,906	8,748,212
4	1,215,506	1,039,126	6,850,000	978,443	8,748,212
5	1,276,281	1,120,336	6,850,000	1,058,949	8,748,212
6	1,340,095	1,209,246	6,850,000	1,147,469	8,748,212
7	1,407,100	1,289,812	6,850,000	1,223,353	8,748,212
8	1,477,455	1,380,916	6,850,000	1,310,751	8,748,212
9	1,551,328	1,470,459	6,850,000	1,394,178	8,748,212
10	1,628,894	1,572,504	6,850,000	1,491,457	8,748,212
11	1,710,339	1,678,048	6,850,000	1,590,692	8,748,212
12	1,795,856	1,781,194	6,850,000	1,684,212	8,748,212
13	1,885,649	1,895,409	6,850,000	1,788,932	8,748,212
14	1,979,931	2,014,234	6,850,000	1,896,362	8,748,212
15	2,078,928	2,138,682	6,850,000	2,007,607	8,748,212
16	2,182,874	2,268,654	6,850,000	2,122,188	8,748,212
17	2,292,018	2,403,264	6,850,000	2,238,416	8,748,212
18	2,406,619	2,549,930	6,850,000	2,365,379	8,748,212
19	2,526,950	2,694,646	6,850,000	2,484,579	8,748,212
20	2,653,297	2,881,304	6,850,000	2,613,144	8,748,212

Bank money usually in estate and cut in half at death by estate taxes.
Investment Alternative usually out of estate and tax free.

*All figures are based on current assumptions.

* Plan 1 – Buying for larger cash values to compare with savings.
† Plan 2 – Buying the maximum death benefit with the least cash value.

Bank vs. Insurance Policy

The Power of Compound Interest and The Investment Alternative

Age 60	Bank	Insurance			
		Plan 1*		Plan 2†	
Year	Life or Death at 5% Tax Free	In Life Cash Value	At Death Policy Pays	In Life Cash Value	At Death Policy Pays
21	2,785,962	2,990,835	6,850,000	2,712,755	8,748,212
22	2,925,260	3,133,599	6,850,000	2,808,358	8,748,212
23	3,071,523	3,279,170	6,850,000	2,898,055	8,748,212
24	3,225,099	3,428,864	6,850,000	2,982,514	8,748,212
25	3,386,354	3,582,103	6,850,000	3,059,060	8,748,212
26	3,555,672	3,738,796	6,850,000	3,125,381	8,748,212
27	3,733,456	3,898,716	6,850,000	3,178,395	8,748,212
28	3,920,129	4,062,389	6,850,000	3,215,679	8,748,212
29	4,116,135	4,228,497	6,850,000	3,230,368	8,748,212
30	4,321,942	4,397,874	6,850,000	3,218,402	8,748,212
31	4,538,039	4,571,741	6,850,000	3,175,111	8,748,212
32	4,764,941	4,751,514	6,850,000	3,094,433	8,748,212
33	5,003,188	4,939,593	6,850,000	2,970,299	8,748,212
34	5,253,347	5,139,148	6,850,000	2,795,969	8,748,212
35	5,516,015	5,353,664	6,850,000	2,562,022	8,748,212
36	5,791,816	5,587,795	6,850,000	2,258,057	8,748,212
37	6,081,406	5,847,024	6,850,000	1,870,452	8,748,212
38	6,385,477	6,137,912	6,850,000	1,380,981	8,748,212
39	6,704,751	6,468,894	6,850,000	768,039	8,748,212
40	7,039,988	6,850,386	6,850,000	2,973	8,748,212

Bank money usually in estate and cut in half at death by estate taxes.
Investment Alternative usually out of estate and tax free.

*All figures are based on current assumptions.

* Plan 1 – Buying for larger cash values to compare with savings.
† Plan 2 – Buying the maximum death benefit with the least cash value.

Bank vs. Insurance Policy

The Power of Compound Interest and The Investment Alternative

Age 70	Bank	Insurance			
		Plan 1*		Plan 2†	
Year	Life or Death at 5% Tax Free	In Life Cash Value	At Death Policy Pays	In Life Cash Value	At Death Policy Pays
1	1,050,000	816,609	3,970,000	745,758	5,247,211
2	1,102,500	890,494	3,970,000	820,883	5,247,211
3	1,157,625	958,198	3,970,000	885,522	5,247,211
4	1,215,506	1,026,735	3,970,000	948,540	5,247,211
5	1,276,281	1,099,371	3,970,000	1,014,980	5,247,211
6	1,340,095	1,172,435	3,970,000	1,079,844	5,247,211
7	1,407,100	1,251,545	3,970,000	1,150,403	5,247,211
8	1,477,455	1,331,552	3,970,000	1,219,686	5,247,211
9	1,551,328	1,420,747	3,970,000	1,298,472	5,247,211
10	1,628,894	1,511,568	3,970,000	1,376,576	5,247,211
11	1,710,339	1,607,745	3,970,000	1,457,491	5,247,211
12	1,795,856	1,701,769	3,970,000	1,530,806	5,247,211
13	1,885,649	1,798,086	3,970,000	1,601,839	5,247,211
14	1,979,931	1,901,126	3,970,000	1,675,796	5,247,211
15	2,078,928	2,002,654	3,970,000	1,740,700	5,247,211
16	2,182,874	2,106,198	3,970,000	1,797,886	5,247,211
17	2,292,018	2,211,199	3,970,000	1,846,381	5,247,211
18	2,406,619	2,321,964	3,970,000	1,889,978	5,247,211
19	2,526,950	2,435,053	3,970,000	1,921,896	5,247,211
20	2,653,297	2,555,177	3,970,000	1,945,714	5,247,211

Bank money usually in estate and cut in half at death by estate taxes.
Investment Alternative usually out of estate and tax free.

*All figures are based on current assumptions.

* Plan 1 – Buying for larger cash values to compare with savings.
† Plan 2 – Buying the maximum death benefit with the least cash value.

Bank vs. Insurance Policy

The Power of Compound Interest and The Investment Alternative

Age 70	Bank	Insurance			
		Plan 1*		Plan 2†	
Year	Life or Death at 5% Tax Free	In Life Cash Value	At Death Policy Pays	In Life Cash Value	At Death Policy Pays
21	2,785,962	2,657,511	3,970,000	1,923,496	5,247,211
22	2,925,260	2,762,872	3,970,000	1,877,989	5,247,211
23	3,071,523	2,872,706	3,970,000	1,805,473	5,247,211
24	3,225,099	2,988,922	3,970,000	1,701,798	5,247,211
25	3,386,354	3,113,659	3,970,000	1,561,254	5,247,211
26	3,555,672	3,249,728	3,970,000	1,377,480	5,247,211
27	3,733,456	3,400,441	3,970,000	1,142,118	5,247,211
28	3,920,129	3,569,757	3,970,000	844,012	5,247,211
29	4,116,135	3,762,744	3,970,000	469,887	5,247,211
30	4,321,942	3,985,644	3,985,644	2,039	5,247,211

Bank money usually in estate and cut in half at death by estate taxes.
Investment Alternative usually out of estate and tax free.

*All figures are based on current assumptions.

* Plan 1 – Buying for larger cash values to compare with savings.
† Plan 2 – Buying the maximum death benefit with the least cash value.

Bank vs. Insurance Policy

The Power of Compound Interest and The Investment Alternative

Age 80	Bank	Insurance			
		Plan 1*		Plan 2†	
Year	Life or Death at 5% Tax Free	In Life Cash Value	At Death Policy Pays	In Life Cash Value	At Death Policy Pays
1	1,050,000	894,963	2,420,000	829,158	3,571,408
2	1,102,500	947,139	2,420,000	864,929	3,571,408
3	1,157,625	1,000,180	2,420,000	897,458	3,571,408
4	1,215,506	1,059,366	2,420,000	935,124	3,571,408
5	1,276,281	1,117,756	2,420,000	967,350	3,571,408
6	1,340,095	1,178,119	2,420,000	997,852	3,571,408
7	1,407,100	1,242,804	2,420,000	1,029,702	3,571,408
8	1,477,455	1,310,003	2,420,000	1,059,796	3,571,408
9	1,551,328	1,381,860	2,420,000	1,090,247	3,571,408
10	1,628,894	1,457,781	2,420,000	1,118,460	3,571,408
11	1,710,339	1,534,425	2,420,000	1,133,984	3,571,408
12	1,795,856	1,612,437	2,420,000	1,134,945	3,571,408
13	1,885,649	1,692,242	2,420,000	1,117,847	3,571,408
14	1,979,931	1,774,536	2,420,000	1,078,439	3,571,408
15	2,078,928	1,861,133	2,420,000	1,014,615	3,571,408
16	2,182,874	1,950,085	2,420,000	904,634	3,571,408
17	2,292,018	2,049,255	2,420,000	758,590	3,571,408
18	2,406,619	2,156,666	2,420,000	562,152	3,571,408
19	2,526,950	2,290,272	2,420,000	327,764	3,571,408
20	2,653,297	2,425,172	2,425,173	1,209	3,571,408

Bank money usually in estate and cut in half at death by estate taxes.
Investment Alternative usually out of estate and tax free.

*All figures are based on current assumptions.

* Plan 1 – Buying for larger cash values to compare with savings.
† Plan 2 – Buying the maximum death benefit with the least cash value.

Caveats

BOCA

Based On Current Assumptions

All figures are based on current assumptions of mortality and interest; any change could affect the cash value, death benefit, or outlay as indicated on the proposal.

BOCT

Based On Current Taxes

All figures are based on current income and estate taxes. Any change in the tax laws will impact this program, producing higher or lower after tax yield.

BOLE

Based On Life Expectancy

All figures are based on current life expectancy. This term denotes a period for which the annuitant will be taxed on the interest alone. After such period the annuitant will be taxed on the entire income.

FAT - POLICY-THIN

The Most Insurance For The Least Money

Give the insurance company the least amount of money for the most insurance. Only if you are sophisticated and understand you have left no margin for interest drop. Any rise in interest can make a thin policy fat and a fat policy obese.

All figures are based on current assumptions. Charts are for illustrative purposes only.

Index